ANTIQUES *at* AUCTION *in* AMERICA

by Dorothy Hammond

ALL NEW ENTRIES, ALL NEW PRICES, ALL NEW PHOTOGRAPHS

TWENTY-SIXTH EDITION

First published 2009
© Dorothy Hammond
World copyright reserved

ISBN 978-1-85149-594-8

British Library Cataloguing-in-Publication Data
A catalogue record for this book is available from the British Library

Printed in China
Published in England by the Antique Collectors' Club Limited

Contents

This twenty-sixth edition is affectionately dedicated to my family
"on the home front"
whose deep and abiding interest in all of my ventures
is very meaningful to me

Introduction

Change in our lives is inevitable. As the result of an accident last year, I was unable to finalise this edition as scheduled. During this interval the title was changed to *Antiques at Auction in America*, but the format remains the same, twenty-one categories featuring over 4,000 illustrated objects in color that have sold during the past two years. Each entry is keyed to the auction house where the item sold, with the state abbreviation. As we all know, prices vary due to geographic differences. An introductory essay provides background information to each chapter with the exception of Miscellaneous.

As always, serious dealers and collectors look to auctions as the ultimate price determinant because they reflect market trends. When comparing similar pieces within this edition, the reader must take into consideration that fluctuations in the market, in addition to quality, the region in which an item sold and its popularity will always determine the hammer price.

Collecting is a process of acquiring and possessing objects with eye appeal. There continues to be much interest in all fields these days, even faithful reproductions... especially furniture from the "Centennial" period ca.1876 and beyond. The best examples have been solidly made and have great character and individuality. Reproductions in all fields, especially if they are faithful copies, have become more popular because of the diversity of forms, and they sell for a fraction of the cost of an original period piece. They are out there, just waiting to be found and treasured. All agree, however, that the best investment is in quality. Design and workmanship will always surpass the mediocre in its rate growth... and the past will continue to hold its allure and command respect. Objects produced during the late nineteenth century and well into the twentieth continue to dominate a large segment of the market because of their availability.

Craft items, although commonly defined as unique, have become popular collectibles. Many fine examples are finding their way into the marketplace in almost every price range. Among the current trends is to blend these items with period or modern interiors... and the combinations are endless.

Knowledge and perseverance are the keys to discovering great finds when forming a collection... especially pieces that serve a purpose

Good hunting!

A-NH   Northeast Auctions
960 **Hooked Rug with Floral Urn and Fronds,** worked in polychrome yarns on black ground. Mounted on stretcher, 27 x 46in. **$9,280**

Acknowledgments

No undertaking of this magnitude could possibly be accomplished without the assistance of others. The author wishes to express her gratitude to her Publisher, Diana Steel, Managing Director of Antique Collectors' Club Ltd., Woodbridge, Suffolk, England, for her assistance in the preparation of the book, and her dedication to a quality publication. To those on her staff, my heartfelt thank you goes to Tom Conway, Primrose Elliott, Stephen Farrow, Pam Henderson, Sandra Pond and Anna Morton for their dedication to the project. And I am very grateful to Dan Farrell, Managing Director of Antique Collectors' Club, North America, for his assistance and continued commitment to the book.

I wish to express my sincere gratitude to the following individuals and auction houses who have so generously provided both pictorial and textual material from the beginning for this edition. Without their support, the book would not have been possible.

Front Cover Image:
Northeast Auctions, Portsmouth, NH
The Kilcup Collection
Photo by: Ellen McDermott

Back Cover Image:
Skinner Inc., Boston, MA

Alderfer's Fine Art & Antiques
501 Fairgrounds Road
Hatfield, PA 19440
215-393-3000
www.alderferauction.com

Noel Barrett Antiques & Auction Ltd.
6183 Carversville Road
Carversville, PA 18913
215-297-5109

Bertoia Auction Gallery
2141 DeMarco Drive
Vineland, NJ 08360
856-692-1881
www.bertoiaauctions.com

Brunk Auction Services, Inc.
P.O. Box 2135
Asheville, NC 28802
828-254-6846
www.brunkauctions.com

Charlton Hall Galleries, Inc.
912 Gervais Street
Columbia, SC 29201
803-779-5678
www.charltonhallauctions.com

Conestoga Auction Company, Inc.
768 Graystone Road
Manheim, PA 17545
717-898-7284
www.conestogaauction.com

Crocker Farm
P.O. Box 725
Riderwood, MD 21139
410-337-5090
stoneware @crockerfarm.com

David Rago Auctions
333 North Main Street
Lambertville, NJ 08530
609-397-9374
www.ragoarts.com

Early Auction Company
123 Main Street
Milford, OH 45150
513-831-4833
www.earlyauctionco.com

Robert C. Eldred Company, Inc.
1483 Route 6A
P.O. Box 796
East Dennis, MA 02641
508-385-3116
www.eldreds.com

Fontaines Auction Gallery
1485 West Housatonic Street
Pittsfield, MA 01201
413-448-8922
www.fontaineauction.com

Samuel T. Freeman & Company
1808 Chestnut Street
Philadelphia, PA 19103
215-563-9275
www. freemansauction.com

Garth's Arts & Antiques
2690 Strataford Road
P.O. Box 369
Delaware, OH 43015
740-362-4771
www.garths.com

Glass Works Auctions
P.O. Box 180
East Greenville, PA 18041
215-679-5849
www.glswrk-auction.com

Guyette & Schmidt. Inc.
P.O. Box 522
West Farmington, ME 04992
207-778-6256
www.guyetteandschmidt.com

Horst Auction Center
50 Durlach Road
Ephrata, PA 17522
717-738-3080
www.horstauction.com

Jackson's International Auctioneers, Inc.
2229 Lincoln Street
Cedar Falls, IA 50613
319-277-2256
www.jacksonsauction.com

James D. Julia, Inc.
P.O. Box 830
Fairfield, ME 04937
207-453-7125
www.juliaauctions.com

Northeast Auctions
93 Pleasant Street
Portsmouth, NH 03801
603-433-8400
www.northeastauctions.com

Pook & Pook, Inc.
P.O. Box 268
Downingtown, PA 19335
610-269-0695
www.pookandpook.com

Skinner, Inc.
63 Park Plaza
Boston, MA 02116
617-350-5400
www.skinnerinc.com

Treadway Gallery, Inc.
2029 Madison Road
Cincinnati, OH 45208
513-321-6742
www.treadwaygallery.com

Willis Henry Auctions, Inc.
22 Main Street
Marshfield, MA 02050
781-834-7774
www.willishenry.com

The above auction houses charge a buyer's premium which is a surcharge on the hammer or final bid price at auction), which will vary. For readers' convenience, the author has included a complete address and website.

In conclusion, every effort has been made to ensure that all information presented in this book is accurate.

However, neither the author, publisher nor any of its staff is responsible for omissions or information that has been misrepresented. And they accept no liability for any financial or other loss, or for errors that might have occurred as a result of typographical or other errors.

– Dorothy Hammond

Abbreviations

Am.	American	hdw.	hardware	pat.	patent
approx.	approximately	ht.	height	patt.	pattern
att.	attributed	illus.	illustrated	pc./pcs.	piece/pieces
C.	century	imp.	impressed	pr.	pair
ca.	circa	imper.	imperfect/imperfections	prof. restor.	professional restoration
comp.	composition	in.	inches	ptd.	patented
cond.	condition	incl.	including	Q.A.	Queen Anne
const.	construction	incor.	incorporating	qt.	quart
dec.	decorated/decoration	int.	interior	ref.	refinish
dia.	diameter	L.	left	repl.	replaced/replacement
dov.	dovetail/dovetailed	lb.	pound	repr.	repair, repaired
dp.	depth	lg.	length	rest.	restored/restoration
D.Q.	diamond quilted	litho.	lithograph	sgn.	signed
ea.	each	mah.	mahogany	sq.	square
emb.	embossed/embossing	mini	miniature	unmkd.	unmarked
Eng.	England/English	mkd.	marked	w/	with
est.	established	m.o.p.	mother-of-pearl	wd.	width
exc.	excluding	mts.	mounts	wt.	wrought
Fr.	France	N. Eng.	New England	yrs.	years
gal.	gallon	n/s	no sale	The common and accepted	
Ger.	Germany	orig.	original	abbreviations are used for states.	

A-PA

123 Winter Landscape with Sleigh sgn. E.W. Redfield, 1869-1965, oil on canvas, 23 x 32in.
$77,675

The word advertising comes from the French word "avertir" meaning to notify. Advertising is actually as old as trade, probably beginning with what present day businessmen call personal selling. In essence, it informs people of the various advantages of a product, an idea, or a service. When manufacturing developed, few persons could read, as universal free education did not exist until the 1800s. Therefore, businessmen used symbols such as a shoemaker used a sign shaped like a shoe over his shop door, or a jeweler displayed a dummy clock. Later, when words were added, the symbols became trade signs.

Today, with new collectors appearing on the scene daily, the serious collecting of early advertising mementos has become widespread throughout the country. Searching out these collectibles is an endless adventure... and values have escalated which forces the serious collector to be more discriminating and build a more meaningful collection.

Nostalgia has created the current craze to acquire early advertising memorabilia because, in our hectic, parlous, plastic world today, the older generation, as well as the young, are fascinated by advertising collectibles in every media.

A-ME   James D. Julia, Inc.
1240 **Brownie Soda Cardboard Sign** w/soiling, ht. 59, wd. 20½in. **$230**

A-ME   James D. Julia, Inc.
1277 **Hercules Powder Co.,** Gunpowder Lithograph used to advertise Infallible & E.C. brands, ht. 18, wd. 22in. **$1,380**

A-ME   James D. Julia, Inc.
1273 **Ballistite & Empire Shotgun Powders Lithograph,** ca.1910 by Noble's Explosive Co., Ltd., ht. 26¾, wd. 13¾in. **$2,070**

A-ME   James D. Julia, Inc.
1248 **King's Candies Porcelain Sign** "For American Queen", ca.1919, ht. 20, wd. 16in. **$2,185**

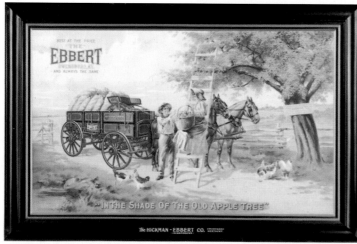

A-ME   James D. Julia, Inc.
1361 **Tin Sign** "In The Shade Of The Old Apple Tree" by Hickman-Ebbert Wagon Co., ca.1906, ht. 25½, wd. 37½in. **$3,162**

A-ME   James D. Julia, Inc.
1285 **Wales-Goodyear Rubbers Cardboard Sign,** 3-panel store display, ca.1906, ht. 20, wd. 30in. **$2,875**

A-ME   James D. Julia, Inc.
1249 Russell's Chocolates Tin
Sign, ca.1909 by Meek
Company, ht. 14½, wd. 14½in.
$258

A-ME
James D. Julia, Inc.
1177 Coca-Cola
1916 Serving
Tray w/image of
Elaine, ht. 19,
wd. 8½in. $172

A-ME
James D. Julia, Inc.
1447 Rockford
Watch Sign,
decal applied to
wood panel, mfg.
by U.S. Decal
Co., ht 21, wd.
15in. $402

A-ME   James D. Julia, Inc.
1292 Diamond Dyes Balloon
Display Cabinet, oak
w/storage dividers & emb.
front panel, image size ht.
20, wd. 15in. $1,265

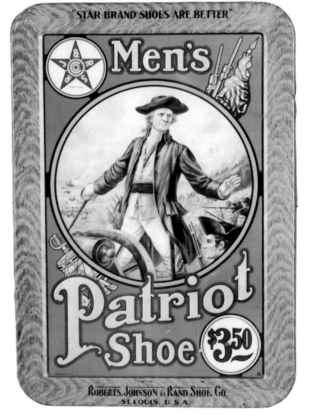

A-ME   James D. Julia, Inc.
1287 Patriot Shoe Tin Sign, depicting Prescott
at the Battle of Bunker Hill. Litho. by Meek
Co., ht. 26, wd. 18in. $2,012

A-ME   James D. Julia, Inc.
1309 Hanover Insurance Paper Sign,
litho., 19th C., image size 23½, wd.
23½in. $1,680

A-ME   James D. Julia, Inc.
1374 Prang's Christmas & New Years Cards
early stone lithograph from the Louis Prang
Co., of Boston. The poster features separate
Christmas & New Years card samples inserted
under the die cut fingers of its blond
messenger. With Prang family provenance
included, image size ht. 27¾, wd. 10½in.
$420

ADVERTISING

A-ME   James D. Julia, Inc.
1235 Ward's Lemon-crush Syrup Dispenser, missing pump, ht. 9, wd. 10½in. **$460**

A-PA
    Conestoga Auction Co., Inc.
227 Tin Tip Tray w/litho. center scene for Hoffman House, 5 x 3⅜in. **$44**

A-PA   Conestoga Auction Co., Inc.
239 Winchester Folding Advertising Screen w/five cardboard panels, first panel missing, w/black painted frame, ht 48, wd. 20in. **$605**

A-ME   James D. Julia, Inc.
1282 DuPont Explosives 1908 Calendar by Osthaus for the powder company, ht. 30, wd. 20in. **$2,300**

A-ME   James D. Julia, Inc.
1308 Tin Litho. For Overholt Whiskey titled It's Old Overholt, incl. frame ht. 27¾, wd. 37in. **$2,070**

A-ME   James D. Julia, Inc.
1275 DuPont Infallible Shotgun Powder Poster, 20 x 36in. **$4,887**

A-PA Freemans
54 **The Jarden Lithographic Company Catalog** w/orig. label designs, light edge wear w/many sheets of chromolithographic samples & die cut labels in envelope mounted to inside back cover. **$598**

A-ME James D. Julia, Inc.
297 **Coca-Cola Welsh Clock** w/Calendar Insert, Ingraham schoolhouse by. E.N. Welch Mrf. Co., ca.1901. This example includes a cropped 1901 Hilda Clark calendar top, pendulum & weight key. The oak case appears ref. w/a repl. front glass face, ht. 26, wd. 17¾in. **$3,162**

A-PA Freemans
791 **Hand-painted Trade Sign**, late 19th C., sgn. Dortreus, ink & ink wash on heavy stock, framed, sight 13 x 9¾in. **$418**

A-ME James D. Julia, Inc.
302 **Two Sided Display** promoting Red Seal White Lead Paint, complete w/bucket & hanger chain, w/scattered surface chips, ht. 25½, wd. 14½in. **$1,380**

A-ME
James D. Julia, Inc.
300 **Two Sided Cardboard Fan Hanger** promoting Schultz & Co., Zanesville, OH, Star Soap, ht. 8½, wd. 5¾in. **$840**

A-PA
Pook & Pook, Inc.
309 **Ghirardelli's Chocolate Tin Sign**, painted, depicting a girl & her doll having a party, image 23 x 17in. **$10,980**

ADVERTISING

A-ME   James D. Julia, Inc.
Advertising Clocks
678 Cast Iron & Sheet Metal Clockmaker's Trade Sign, late 19th C., w/double sided inscription, ht. 44, wd. 28in. **$1,265**
679 Two Jeweler's & Clockmaker's Trade Signs w/double sided inscriptions, ht. 25¼ & 25¾in. **$1,840**
680 Cast Metal Watchmaker's Sign, late 19th C., ht. 41in. **$1,265**

A-ME   James D. Julia, Inc.
676 Cast Iron Optician's Trade Sign, late 19th C. w/inscription, ht. 22, wd. 58in. **$1,495**

A-ME   James D. Julia, Inc.
1263 Jolly Tar Pastime Baird Clock w/papier mâché adv. bezels & orig. label by Baird Clock Co., ht. 30, wd. 18in. **$1,020**

A-ME   James D. Julia, Inc.
1262 Mayo's Tobacco Advertising Clock w/wood case. Clock includes pendulum weight, key & fragments of orig. label. **$2,530**

A-ME   James D. Julia, Inc.
1180 Coca-Cola Gilbert Clock, ca.1910, oak case w/paper dial, w/very minor discoloration, top glass panel repainted & case appears to have been revarnished, ht. 37, wd.19in. **$4,370**

A-ME   James D. Julia, Inc.
1362 Sidney Advertising Wall Clock manu. by the company, Owego, NY, ca.1885 w/separate movement for rotating the bottom drums every five minutes by ringing bell which allowed the clock to display up to 13 separate ads, ht. 69, wd. 28in. **$11,500**

BANKS, Still & Mechanical

Small banks for depositing coins became popular in the United States when hard currency was introduced in the 18th century. The adage "a penny saved is a penny earned" has represented an important part of Americana from the time of Benjamin Franklin. It was a time when parents taught their children the art of saving at a very early age, by giving them "penny" banks. Almost every substance has been used to make a still bank, all of which are very collectible. Hundreds of different types have been produced.

Still banks, so called to differentiate them from banks with mechanical parts, have been produced in quantities since the 19th century. They depict a range of buildings, animal and human figures. The most elaborate were made by leading manufacturing companies including Arcade, A.C. Williams, J. & E. Stevens and Kenton.

The most complex banks were mechanical cast-iron models produced from the 1870s. These banks operate on two principles: the weight of the deposited coin will cause the action to begin, or a person, after inserting a coin, presses a lever that activates a spring, setting the bank in motion. There were hundreds of different types of mechanical banks made until the 1930s by J. & E. Stevens and W.J. Shepard Hardware Company.

A-ME   **James D. Julia, Inc.**
421 **Hubley Trick Dog Mechanical Bank**, ca.1930s w/orig. trap, ht. 7, lg. 8in. **$360**

A-ME   **James D. Julia, Inc.**
424 **Mule Entering Barn** by J.& E.Stevens, ca.1880. When coin is placed behind mule's rear feet, push lever & mule kicks coin into barn, lg. 8¼in. **$517**

A-PA   **Pook & Pook, Inc.**
Cast Iron Mechanical Banks
First Row
109 **I Always Did Spise A Mule**, pat. 1897 w/orig. poly surface, ht. 9¾in. **$633**
110 **Dog On Turntable**, ca.1900 by H.L. Judd Mfg. Co., w/orig. poly. dec. surface, ht. 5in. **$7,474**

111 **Tammany Bank**, pat. 1873 by J. & E. Stevens Co., w/double sided Tammany inscription & orig. dec. surface, ht. 5¾in. **$403**
112 **Mule Entering Barn**, pat. 1880 by J. & E. Stevens, retaining its orig. poly. dec. surface, ht. 5¼in. **$2,760**
Second Row
113 **William Tell**, pat. 1896 by J. &

E. Stevens Co., w/orig. poly. surface, ht. 6½in. **$460**
114 **Boy On Trapeze**, by. J. Barton Smith, ca.1888, w/orig. dec., ht.9¼in. **$4,080**
115 **Teddy & the Bear**, pat. 1907 by J. & E. Stevens Co., retaining its orig. poly. dec. surface, ht. 9¼in. **$1,265**

A-ME   James D. Julia, Inc.
427 **Boy Scout Camp Mechanical Bank** by J.& E.Stevens,
w/wear & re-soldered flag pole attached to boy's hands, lg.
9⅝in. **$2,817**

A-ME   James D. Julia, Inc.
407 **Dentist Mechanical Bank** by J.& E.Stevens, mint.
When bank is activated the dentist rears back with
molar in hand & the patient falls backwards flinging
arms & legs in air, lg. 9in. **$23,000**

A-ME
James D. Julia, Inc.
413 **Elephant & 3
Clowns
Mechanical Bank**
by J.& E. Stevens,
pat. 1882, ht.
6in. **$805**

A-ME   James D. Julia, Inc.
430 **Darktown Battery Mechanical Bank** by J.& E.
Stevens, pat. 1888, lg. 9¾in. Heavy wear
throughout & repl. trap. **$1,080**

A-ME   James D. Julia, Inc.
433 **Mechanical Bank Trade Cards** incl. Humpty Dumpty, Uncle Sam & Trick Pony. **$747**
433A **Two Mechanical Bank Trade Cards** incl. Punch & Judy & Speaking Dog card. **$540**

A-IA
Jackson's International Auctioneers, Inc.
847 **Hall's Excelsior Cast Iron Still Bank,** late 19th C. w/orig. paint, missing parts, ht. 5in. **$94**

A-IA   Jackson's International Auctioneers
Cast Iron Still Banks
848 **Jolly Nigger,** ca.1900, ht. 6¼in. **$352**

A-PA   Conestoga Auction Co. Inc.
Still Banks
76 **Redware Bank** in shape of apple, dia. 3½in. **$209**
75 **Moravian Melon or Gourd Bank** ca.1825-50, ht. 5½, dia. 4in. **$1,402**
78 **Stoneware Bank** in shape of pear, ht. 5½in. **$412**
77 **Redware Bank** in shape of peach, ht. 3in. **$143**

A-ME   James D. Julia, Inc.
409 **Mason Mechanical Bank** by Shepherd Hardware Co., pat. 1887, lg. 7¼in. **$3,162**

A-ME   James D. Julia, Inc.
415 **Pelican Bank by Trenton Hdw.** When coin is inserted in pelican's head, beak pops open revealing obstinate figure w/old repl. to hinged part containing eyes, ht. 7⅞in. **$2,127**

A-IA

Jackson's International Auctioneers

Cast Iron Still Banks

850 **Toy Dresser**, ca. 1900 by J. & E. Stevens w/orig. finish, ht. 6in. **$176**

851 **Aunt Jomima Bank**, early 20th C., ht. 6in. **$205**

852 **State Bank**, late 19th C. w/orig. painted surface, ht. 4¼in. **$117**

A-PA   Pook & Pook, Inc.

Mechanical Banks, Cast Iron

First Row

118 **Trick Dog**, ca. 1900 by Hubley w/orig. poly. surface, ht. 7⅛in. **$1,725**

119 **Owl Turns Head**, pat. 1880 by J.& E. Stevens Co., w/orig. poly. dec. surface, ht. 7¼in. **$460**

120 **Eagle & Eaglets**, pat. 1883 by J.& E. Stevens Co., w/orig. poly. surface, ht. 5½in. **$575**

Second Row

121 **Lion & Two Monkeys**, pat. 1883 by Kyser & Rex w/orig. poly. surface, ht. 8¾in. **$1,610**

122 **Uncle Sam**, pat. 1886 w/orig. dec. surface, ht. 11in. **$2,070**

123 **Speaking Dog**, pat. 1885 by Shepard Hardware Co., w/orig. dec. surface, ht. 7in. **$978**

BASKETS

The art of basketry was one of our earliest crafts and is recognized today as yet another interesting form of folk art. Because basketry was common on the Continent, many of the first settlers were experienced basketmakers and quickly adopted new techniques from the Indians, who were excellent basketmakers.

During the decades following the first colonization, the need for containers and storage facilities was immense. Materials were abundant, so the art of basketmaking literally flourished until around the late 1800s when basket factories became established.

Among the most desirable baskets of interest to collectors these days are the Shaker, American Indian, the so-called Nantucket Lightship baskets, and the coiled rye straw baskets that are characteristically Pennsylvania Dutch.

Baskets continue enjoying much popularity among collectors, regardless of vintage. After all, everything collected these days was "new" once. An interesting collection can still be assembled inexpensively, unless one's taste preference includes one of the above types.

A-ME   James D. Julia Auctions, Inc.
438 Nantucket Basket w/squared wood swing handle, wood oval bottom & base sgn. w/label Made by Mitchell Ray, Nantucket, Mass., shows wear. A 4in. section of top edge wrap is missing. **$4,025**

A-MA   Skinner, Inc.
431 Southwest Coiled Basketry Bowl, Apache, ca. late 19th C., w/black & dark red maze patt. Minor stitch loss, ht. 3¾, dia. 15in. **$2,938**

A-MA   Skinner, Inc.
California Indian Basketry
476 Coiled Bowl, ca.1900 w/flared sides & dec. w/three banded two-color meandering patt., ht. 7¼, dia. 7¾in. **$1,410**
477 Coiled Bowl, Pomo, ca. late 19th C., globular form w/petal patt., w/white seed beads & clamshell dec. w/minor stitch loss, ht. 5¼, dia. 11in. **$1,763**
478 Coiled Bowl, Yokuts, ca. early 20th C., flared form w/two bands of dec. & minor stitch loss, ht. 4¼, dia. 14in. **$764**
479 Porno Coiled Bowl, ca.1900 w/multi. feathers in triangle patt., ht.1¾, dia. 4¼in. **$1,116**
480 Columbia River Twined Bowl, flared form w/clamshell dec., ht. 4, dia.12in. **$999**
481 Columbia River Pictorial Twined Bowl, Klikitat, ca.1900 w/two-color geometric & animal patt., ht. 2¾, dia. 3¼in. **$646**

A-PA   Conestoga Auction Co., Ind.
314   Northeast Algonkin Split Ash Lidded Indian Basket w/poly. dec. & paper lined, breaks, 12 x 12in. **$385**

A-IA   Jackson's International Auctioneers
1510   Pima Basket Tray, ht. 5¼, dia. 16in. **$1,175**

A-IA   Jackson's International Auctioneers
1515   Northern California Indian Basket, ht. 4¼, dia. 7¼in. **$528**

A-ME   James D. Julia, Inc.
517X   Splint Wall Basket, late 19th C. w/old salmon paint & curlicue dec., shows wear & soil, ht. 19, wd. 12in. **$920**

A-ME   James D. Julia, Inc.
517W   Old Splint Wall Basket w/very old black painted surface, possibly Passamaquoddy, ht. 9½, wd. 10in. **$431**

A-MA   Skinner, Inc.
102   Shaker Woven Splint Basket, possibly Mt. Lebanon, NY, 19th C. w/slightly domed base, carved wooden handles & single lashing around rim, w/minor breaks on base, ht. 7⅞, dia. 14in. **$2,585**

A-PA   Conestoga Auction Co., Inc.
First Row
69   Gathering Basket w/fixed handle & God's eye wrap, ht. 11¼in. **$50**
Second Row
66   Gathering Basket in old red paint w/fixed handle & breaks, ht.9in. **$137**
67   Gathering Basket w/fixed bent wood handle, ht. 8½in. **$77**
68   Large Gathering Basket w/fixed handle, ht. 11¼in. **$50**

A-PA   Conestoga Auction Co., Inc.

First Row

55 Miniature Splint Buttocks Basket w/minor breaks, wd. 3in. **$385**

56 Two Miniature Baskets, one buttocks w/fixed handle, ht. 1⅞in.; the second w/swing handle & breaks, **$357**

Second Row

51 Miniature Splint Basket w/minor breaks, ht. 4½in. **$110**

52 Small Splint Buttocks Basket w/fixed handle, ht. 4½in. **$55**

53 Miniature Splint Buttocks Basket w/fixed bent wood handle w/God's

eye wrap, ht. 4in. **$412**

54 String Basket w/dyed bands & open work w/central hole in lid & minor breaks, ht. 4¼in. **$22**

Third Row

63 Painted Splint Basket w/secondary attached internal basket w/minor breaks, ht. 4¾in. **$110**

64 Round Splint Basket w/small loop side handles, ht. 4½in. **$49**

65 Gathering Basket w/fixed handle & God's eye wrap, ht. 9 in. **$110**

Second Row

60 Small Splint Basket w/fixed wood carry handle, ht. 5½in. **$137**

61 Wall Basket w/fixed bent wood handle & breaks, ht. 8½in. **$77**

Third Row

57 Splint Gathering Basket w/swing handle, ht.6¼in. **$110**

58 Buttocks Basket w/fixed handle & painted red band on either side, ht. 5½in. **$220**

59 Small Splint Basket w/fixed bent wood handle, minor breaks, ht. 5½in. **$82**

62 Divided Wall Basket w/open work decorative band on each pocket, ht. 12in. **$165**

BASKETS

A-PA　　　Conestoga Auction Co., Inc.
First Row
321 Small Buttocks Trinket Baskets of splint oak, minor breaks, **$165**
322 Miniature Splint Oak Basket w/fixed handle, ht. 3¼in. **$220**
324 Miniature Splint Buttocks Basket w/black paint & poly. accents, ht. 2¾in.w/handle. **$27**

325 Shaker Berry Basket w/tin rim & base band w/breaks, ht. 3⅞in. **$93**
Second Row
317 Nantucket Lightship Basket w/wood floor & inscribed on bottom Made in Nantucket, Jose Formoso Reyes, 1902-1980, ht. 4, dia. 9in. **$1,430**
318 Splint Ash Lidded Trinket Basket

w/swelled body, ht. 4½in. **$412**
319 Shaker Kitten Head Berry Basket w/washed surface, overall ht.7¼, dia.5⅜in. **$1,540**
320 Splint Gathering Basket w/tooled circular & floral dec. w/minor breaks, ht. 7¼in. **$93**

A-PA　　Conestoga Auction Company, Inc.
Buttocks Baskets
80 Splint Basket w/fixed bent wood handle w/God's eye wrap & minor breaks, ht. 18in., wd. 22½in. **$247**
81 Splint Basket w/fixed bent wood handle & God's eye wrap & minor breaks, ht. 13½, wd. 16¼in. **$71**
82 Splint Basket w/fixed bent wood

handle, God's eye wrap & minor breaks, ht. 13, wd. 16in. **$44**
83 Flat Splint Basket w/fixed bent wood handle & God's eye wrap, minor breaks, ht. 11¾, wd. 14½in. **$55**
84 Basket w/traces of old painted surface, fixed bent wood handle w/God's eye wrap, ht. 12¼, wd.

14½in. **$104**
85 Varnished basket w/fixed handle & minor breaks, ht. 10¼, wd., 12½in. **$93**
86 Small Basket w/fixed bent wood handle & God's eye wrap, ht. 6½, wd., 8in. **$852**

BOTTLES

The "golden era" of bottle collecting escalated during the 1960s and well into the 1980s. It was a time when there was a steady supply of unusual new finds being discovered, either privately or through auctions which fueled collectors' demands. Bottle price guides were published, and eastern and mid-western auction houses began offering more bottles in their auctions. It was at this time that major auction houses added specialists to their staff as they moved into this "new" collectible field which became a major hobby for many collectors. The most desirable and pricy bottles are historic flasks, bitters, ink, figural and perfume.

A-NH　　　　　**Northeast Auctions**
First Row

46 Masonic-Eagle Pint Flask, two-mold olive green, by Keene Glassworks, Keene, NH. ht. 7¼in. **$300**

47 Masonic Pint Flask, two-mold olive green, att. to Stoddard, NH. Molded on obverse w/all-seeing eye of God & a six-pointed star above initials ·AD, ht. 7⅜in: **$500**

48 Dark Green Masonic-Eagle Half-pint Flask, Keen, NH, ca.1820-30. Molded w/a Masonic arch, pillars, crossbones, trowel, skull, moon & eagle, ht. 6in. **$750**

49 Light Blue-Green Masonic-Eagle Flask, half-pint, Keene Glassworks w/ molded Masonic arch, pillars, cross-bones, trowel, skull, sun, moon & seven stars. The reverse w/eagle holding an E Pluribus Unum banner above conjoined letters IP within oval, ht. 7⅜in. **$550**

Second Row

50 Deep Green Eagle Pint Flask, Willington Glass Works w/molded eagle & shield & inscription Liberty, ht. 8in. **$500**

51 Golden Amber Eagle Pint Flask w/molded eagle, shield and the reverse w/fruit-filled cornucopia, ht. 7in. **$100**

52 Amber Eagle Pint Flask w/molded eagle & five-bar shield w/fruit-filled cornucopia, ht. 7in. **$200**

53 Golden Amber Pint Flask, ca.1820-30 w/molded eagle & five-bar shield, the reverse w/ fruit-filled cornucopia, ht. 7in. **$150**

54 Amber Half-pint Flask w/molded eagle & shield w/inscription Liberty & Willington Glass Co., West Willington Conn. ht. 6⅜in **$300**

Third Row

55 Amber Eagle Half-pint Flask w/ six-bar shield, ht. 6in. **$200**

56 Olive Green Half-pint Flask, Coventry, CT Glass Works, ht. 6in. **$450**

57 Mid-Atlantic Aquamarine Eagle Quart Flask w/molded eagle clutching in its talons a thunderbolt & olive branch beneath 13stars, ht. 7in. **$100**

58 Two Golden Amber Eagle Pint Flasks, Granite Glass Works w/molded eagle & seven bar shield, the reverse molded Stoddard, NH, ht. 7½in. **$250**

59 Aquamarine Eagle Pint Flask, two-mold w/a molded eagle on each side. ht. 7¾in. **$100**

60 Aquamarine Eagle Pint Flask, two-mold w/a molded eagle & seven-bar shield beneath fourteen stars. ht. 6¾in. **$200**

A-VA   Green Valley Auctions, Inc.

Cologne Bottles

1441 **Cobalt blue to colorless** w/punty cuttings, star-cut base w/orig. hollow stopper & star cut top, ca.1845-1860, Boston & Sandwich Glass Co., ht. 5in. **$385**

1442 **Cut Double Overlay Bottle,** deep blue to white to colorless w/star-cut base, orig. hollow stopper & star-cut top, Boston & Sandwich Glass, ht. 5in. **$198**

1443 **Cut Overlay Bottle,** white to colorless w/punty cuttings, star-cut base, orig. hollow stopper, Boston & Sandwich Glass, ht. 5½in. **$231**

A-VA   Green Valley Auctions, Inc.

Cologne Bottles

1444 **Cut Overlay Bottle,** white to colorless w/cranberry cased interior & gilt dec., polished pontil mark, ca.1850-1870, ht.7in. **$715**

1445 **Cut Overlay,** white to colorless w/gilt dec., trefoil & Moorish window cuttings w/orig. hollow stopper & polished pontil mark, ca.1850-1870, ht. 7½in. **$242**

1446 **Cut Overlay Bottle,** white to jade green w/pointed quatrefoil, loop & pointed punty cuttings w/orig hollow stopper numbered to match bottle, ca.1850-1870, ht. 7½in. **$660**

Opposite

A-MA   Skinner, Inc.

First Row

651 **Blown-molded Historical Glass Flasks,** Am., 19th C. The first light aqua calabash qt. flask w/bust of Washington; the second light aqua w/Union shield w/ clasped hand on one side & an eagle shield on reverse; the first amber pint flask w/a sheaf of grain crossed w/a rake & pitchfork, mkd. Westford Glass Co. on reverse; the second amber pint flask w/handle w/portrait of trotting horse Flora Temple; and the third an olive green flask w/a horse pulling cart, lettering Railroad & Lowell, and on the reverse, a spreadwing eagle & stars. **$940**

Second Row

652 **Aqua Blown-molded Glass Flasks,** Am., early 19th C., the first featuring a leafy tree w/bird & lettering Summer; the second pint flask depicts a full-rigged frigate, Franklin & Free Trade Sailors Rights w/Kensington Glass Works Phil. above a Masonic arch w/crack near base; the third a half pint flask depicting a sloop & on reverse an eight-point star w/tiny ornaments. **$353**

653 **Four Aqua Blown-molded Flasks,** Am., the first qt. flask w/profile bust of Washington w/raised lettering The Father of His Country & bust of General Taylor on reverse; the second pint flask w/Columbia on one side & on the reverse B&W in script; the third pint scroll flask w/lip chips; the fourth w/an eagle & stars on both sides. **$588**

Third Row

654 **Three Olive/Amber Blown Flasks,** Am., the first w/ sunburst on both sides & letters KEEN; the second pint w/both sides featuring an eagle; the third with both sides depicting an eagle w/tiny nick. **$940**

655 **Amber Glass Whiskey Bottle,** Whitney Glass Works, Glassboro, NJ, ca.1850,w/emb. lettering & rim chips. **$499**

656 **Three Blown-molded Cornucopia Glass Flasks** by CT Glass Works, early 19th C. The olive amber flask is cracked. **$470**

Fourth Row

657 **Olive Green Masonic Glass Pint Flask** by Keene Glassworks, early 19th C. One side depicting Masonic columns, archway & symbols, the reverse an Am. flag, w/base crack. **$2,703**

658 **Amber Glass Whiskey Jug,** ca.1840-60 w/applied handle & two flattened label panels w/lettering Griffith Hyatt & Co., Baltimore. **$646**

659 **Amber Blown Bitters Bottle** w/raised lettering Binninger's Regulator/ 19 Broad Street New York. **$499**

660 **Two Olive Blown Glass Pint Flasks,** one a Pitkin type & the other w/a sunburst pattern on each side w/crack. **$3,525**

661 **Aqua Captain Bragg Glass Pint Flask,** att. to Baltimore Glass Works, early 19th C. w/raised lettering A Little More Grape Capt. Bragg. The reverse in a semi-circle Gen'l Taylor Never Surrenders, w/three small lip chips. **$382**

662 **Two Colored Flasks,** the first amber glass mkd. Keene w/one side depicting Washington in profile, the reverse Jackson; the second an olive green pint flask by Willington Glass Works & featuring an Am. eagle on one side. **$823**

665 **Amber Glass Old Kentucky Bourbon Betters Bottle,** by Binneger & Co., distilled in 1848, barrel-form w/ribbed bands, ht. 9½in. **$382**

Sixth Row

664 **Two Olive Amber Pint Flasks,** one w/emb. eagle & a cornucopia on reverse side; the second made in Coventry CT, w/spreadwing eagle on one side & a horse & cart w/lettering Success To The Railroad on reverse. **$118**

663 **Colorless Blown-molded Cologne Bottle,** 19th C., barrel-form, ht. 4¼in. **$323**

A-ME   James D. Julia, Inc.

The following four lots are polychromed paint enamel decorated glass bottles which have been favorites of collectors for many years. The bottles are European in origin, possibly German. They are fitted with a lip mounted pewter neck and cap. Bottles of this form generally date from 1750-1800. Though many German glass makers brought their skills to America during the early years of this country, there is no written or archeological documentation to support or indicate their production in this country. Furthermore, the exact use and purpose of these bottles is not known. However, due to their colorful decoration and inscription on some, they served an ornamental purpose as well as a practical one. These bottles are oftentimes called Steigel-type.

A-PA   Conestoga Auction Company, Inc.

106 **Clear Bottle** w/enamel dec. depicting a woman w/arm raised. German verse on opposite side, ending in floral dec. w/screw cap & pewter collar, ht. 5⅞in. **$330**

107 **Clear Bottle** w/enamel floral dec. & pewter cap, ht. 5¼in. **$110**

108 **Clear Bottle** w/floral dec., ht. 4⅝in. **$247**

109 **Enameled Glass Tumbler** w/enamel dec. of a bird perched on stump & floral surrounded by floral dec., ht. 3in. **$77**

A-PA
Conestoga Auction Company, Inc.
69 **Cobalt Blue Half-post Bottle** w/polychrome enamel floral dec., ht. 5½in. **$300**

A-PA
Conestoga Auction Company, Inc.
74 **Cobalt Blue Half-post Bottle** w/poly.dec. & fitted pewter top, ht. 5½in. **$200**

A-PA
Conestoga Auction Company, Inc.
98 **Two Clear Bottles** w/poly.dec., both missing pewter caps & small areas of enamel, ht. 6 & 4¼in. **$100**

A-PA
Conestoga Auction Company, Inc.
79 **White Half-post Bottle** w/poly.enamel floral dec. as well as a bird on the opposite side w/fitted top, minor enamel loss & missing cap, ht. 7in. **$100**

A-VA   Green Valley Auctions, Inc.

1504 **Facet-Cut Double Scent Bottle,** cased teal green, hinged in center, hinged & screw caps, no hallmarks, ca.1860-1890, ht. 5¼in. **$253**

1505 **Facet-Cut Double Scent Bottle,** cased ruby, hinged & screw repoussé silver caps w/interior stopper, ca.1860-1890, ht. 4in. **$176**

1506 **Panel-Cut Scent Bottle,** cased ruby w/hinged brass cap & orig. stopper, ca.1860-1890, w/imper. , ht. 4⅛in. **$55**

1507 **Concave-Cut Scent Bottle,** deep cobalt blue w/traces of gilt dec.& hinged brass cap set w/blue jewel, ca.1860-1890, imper., ht. 4½in. **$198**

Opposite
A-MA   Skinner, Inc.

536 **Ship In Bottle Wharf Scene,** early 20th C. depicting a rigged three-masted brig, mounted on a painted molded putty sea w/backdrop of houses, bridge, church & lighthouse w/Am. flag. lg. 13in. **$205**

537 **Three Ships Bottles,** Am. & Spain, late 19th/early 20th C. One w/two-masted schooner flying a Spanish flag; a four-masted bark w/sails & rigging flying an Am. flag & a three-masted bark w/rigging on a molded putty sea

w/backdrop, lg. 8, 8 & 10in. **$353**

538 **Carved & Painted Ship in a light-bulb,** early 20th C., w/three-masted vessel mounted on a putty sea w/backdrop depicting a lighthouse, cottage, deck steamer w/funnel floats nearby, lg. 7¾in. **$206**

539 **Carved & Painted Ship in Bottle,** early 20th C. depicting a three-masted brig w/rigging on molded putty sea before an island w/carved & painted house, church, lighthouse & trees, w/imper., lg. 12¼in. **$235**

540 **Carved Wooden Ship in Bottle,** a

three-masted vessel w/rigging flying Am. flag, lg. 12¼in. **$646**

541 **Five-Masted Ship,** probably France, late 19th C. w/painted gun ports & smokestack, lg. 12¾in. **$646**

542 **Wharf Scene in a Bottle,** early 20th C, depicting a rigged three-masted ship flanked by a double-decker steamer w/backdrop of houses, church & lighthouse, lg. 13in. **$235**

543 **Four-masted Ship in Bottle** w/sails & rigging flying an Am. flag w/backdrop of houses on a hillside in a gallon-size bottle, lg. 11¼in. **$382**

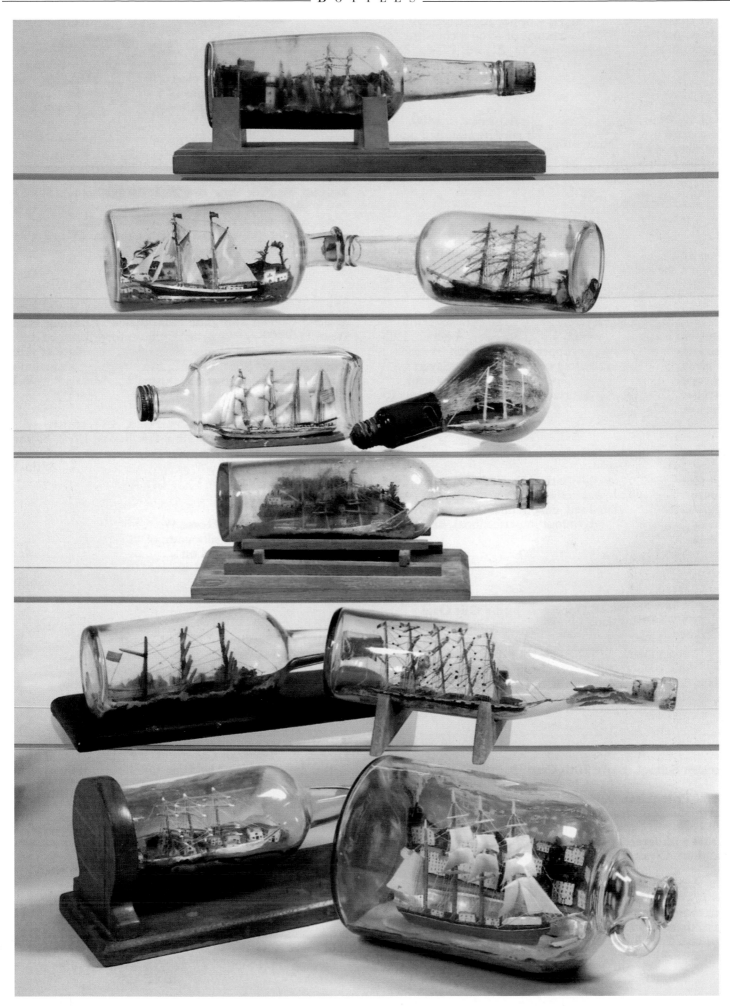

BOXES

Boxes are fascinating collectibles. They come in a variety of shapes, sizes and materials, and have been used for various purposes throughout our recorded history. Finding two early examples exactly alike is almost an impossibility, except for those that were made on molds or in wood factories during the 1800s.

Wooden boxes are favorites of the country collector. Woods used for making these containers are generally pine, birch, maple, ash or beech. For assembling the earliest boxes, short wooden pegs were used to fasten the bottom to the side and top to the rim. Later examples were fastened with copper or iron nails. Round boxes were the most common shape. These were used in pantries and in kitchens for storage, and rarely decorated.

Spice boxes – metal or wooden – are especially favored by collectors, in addition to candleboxes with their sliding covers, salt, pipe, sewing, writing, trinket, and interesting Bible boxes, oftentimes embellished with carving.

Bright and delightfully colorful boxes became popular during the late 1800s. These were common in the Pennsylvania German areas. The interesting band box, oftentimes covered with colorful printed papers depicting well-known sights or historical events, has remained popular. Band boxes were used for storage as well as transporting clothing and personal effects.

Many boxes used in American homes were not originally of American manufacture. Before and after the Revolution, many commercially produced items were imported in exchange for domestic goods sent overseas. Among the 18th and early 19th centuries imports were snuffboxes made of china, silver, tortoiseshell, tin, papier-mâché and leather. Decorative Battersea enamel patch boxes were advertised during the 1760s. Elegant mahogany knife boxes became popular in England during the George III period (ca.1765), and are still available but very pricey. From the late 18th and early 19th centuries, a period without equal in the history of tea caddies, many rare and exciting examples were made in a wide range of shapes, sizes and decorative finishes. During the last decade, tea caddies made in England and Germany in the form of fruits and vegetables during the second half of the 18th century have literally set auction records. This may aptly be referred to as "The Golden Age of the Tea Caddy".

A-PA   Conestoga Auction Company, Inc.
617 Slide Lid Candlebox w/chip carved edge, carved finger notch & dov. const., ht. 4¼, wd. 14⅜in. **$247**
618 Walnut Slide Lid Candlebox w/chamfered lid, dov. const. & carved finger notch, ht. 3⅜, wd. 11¾in. **$104**

A-NH   Northeast Auctions
854 Regency Figured Cutlery Urns, early 19th C., mah. w/dome cover & fully fitted int., ht. 26in. **$5,000**

A-MA   Skinner, Inc.
322 Candlebox, fan carved & paint dec., late 18th C., Am. fans painted olive green on a creamy white painted ground w/salmon-painted scrollwork, ht. 15½, wd. 12in. **$9,400**

A-PA   Freeman's
638 George III Inlaid Knife Boxes, mah., ca.1780, w/fan motifs & ogee bracket feet, ht. 14in. **$5,975**

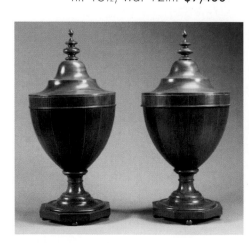

A-NH
Northeast Auctions
835 George III Inlaid Knife Urns, mah., each w/line inlay, int. fitted for flatware & raised on an octagonal base, ht. 27¼in. **$4,500**

A-PA   Pook & Pook, Inc.
671 **Poplar Candlebox,** PA, painted, initialed E + RW, &
dated 1854, ht. 5½, wd. 5½, lg. 9in. **$12,870**

A-PA   Conestoga Auction Company, Inc.
169 **Lift-lid Sewing or Tape Box** w/heart in handle &
sponge dec., PA, ht. 9, lg. 10¼in. **$7,700**

A-PA   Pook & Pook, Inc.
636 **Sailor's Shellwork Valentine,** 19th C.,
w/flowers & heart dec., closed, 10in. sq.
$6,435

A-OH
        Garth's Arts
        & Antiques
102 **Pipe
Box,** walnut
w/pine
secondary,
square nails,
double tiered
w/cutout
slides, single
drawer
w/orig.
brass pull &
red wash.
Minor wear
& scorch
mark, ht.
20⅜in.
$5,750

A-PA   Alderfer's Fine Art & Antiques
1122 **Chinese Treenware Tea Caddy,** eggplant form w/screw-off lid, calligraphy
inscriptions & repair to lid. Late 18th or
early 19th C., ht. 5¾in. **$690**

A-OH   Garth's Arts & Antiques
151 **Pipe Box,** cherry w/orig. finish, pull
and dov. drawer, ht. 18½in. **$8,050**

BOXES

A-PA
Conestoga Auction Company, Inc.**170 Dome-top Box**, bird's eye maple w/red highlights & hearts, dov., ca.1800, orig. hdw., brass pull on top & wooden pins, ht. 6, lg. 10in. **$880**
171 Dome-top Box in orig. painted dec.,dated 1763, PA, Moravian, ht. 5¼, lg. 11¾in. **$5,500**

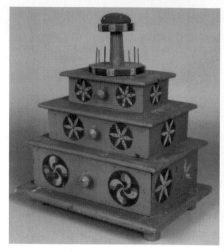

A-PA   Conestoga Auction Company, Inc.
168 Sewing Box, 19th C., in the form of miniature chest-of-drawers w/inlay initials N.H., hearts, flowers & stars. An inscription on bottom of drawer indicates the chest belonged to Nancy Hanks, mother of Abraham Lincoln, 15½in. sq., ht. 9in. **$825**

A-PA Conestoga Auction Company, Inc.
176 Sewing Stand w/tiered drawers & splashy paint dec. Sgn. Roanoke (VA) on one drawer bottom. Pin cushion at top restored, ht. 19, lg. 15, dp. 11in. **$2,530**

A-PA   Conestoga Auction Company, Inc.
183 Sewing Box, PA, mixed woods w/painted dec. & repr. to left ea., ht. 11¾, wd. 6in. **$495**

A-PA   Freeman's
1338 Miniature Pine Chest, green ground & dec. w/flowers & pin-striping, ht. 6¼, wd. 9, dp. 6¼in. **$1,075**
1339 Incised & Decorated Candlebox, PA, 19th C. The raised panel on lid & sides dec. w/stylised tulip-filled urns in red, green & black dots, ht. 5, lg. 14½in. **$2,509**
1340 Document Box, painted black & dec. w/yellow, red & green swags & tassels, ht. 5½, lg. 11¾in. **$2,390**
1341 Pine Candlebox, PA, ca.1840, painted green, white & red w/potted tulips, paisley corners & molded base, ht. 6½, lg. 12¼, wd. 9½in. w/provenance, **$4,825**
1343 Painted & Decorated Bucher Box, PA, dec. w/tulips & inscribed M. Schemel, ht. 2⅜, wd. 8in. **$4,481**

A-PA   Conestoga Auction Company, Inc.
185 **Fruitwood Cutlery Box** in orig. soft-green paint, 19th C., ht. 6½, lg. 7½in. **$165**

A-OH   Garth's Arts & Antiques
482 **Dome-top Box**, pine w/orig. vinegar grained paint in red & yellow to resemble flame grain mah. Brass ring handle, ht. 7¼, wd. 13in. **$575**

A-PA   Conestoga Auction Company, Inc.
630 **Dough Box**, poplar w/old red painted surface & cutout heart handles, lg. 30, wd. 14in. **$880**

A-PA   Freeman's
568 **New England Sewing Box**, early 19th C., mah. w/inlaid lid of exotic wood triangles & swing handle, fitted w/lift lid, ht. 7, wd. 11½, dp. 9in. **$1,350**

A-MA   Skinner, Inc.
682 **Regency Tortoiseshell Veneered Tea Caddy**, early 19th C., panels separated by silver fillets, the sides of body w/brass lion mask pendant handles & on paw feet. Int. fitted w/colorless glass mixing bowl set between two lidded wells, ht. 7⅜, wd. 13¼, dp. 6⅜in. **$4,994**

A-PA   Conestoga Auction Company, Inc.
626 **Hanging Spice Box** w/dry scraped green paint & open shelf, ht. 21½in. **$797**
627 **Wall Box** w/ relief carving of floral & foliate dec., ht. 9⅝in., wd. 11¼in. **$55**
628 **Mechanical Counter Box** w/painted dec, stenciled on end Manufactured by C.L. Nesmith, Washington, Ill. Metal handle activates internal iron wheels, ht. 4¾, wd. 5¼in. **$412**
629 **Softwood Wall Box** w/old surface & initialed on backboard E.J.N. 1894, ht. 12½in. **$275**

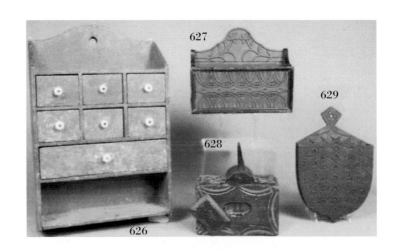

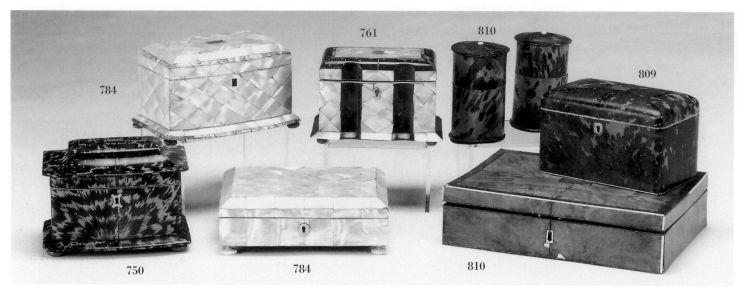

A-PA   Freeman's
Tea Caddies & Boxes
784 Victorian MOP w/rectangular bow front form, two lidded compartments & raised on bun feet, ht 5, wd. 7½in. Together w/a Victorian MOP bijouterie box, wd. 8in. **$2,151**
761 Regency Tortoiseshell & MOP

Caddy, ca.1820 w/two covered compartments raised on bun feet, ht. 4½, wd. 6in. **$2,032**
810 Rectangular Cross Banded Box w/compartmented int., wd. 11in., together w/a pr. of tortoiseshell cylindrical covered boxes, ht. 5in., & a miniature box. **$1,195**

809 Regency Tortoiseshell tea caddy, ca.1820 w/domed lid opening to reveal two lidded compartments. Bun feet missing, ht. 4½, wd. 7in. **$1,673**
750 Tortoiseshell tea caddy w/hinged pagoda lid enclosing a divided int. w/two lids w/squat bun feet. **$3,107**

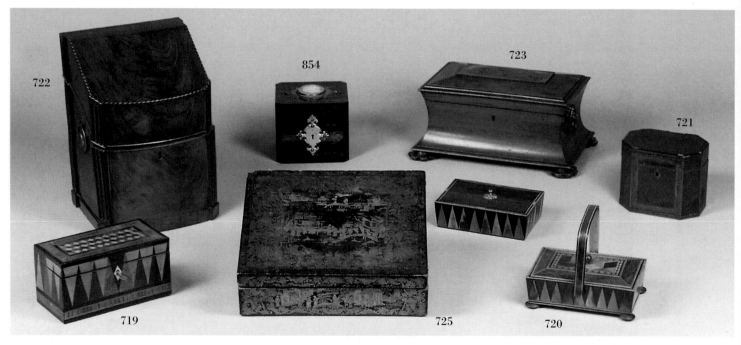

A-MA   Skinner, Inc.
First Row
722 George IV Knife Box w/inlay, mah., early 19th C. w/checker-banded perimeter & fluted pilasters to front corners, fitted int., ht. 13⅜, wd. 9in. **$734**
854 Jasper-mounted Calamander Four-Bottle Scent Box, late 19th C., the lid set w/a blue & white jasper plaque of cupid & swan, metal escutcheon & fitted velvet-lined int. w/four colorless cut glass bottles w/lids & stoppers, ht. 3⅜, wd 5in. **$529**

723 Regency-style Tea Caddy, late 19th C., w/side pendant lion mask handles, on platform flattened feet & fitted int. w/two lidded wells & well for mixing bowl, ht. 7, wd. 13in. **$1,203**
Second Row
719 Georgian-style Parquetry Inlaid Tea Caddy, late 19th/ early 20th C.,w/specimen wood diamond inlay to lid & inlay to three sides. Int. fitted w/two foil-lined wells w/inlaid lids, ht. 4⅛, wd. 7in. **$411**
725 Chinese Lacquer Game Box, late 18th/early 19th C., gilt dec.

throughout w/figures. Int. w/four removable boxes, all with dec. lids w/central monograms, enclosing group of engraved MOP loo counters, box 12⅛ x 10in. **$411**
720 Two Georgian-style Parquetry Inlaid Work Boxes, late 19th/early 20th C., one w/swing handle & velveteen lined int., wd. 7¼in., together w/plain flat lid box w/gilt-metal finial & small MOP inlay panels, wd. 7in. **$705**
721 George III Tea Caddy, mah. w/inlay & two foil-lined compartments, ht. 5⅛, wd. 6in. **$382**

A-SC   **Charlton Hall Galleries, Inc.**

011 English Inlaid Satinwood Tea Caddy, octagonal paneled form w/ovals of flowers & hinged lid over fitted int., ht. 4¾, wd. 5¼in. **$200**

012 English Rosewood Brass-bound Letter Box, late 19th C., fabric lined w/etched brass ornaments & hinged dome cover, ht. 3⅜, lg. 9in. **$200**

013 English Brass & Ivory Bound Gentleman's Box, ca.1900 w/burl wood case, w/some losses to ivory & brass, ht. 4½, wd. 10¼n. **$275**

014 English Inlaid Tea Caddy, 19th C., mah. w/hinged lid & canted corners, ht. 4¾, wd. 7¼in. **$225**

A-SC   **Charlton Hall Galleries, Inc.**

009 Victorian Tea Caddy, octagonal paneled form w/ovals of flowers, hinged lid & fitted int., ht. 4¾, wd. 5¼in. **$200**

010 English Rosewood Dressing Box w/fitted int., lift-out trays & silver mounts, ht. 8¼, wd. 15¼in. **$800**

A-SC   **Charlton Hall Galleries, Inc.**

015 Victorian Tea Caddy dec. w/inlaid MOP. & tortoiseshell, 19th/early 20th C. w/hinged top concealing double lidded int. compartments & round ivory feet, ht. 6⅝, wd. 7½in. **$1,300**

A-PA   **Pook & Pook, Inc.**

623 Pair of English Knife Boxes, ca.1790, mah. w/serpentine fronts, fitted int., silver mounts & bookend inlays, ht. 14⅛, wd. 9½, dia. 11⅛in. **$5,520**

A-PA   **Pook & Pook, Inc.**

First Row

583 Three Georgian Enamel Pill Boxes, length of each approx. 2in. **$497**

Second Row

584 Three Oval Enamel Pill Boxes, one inscribed Washington, dia. 1⅜in., the second inscribed Amans Fidelle, dia. 2in. & the third Keep this for my sake, dia. 1½in. **$936**

Third Row

585 Three Georgian Enamel Pill Boxes, the first dia. 1¾in., the second inscribed A friends gift, dia. 1⅞in., & the third inscribed Love for Love, dia. ¾in. **$761**

The earliest clocks came to America with the first settlers. At that point in our history, a clock had more prestige than practical value because time meant very little to the colonist who spent his daylight hours building a homestead or tilling the soil.

Over the years, America has added its fair share of illustrious names to the world's great clockmakers. Some craftsmen were working here as early as the 17th century and, during the 18th century, every colony had a clockmaker. It took months to produce a single clock because each of its innumerable parts was carefully made by hand.

The two main district communities producing clocks during the 18th century were Philadelphia and Boston. The early craftsmen – English, Dutch and German descendants – followed the traditional styles they had learned while apprentices; therefore, at first sight it was oftentimes difficult to distinguish the colonial tall-case clock from its progenitor in Europe. But, with the passage of time, American clockmakers developed their own recognizable styles. They chose for their cases the finest of hardwoods – walnut, mahogany and cherry preferred, with satinwood and other exotic hardwoods used.

Clocks did not become common in American homes until after the 1800s. Their manufacture in quantity began in 1840, fathered by Chauncey Jerome, a Waterbury clockmaker. His new methods of manufacture quickly replaced wooden movements with rugged interchangeable brass-geared works which eventually led to mass production. Surviving examples of the early tall case clocks, wall and shelf in addition to watches, are very collectible these days… and those in fine original condition and in good running order are very much in demand.

A-MA   **Skinner, Inc.**
62 Cherry Tall Case Clock w/inlay, probably MA, ca.1800 w/poly. & gilt iron dial showing three sailing ships in the arch, weight movement, rest. & ref., ht. 92¾in. **$9,988**

A-PA
Alderfer's Fine Art & Antiques
1438 Walnut Tall Case Clock, sgn. Peter Stretch Philadelphia, eight-day, ca. early 18th C., ht. 92in. **$19,550**

A-NH   **Northeast Auctions**
700 Federal Cherry Clock w/brass works, attrib. to workshop of Abel Hutchins, w/painted enamel face & calendar dial, ht. 93in. **$6,500**

A-NH   **Northeast Auctions**
288 Chippendale Clock by William Cummens w/mah. case, scalloped bracket feet, brass works & enameled dial w/floral spandrels, ht. 85in. **$18,000**

A-PA   Pook & Pook, Inc.
158 **Acorn Clock**, CT, ca.1840, mah., by Forestville w/white painted face over eglomisé panel of landscape, ht. 24½in. $18,720

A-PA   Pook & Pook,Inc.
703 **George III Clock**, mah. case, ca.1800, 8-day musical works, ht. 95¾in. **$8,775**
704 **George III Clock**, mah. case, late 18th C. w/brass musical 8-day works, sgn. Jane Pepper Biggles Wade, w/overall marquetry & bellflower chain inlay, ht. 101in. **$11,700**

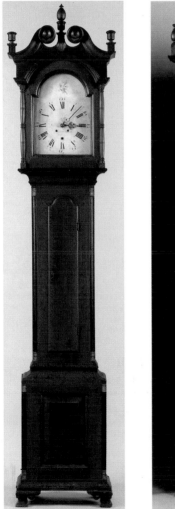

A-PA
        Pook & Pook, Inc.
125 **Bucks Co. PA Chippendale Clock**, ca.1780, walnut w/painted face inscr. Benjamin Morris & retains its orig. finish, ht. 94in. **$8,775**

A-PA Pook & Pook, Inc.
518 **PA Chippendale clock**, walnut, ca.1805, 30 hour works, sgn. Solomon Yeakle, ht. 95in. **$7,020**

A-PA
        Pook & Pook, Inc.
89 **New Jersey Tall Case Clock**, ca.1795, mah. case, attrib. to Matthew Egerton Jr., 8-day works w/painted face & moon phase, ht. 96½in. **$28,000**

A-PA   Freeman's
817 **Regency Tortoiseshell Bracket Clock** ca.1820, sgn. Levy, Birmingham, ht. 27, wd. 16, dp. 11½in. **$4,183**

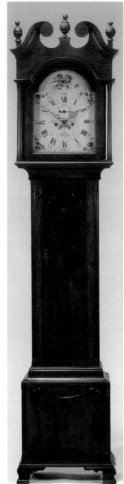

A-PA   **Freeman's**
178   **Federal Clock by John Hall**, Phil., ca.1806 w/painted face, displaying phases of the moon & Arabic numerals, ht. 94¼in. **$6,573**

A-PA   **Freeman's**
203   **Cherry Tall Case Clock** by Thomas Norton, Phil., ca.1800 w/ Roman & Arabic numerals. **$14,340**

A-PA   **Freeman's**
204   **Late Federal Clock**, cherry, ca.1815 w/Arabic numeral chapter ring & phases of the moon. **$3,346**

A-PA   **Pook & Pook, Inc.**
899   **Chippendale Tall Case Clock**, PA, ca.1790, applewood, 8-day works w/ painted dial inscr. Thom Lindsey, Frankford, ht. 97in. **$10,530**

A-NH   **Northeast Auctions**
938   **English Bracket Clock**, mah. w/two chapter rings inscr. Slow/Fast & Chime On Eight Bells/Westminster On Gongs, ht. 16½in. **$400**

A-PA   **Freeman's**
1508   **PA Tall Case Clock**, early 19th C., w/painted face & line inlay, ht. 97½in. **$16,730**
1509   **Federal Clock**, ca.1800, mah. w/bellflower inlays & painted face, ht. 98in. **$15,535**
1510   **PA Cherry Tall Case Clock**, early 19th C., painted face, phases of the moon & pencil line inlay, ht. 96¼in. **$8,962**

A-PA

Alderfer's Fine Art & Antiques
1174 French Brass Carriage Clock w/silvered top dial for Raumur/Fahrenheit thermometer w/curved mercury tube. The barrel movement w/strike on gong & pierced flower at back stamped Made in France 2629, ca.1890, ht. 10½in. to top of handle. **$2,875**

A-OH

Garth's Arts & Antiques
645 Federal Pillar & Scroll Mantel Clock, mah. & mah. veneer w/old finish. Face w/floral spandrels, & reverse painted glass panel of George Washington mounted on horse overlooking the red-coats across the river. Minor flaking on glass panel, some repr. to base, key, weights & pendulum orig., ht. 32in. **$13,800**

A-NH   Northeast Auctions
937 English Table Clock w/gilt-metal Westminster chimes w/ tulip finials, ht. 26in. **$2,200**

A-OH   Garth's Arts & Antiques
315 Arts & Crafts Tall Case Clock, oak w/beveled glass panels & convex dial lens. Brass works mkd. Gustav Becker, Freiburg, and chimes behind dial mkd. Harfen-Gong, GV,DRP, ht. 84½in. **$747**

207

208

209

210

211

212

213

A-IA   Jackson's International Auctioneers
207 German Oak Wall Clock, 19th C. w/butterfly pendulum, ht. 30in. **$381**
208 Shelf Clock by Seth Thomas, walnut w/alarm & gilt dec. door, ht. 22in. **$176**

209 Waterbury Walnut Shelf Clock w/alarm & silvered enameled door, ht. 20in. **$117**
210 Waterbury Walnut Calendar Clock w/two dials, ht. 23in. **$499**
211 Mantel Clock by Waterbury, ca.1900 in cherrywood case, ht.

12in. **$82**
212 German Mantel Clock, early 20th C. in wooden case, ht. 10in. **$35**
213 Seth Thomas Mantel Clock, ca.1900 w/burled finish & Sonora chimes, ht. 14in. **$323**

858 English Wheel Barometer, mah. w/various measuring tubes & dials w/mirror & ebonised borders, ht. 39in. **$300**

859 English Stick Barometer by F. Amadio & Son, ca.1829-44 w/brass finial above the concealed tube & bone plates, string-inlaid throat & circular cistern cover, ht. 38½in. **$2,200**

860 English Wheel Barometer, mah. by Gobbi, Liverpool, ht. 37in. **$500**

861 George III Wheel Barometer, sgn. P & P Gally, Ltd. London, w/a hygrometer, silvered rondel thermometer, barometer & level, mah., ht. 38½in. **$900**

7 Silver & Gold Pocket Watch sgn. John Carrell, Phil., late 18th C. w/English silver cases & key. **$1,300**

1032 Brass & Glass Carriage Clock, Waterbury Clock Co., w/time & strike, together w/a French brass carriage clock, hts. 4½ & 4¼in. **$200**

1033 French Brass & Crystal Regulator Clock w/oval case, circular dial painted w/floral swags, ht. 10in. **$300**

1034 English Brass & Glass Carriage Clock, Quincy, ht. 4½in. **$200**

1035 Miniature Carriage Clock, Waterbury Clock Co., & two brass glass globe timepieces, hts. 3 & 2¼in. **$200**

A-PA   Frank H. Boos Gallery
54 Elgin Yellow Gold Pocket Watch w/inset ruby & inscr. dated 1886. **$779**

A-ME   James D. Julia, Inc.
542 Pillar & Scroll Shelf Clock by Eli & Samuel Terry w/orig. label, key & pendulum. Panel scene may be a repl., small crack & chip in dial, ht. 31¼in. **$1,035**

A-NH   Northeast Auctions
848 English Satinwood Balloon Mantel Clock by Milius of London, ht. 12½in. **$1,000**

A-PA   Pook & Pook, Inc.
Watches
First Row
1186 Pierre Simon Gounouilhou, Geneva, early 19th C. gold repeating pocket watch w/silver engine-turned dial. **$3,450**
1187 Austrian Verge Fusee Triple-case watch, ca.1750, mkd. F.M.S. in Gratz on backplate, tortoiseshell outer case. **$920**
1188 Swiss Paperweight Clock, ca.1900 w/blue enameled moon phase dial & 3 subsidiary dials w/seconds, day & date; together w/a Swiss paperweight clock, ca.1890, & a smaller example w/second dial not illus. **$546**
1189 Swiss or French verge fusee, silver case watch, ca.1790, w/front & reverse side dials, calendar & key. **$1,150**
1190 Duchene & Fils, Geneva watch, gold musical, repeating w/enamel

face. Backplate inscr. Musique, Montre, Silence No. **$2,990**
Second Row
1191 C. Charleson, London, ca.1720, verge fusee, signed, chased silver dial, bull's-eye crystal w/signed movement. **$1,495**
1192 Swiss Automation Nickel Case watch, ca.1900, stem wind & pin set. **$489**
1193 Helmstine, mid/late 18th C., verge fusee pair case pocket watch w/backplate mkd. 3400 Stockholm. The reverse of the outer tortoiseshell case w/China Trade harbor scene. **$920**
1194 Sterling Silver Hunting Case, jump hour & minute watch w/enameled dial, inscr. Patent Automatic Timekeeper. **$489**
Third Row
1195 Gold Quarter-hour Repeating watch, early 19th C. w/enameled face, case mkd. K18. **$840**

1196 Swiss or French verge fusee, silver case watch, ca.1790 w/small dial on chased silver & key wind. **$863**
1197 John Walker, London, ca.1880, w/engraved case inscr. verso London & North Western Railway, together w/brass watchman's clock, J. Burk & a Swiss framed watch w/enamel dial, key wind. **$1,380**
1198 Swiss or French verge fusee, silver case watch, ca.1790, key wind w/advance-retard index & dec. coin silver chain. **$920**
1199 Pieter Klock, Amsterdam, mid/late 18th C., verge fusee silver pair case watch, sgn. w/bull's-eye crystal. **$2,760**
1200 Swiss Repeating Watch, quarter-hour, 19th C. w/enameled dial & sunken subsidiary second dial, stem wind-lever set in worn gold filled case. **$345**

A-PA   Pook & Pook, Inc.

251 Pincushion & Watch Holder, 19th C., w/Gala pocket watch, ht. 5½in. **$556**

252 Watch Hutch w/red stain, 19th C , together w/a pocket watch by American Watch Co., ht. 7in. **$1,287**

A-MA   Skinner, Inc.

264 Classical Carved Mantel Clock, mah.& mah. veneer, ca.1825 w/label reading: Manufactured by Moses Barrett, Amherst, Nova Scotia, wooden dial & thirty-hour wooden movement & imper. ht. 33½in. **$3,173**

265 Federal Pillar & Scroll Mantel Clock, mah., by Ephraim Downes, Bristol, CT, ca.1825, w/thirty-hour wooden weight-driven movement w/rest., ht. 31¾in. **$1,410**

A-PA   Frank H. Boos Gallery

51 Seth Thomas Double Dial Mantel Clock, time-and-strike w/calendar dial & Roman chapters. **$899**

A-MA   Skinner, Inc.

266 Federal Banjo Clock, mah. & eglomisé, ca.1820, w/eight-day brass weight-driven movement & tablet w/grapevine borders & lower tablet shows Lady Liberty, an eagle & shield, w/imper. ht. 30in. **$2,233**

267 Federal Banjo Clock, mah & eglomisé, ca.1820 by Elnathan Taber, Roxbury, MA, dial sgn. w/brass eight-day weight-driven movement & tablet showing a female in chariot, imper. ht. 38in. **$5,288**

268 Federal Banjo Clock, mah. gilt-gesso & eglomisé, ca.1820 w/eight-day brass weight-driven movement; the lower tablet showing a fly-fishing scene, imper.& res., ht. 34¼in. **$1,645**

A-ME   James D. Julia, Inc.
**1192 Jigsaw Worked
Wall Clock** w/fancy
cutout case fitted
w/Waltham movement
& chime, no key, ht. 49,
wd. 14in. **$632**

A-IA
Jackson's International
Auctioneers, Inc.
**860 French Louis XV Style
Desk Clock,** ormolu
mounted & tortoiseshell
case, w/Japy Frères
stamped movement, ht.
18in. **$411**

A-IA   Jackson's International Auctioneers, Inc.
1074 Swiss Black Forest Carved Wood Figural Clock, late
19th C. w/enameled numerals, ht. 24in. **$3,760**

A-IA
Jackson's International Auctioneers, Inc.
857 Austrian Desk Clock, ca.1900 in
rouge marble case w/bronze mounts,

works stamped M&Sohn, ht. 9¾in. **$705**
**858 French Figural Bronze & Marble
Clock,** 19th C. w/marble veneered case
& gilt bronze bezel, ht. 20in. **$499**

**859 Napoleon III Gilt Bronze &
Ebonized Portico Clock,** late 19th C.,
suspended drum case, ht. 20in. **$587**

CLOCKS

A-IA
Jackson's International Auctioneers, Inc.
1075 Game Clock, Swiss Black Forest, carved oak, 19th C., w/enameled Roman numerals, ht. 37in. **$1,880**

A-NJ   Craftsman
416 Mantel Clock w/tiles on each side & top, emb. w/bees & foliage under green glossy glaze. Case made of carved wood w/New Haven Clock Co., works w/ivory enameled face. Complete w/weight & key. Tiles stamped J&J.G.Low Patent, ht. 14¼in. **$4,750**

A-PA   Pook & Pook, Inc.
313 Late Federal Miniature Shelf Clock, ca.1830, inscribed J.D. Custer w/carved lyre-form mah. case & rectangular plinth supported by brass ball & claw feet, ht. 14¾in. **$3,416**

A-PA   Pook & Pook, Inc.
312 Banjo Clock, PA, ca.1835, the face inscribed Joseph Fix Maker, Reading, PA, ht. 39in. **$2,574**

A-MA   Skinner, Inc.
102 Federal Tall Case Clock by Aaron Willard, Boston, ca.1800, mah. w/inlay, poly. & gilt moon-phase dial w/seconds hand & calendar aperture, eight-day brass weight-driven movement & old finish. Imperfections & rest., ht. 92in. **$47,000**
Note: Maker's engraved label affixed to the interior.

DECOYS

Decoys are choice items of collectors and decorators these days. They diligently search for these pieces of floating and sitting sculpture, realizing that many have found their way into antique shops, or are still roosting quietly in old abandoned sheds, waterfront shacks and barns. Floaters are the most popular, followed by shorebird stickups which were never widely made beyond the Atlantic coastal area. In 1918 a Federal law prohibited shooting these diminutive shorebirds; therefore, early stickups are rare. Fish decoys have also become choice collectibles. They are used for ice fishing during the winter months, especially around the Great Lakes.

Many producers of decoys claimed that the most effective decoy was a realistic one, carved and painted to resemble a particular type of bird, while others believed that details didn't really matter; so the difference of opinions resulted in a great variety of decoy styles made from wood, metal, papier mâché, canvas and rubber. Most found today were made during the late 19th and 20th centuries. Wooden and tin decoys were produced by small manufacturers such as the Mason and Dodge factories.

Most professional carvers marked their birds and examples of their work is extremely valuable. Although many decoys are unsigned, carvers can oftentimes be identified by their style, while others will remain anonymous. Serious collectors prefer to collect the early hand-carved varieties which have become very scarce and expensive.

A-ME James D. Julia, Inc.
485K Ward Brothers Redhead Drake, sgn. Lem at a later time, a standard practice, also sgn. LT Ward-Bro. Chrisfield, MD 1929, lg. 16in. **$5,462**

A-ME James D. Julia, Inc.
485L Mason Premiere Mallard Decoy w/glass eyes & orig. paint, lg.18in. **$1,495**

A-PA Conestoga Auction Company, Inc.
11 Golden Eye Drake by Lebouf, Quebec, w/old working repaint, lg. 13¼in. **$176**

A-PA Pook & Pook, Inc.
First Row
801 Carved & Painted Mallard Drake mid-20th C., mkd. Madison Mitchell, lg. 17½in., together w/two carved & painted canvas-back decoys, the hen mkd. Paul Gibson Havre de Grace, made in Maryland, lg. 14 & 16in. **$633**
Second Row
802 Two Canvas-back Decoys, mid-20th C., lg. of drake 18½, hen 18in.; together w/a small carved painted winged surf scooter, lg. 13in. **$633**
Third Row
803 Two Canvas-back Decoys, mid-20th C., lg. 18½ & 16½in. **$748**
Fourth Row
804 Carved & Painted Canada Goose, mid-20th C., stamped Pete #276, lg. 21in. **$316**
805 Canada Goose, mid-20th C., ht. 15, wd. 22in. **$345**

A-PA   Conestoga Auction Company, Inc.
9 **Brant Duck Decoy** attrib. to Barneget Bay, NH, hollow body w/old working repaint, lg. 16¼in. **$154**
10 **Black Duck,** attrib. to NJ, hollow body const. w/orig. paint & neck crack, lg.15¼in. **$93**

A-PA   Conestoga Auction Company, Inc.
26 **Susquehanna River Canvas-back Drake,** working repaint, ca.1930, lg. 17½in. **$176**

A-PA   Conestoga Auction Company, Inc.
16 **Bluebill Drake Decoy,** attrib. to Ira Hudson, w/old working repaint & tack eye. Small chip to tail, lg. 13¾in. **$110**

A-PA   Conestoga Auction Company, Inc.
42 **Canvas-back Drake,** Susquehanna River w/working repaint, lg. 15½in. **$154**
43 **Canvas-back Hen,** attrib. to Michigan, branded LR, lg. 17¾in. **$49**
44 **Redhead Drake Decoy** w/factory working repaint, lg. 13¼in. **$132**

A-PA
Conestoga Auction Company, Inc.
25 **Early Shorebird,** attrib. to NJ, worn orig. paint, ca.1910, ht. 10in. **$522**

A-PA
Conestoga Auction Company, Inc.
49 **Pintail Drake,** signed on base 1948 Lem & Steve Ward, repainted 1972 by Lem, lg. 16¾in. **$2,530**

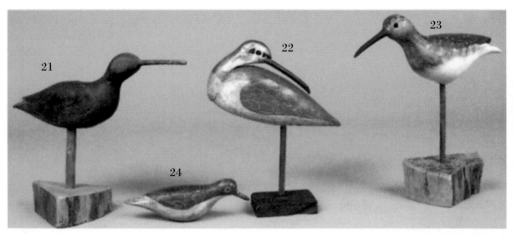

A-PA   Conestoga Auction Company, Inc.
21 **Shorebird,** unknown w/wood inserted bill & loss to wood at wing tips, ht. 12in. **$99**
22 **Curlew Shorebird** w/orig. paint & crack at neck, cont., ht. 8in. **$27**
23 **Dowitcher Decoy** w/orig. paint, cont., ht. 11in. **$66**
24 **Peep Yellow Legs Shorebird Decoy** w/orig. paint & carved wing detail, ht. 7in. **$660**

A-PA   Conestoga Auction Company, Inc.
87 **Blue Wing Teal Drake,** Mason Detroit Grade w/old working paint touch-up, lg. 11in. **$2,090**

A-PA   Conestoga Auction Company, Inc.
86 **Black Duck,** Mason Detroit Grade, stamped Mackey Collection on bottom, lg. 15½in. **$407**

A-PA   Conestoga Auction Company, Inc.
60 **Bluebill Duck** attrib. to Ira Hudson, w/working repaint & split in body, lg. 13¼in. **$412**

A-PA   Conestoga Auction Company, Inc.
50 **Canada Goose,** sgn. on base made by Steve Ward 1931 & repainted by Lem 1971, lg. 26½in. **$1,650**

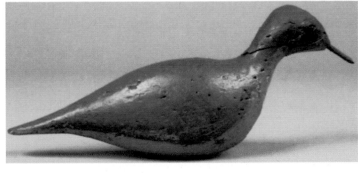

A-PA   Conestoga Auction Company, Inc.
118 **Shorebird,** branded Accomack Gun Club, VA, w/old working repaint, reprs. lg. 8¾in. **$302**

A-PA   Conestoga Auction Company, Inc.
204 **Canvas-back Drake** attrib. to Ira Hudson, w/remains of orig. paint, split on underside of body & crack in neck, lg. 16in. **$1,320**

A-PA   Conestoga Auction Company, Inc.
169 **Canada Goose,** sgn. on bottom Ward Brothers, Crisfield, MD, 1936 w/old working repaint & minor neck filler loss, lg. 23½in. **$8,800**

A-PA   Conestoga Auction Company, Inc.
205 **Pintail Duck Decoy** w/old repaint, lg. 18½in. **$302**
206 **Merganser Duck Decoy,** unknown w/old working repaint, lg. 19in. **$203**

A-PA

Conestoga Auction Company, Inc.

A-PA

Conestoga Auction Company, Inc.

114 **Shorebird Decoy** attrib. to Eastern Shore of VA, w/minor shot damage, ca.1890s, lg. 10¼in. **$962**

110 **Folk Art Shorebird Decoy** w/old working repaint, mounted to driftwood, lg. 9½in. **$82**

111 **Plover Shorebird**, attrib. to Stevens Decoy Co., w/old working repaint & mounted to wood block, lg. 10½in. **$187**

112 **Shorebird**, unknown w/old working repaint & repl. bill, lg. 10½in. **$11**

113 **Black Belly Plover Shorebird** w/old working repaint & repl. bill, lg. 10¾in. **$357**

A-PA   Conestoga Auction Company, Inc.

45 **Canvas-back Duck** attrib. to Jess Urie w/working repaint, lg. 14¼in. **$77**

46 **Black Duck,** unknown, canvas over wood frame w/wood head & tack eyes, w/working repaint, lg. 14¼in. **$66**

47 **Canvas-back Duck,** attrib. to Wildfowler w/balsa body & paint loss, lg. 15in. **$44**

48 **Merganser Duck,** cont. by unknown maker & orig. paint, lg 14in. **$55**

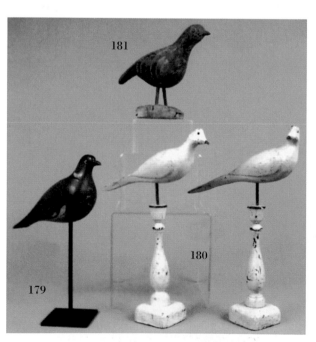

A-PA   Conestoga Auction Company, Inc.

179 **Pigeon Decoy** w/orig.paint, mounted to steel stand, lg. 12in. **$104**

180 **Dove Decoys,** pr., branded BBD w/orig. paint & mounted to baluster turned stands, overall ht. 16¾in. **$110**

181 **Quail Carving** w/orig. paint & mounted to wood block, lg. 9¾in. **$132**

A-PA   Conestoga Auction Company, Inc.

182 **Shorebird** attrib. to Eastern Shore of VA, w/traces of orig. paint, lg. 8½in. **$1,100**

186 **Robin Snipe Shorebird** w/old working repaint & shot damage, lg. 7¾in. **$880**

A-PA   Conestoga Auction Company, Inc.
194A **Large Swan Decoy** branded SW w/orig.
paint, lg. 37in. **$660**

A-PA   Conestoga Auction Company, Inc.
208 **Bluebill Hen Decoy** sgn. R. Madison Mitchell, Havre-de-
Grace, MD, 1962, w/orig. paint & minor shot damage, lg.
13¾in. **$275**

A-PA   Freeman's
207 **Carved & Painted Whistler Golden Eye Decoy,**
early 20th C. w/carved bill leather rig strap & lead
weights, inscribed Frank Parker Barnegat, lg.
12½in. **$1,100**

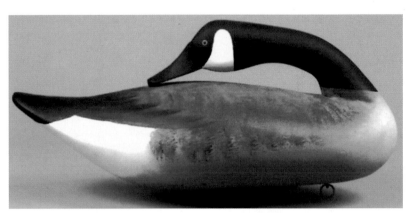

A-PA   Conestoga Auction Company, Inc.
174 **Canada Goose Decoy,** sleeper, attrib. to R. Madison Mitchell
w/orig. paint, 21¾in. **$962**

A-PA   Freeman's
Fish Decoys
309 **Four Painted & Carved Decoys,** 20th C,
variously painted w/tin fins, two w/glass eyes &
one sgn. J. Bingaman '98, lg. 6½ to 8½in. **$650**
310 **Two Patriotic Carved & Painted Decoys,** 20th
C., each painted red, white and blue w/tin fins &
one w/glass eyes, lg. 10½ & 7½in. **$325**

A-NH   Northeast Auctions
443 **Pair of Redhead Decoys** by H. Keyes, each w/glass eyes &
circular weight on underside, lg. 14½in. **$3,480**
444 **Merganser Hen Decoy** w/carved feet, painted eyes &
applied carved & painted legs, probably Wacquoit, MA, lg.
16¼in. **$1,160**
445 **Two Keyes Decoys,** a widgeon & a blue bill, Martha's
Vineyard, each w/glass eyes & circular weight, approx. lg. 15in.
$2,436

Dolls come in an incredible variety ranging from the exquisitely dressed French fashion dolls to the fine German bisque dolls made in Meissen, Germany, to humble American folk dolls. Only in recent years have collectors' tastes broadened to include these charming old whimsical dolls which have a timeless quality.

Most dolls sold in America from 1900 to 1910 came from Europe. The First World War practically halted the production of French and German dolls and again during the Second World War dollmaking was disrupted. It wasn't until 1949 that a breakthrough invigorated the doll industry with the invention of hard plastic which quickly solved many problems that had plagued dollmakers. By the 1950s the introduction of soft vinyl resulted in the production of even more realistic dolls.

Modern and vintage dolls, like many toys these days, are throwbacks to dolls made years ago. Trends have a tendency to become fashionable again, only to lose their popularity after a few years and then reappear years later, different but reminiscent of the originals. An example would be cloth advertising dolls that became popular during the early 1900s.

Dolls delight children, but they serve primarily as a very gentle friend on whom they can project their fantasies and to whom they can turn in times of adversity. Today these childhood memories literally set records at auctions across America. Pristine condition contributes significantly to their value.

The earliest doll-houses were made in Germany and Holland. American doll-houses date from the late 1800s and were generally modeled after popular contemporary styles of architecture. The invention of lithography during the mid-19th century supplied manufacturers of doll-houses with an inexpensive means of mass-producing these toys. The R. Bliss Manufacturing Co., Pawtucket, RI, became a major manufacturer round 1904, and the Morton E. Converse Co, Winchendon, MA, one of America's largest manufacturers of toys during the early 1900s, produced a few doll-houses which appeared in the company's 1913 catalog. During the late 1920s A. Schoenhut & Co., Philadelphia, offered an array of colorful doll-houses in various styles and sizes, all of which are prized collectibles these days.

A-ME   James D. Julia, Inc.
107 **German Handwerck Halbig Doll** w/fully jointed body, redressed & wearing blond synthetic wig., ht. 33in. **$805**

A-ME   James D. Julia, Inc.
105 **Simon & Halbig Dressel Doll** w/orig. fully jointed body, antique outfit & brown human hair wig w/bangs, ht. 28½in. **$690**

A-ME   James D. Julia, Inc.
104 **Kestner Shoulder Head Doll** w/ jointed leather body & bisque forearms, orig. clothing & repl. human hair wig w/ coiled braids at side, ht. 16½in. **$287**

Opposite
A-MA   Skinner, Inc.
First Row
596 **Roullet et Decamps Clockwork Walking Doll** w/bisque head mkd. Simon & Halbig, 1078, Germany, S&H w/jointed papier-mâché body, straight legs, voice box & clockwork mechanism in torso, lacking stop/start rod & stringing loose, ht. 23in. **$1,500**
624 **Tête Jumeau Closed Mouth Doll, Paris,** ca.1886 w/paperweight eyes, blond human hair wig, composition body & period undergarments, later taffeta dress & worn shoes, ht. 22in. **$4,583**
Second Row
694 **Bisque Head E.D. Bébé,** Paris,

ca.1880s, light speckling in bisque, straight limb comp. body w/human hair wig, brown cotton dress w/lace trim, att. to Etienne Denamur & imp. mark E7D Deposé, ht. 17½in. **$2,350**
700 **Small Tête Jumeau Bisque Head Bébé,** Paris, ca.1880s, w/orig. blond wig, cork pate, fully articulated comp. body in orig. finish w/ecru wool challis dress, red stockings & brown leather shoes, ht. 14½in. **$2,115**
702 **Tête Jumeau Bisque Head Bébé,** Paris, ca.1880s w/old breaks on forehead repainted, comp. body w/cotton undergarments & newer dress w/pink cotton stockings w/orig. brown leather shoes mkd. #9 Bébé Jumeau Deposé, ht. 20½in. **$1,645**

Third Row
703 **Tête Jumeau Bébé,** Paris, ca.1880s w/red stamp, cork pate, repl. brown wig, comp. body, light wear to joints, newer pink lace-trimmed silky dress & oval paper label Bébé Jumeau Diplome d'Honneur, ht. 16½in. **$1,763**
845 **Small Size 1 Tête Jumeau Doll,** Paris, ca.1880s, professional rest., w/fully articulated comp. & wood body in orig. finish w/blue stamp on back, white cotton chemise, possibly orig., ht. 9¼in. **$3,525**
829 **Bisque Head Bébé** w/cup & saucer neck att. to Schmitt, France, ca.1880s, unmarked jointed comp. body w/substantial repr. & limbs do not match, ht. 16in. **n/s**

A-MA   Skinner, Inc.

843 **English Wax Doll** w/stationary eyes, ca.1870s, blond wig & orig. cotton undergarments & patriotic gown, ht. 16in. **$1,116**

844 **French Bisque Swivel-neck Lady Doll,** ca.1870s w/human hair wig, period dress w/some deterioration, ht. 15¼in. **$1,528**

905 **Early Brown Mohair Steiff Bear on Wheels,** excelsior stuffed w/black shoebutton eyes, stitched nose w/some damage, no button & on metal wheel frame, ht. 8, lg. 10½in. **$940**

A-MA   Skinner, Inc.

832 **Kestner Bisque Head Doll** w/comp. lady body, Germany, ca.1900, mkd. H Made in Germany w/orig.blond mohair wig, articulated comp. body & white leather flat shoes, ht. 22in. **$1.410**

838 **Kestner Bisque Lady Body,** 162, mkd. Made in Germany w/brown mohair wig, fully articulated comp. body & black leather shoes, ht. 16in. **$1,410**

A-MA   Skinner, Inc.

597 **Gustave Vichy Automaton Representing La Mascotte,** w/an unmkd. Jumeau bisque portrait head. Her torso containing going-barrel movement playing two airs & causing the figure to turn her head from side to side & bow, her left arm proffering flowers as the lid of her basket lifts to reveal a bobbing chick who chirps by means of concealed bellows. Head repr. & repainted, ht. 24in. **$7,050**

A-MA   Skinner, Inc.

788 **French-type Swivel-neck Bisque Doll,** ca.1800 w/solid round dome head, orig. blond mohair wig & apparently orig. dress, ht. 5in. **$2,115**

789 **French-type Swivel-neck Bisque Doll,** ca.1800 w/rosy cheeks, original blond wig, long slender peg-strung limbs, blue two-strap shoes & floral silk faille long train dress, ht. 5in. **$2,115**

A-ME   James D. Julia, Inc.
26 **Composition Shirley Temple Doll**, redressed w/craze lines on face & legs, ht. 18in. **$172**

A-ME   James D. Julia, Inc.
5 **Bisque Baby Doll** mkd. Copyright 1924 by E.I. Horsman & Co. & Germany on rear of torso. Wearing orig. mohair wig & dress. Faint hairline crack in back of head, ht. 6in. **$172**

A-MA   Skinner, Inc.
576 **Roullet et Decamps Jumping Cat Automaton** w/white fur covered body w/ key-wind clockwork movement, ht. 6½in. **$588**
708 **Barrois French Fashion Doll,** ca.1860s w/blond human hair wig, mkd. & wearing an ecru silk wedding gown & net lace veil, ht. 14½in. **$2,115**
709 **Early Bru French Fashion Doll,** Paris, ca.1870s w/blond mohair wig w/braid around head, three-piece pink silk outfit w/lace trim, ht. 15in.

$3,290
788 **French-type Swivel-neck All-Bisque Girl Doll,** ca.1880 w/orig. blond mohair wig, long slender peg-strung limbs & orig. aqua silk dress w/lace trim & covered button detailing, ht. 5in. **$2,115**
840 **French Bisque Swivel-neck Lady Doll by Barrois,** ca.1870s w/new brown curly caracal wig & old blue checkered skirt w/white cotton blouse, ht. 15in. **$4,113**
841 **French Fashion Doll w/Kid-over-Wood Body,** Paris, ca.1860s, orig.

blond mohair wig & wearing an orig. tan silk & wool challis walking outfit piped in French blue silk w/bows. **n/s**
846 **French Bisque Swivel-neck Doll,** Paris, ca.1870s, original blond wig w/green & black silk striped two-piece dress w/black banding & belt, & wearing black leather high button boots, ht. 17in. **$1,998**
852 **Miniature Figured-Walnut Tilt-top Pedestal Table,** 19th C., the top w/36-point star inlay on turned pedestal, ht. 6in. **$558**

A-MA Skinner, Inc.
570 Roullet et Decamps Bébé Rose Automaton Doll w/Jumeau bisque character head mkd. in red HVII, orig. blond mohair wig & cream satin chemise in papier-mâché rose decorated w/petals & painted green leaves. The open-spring motor w/Decamps stop/start causing the lid to lift off as the Bébé slowly rises from the heart of the flower, turns, throws kisses & then suddenly retreats, ht. extended to 10½in. **$5,874**
688 Jumeau Triste Bébé, France, ca.1885 w/imp. #13 on neck, blond wig, fully articulated composition body w/blue Jumeau stamp on back, ht. 28½in. **n/s**

A-MA Skinner, Inc.
594 Automaton of a Shepherdess, by Gustave Vichy, ca.1880, w/François Gaultier bisque head mkd. F.1.G. The going-barrel movement in the base plays two airs, a waltz & a polka, causing the shepherdess to look from side to side & strum her mandolin in time to music, all orig. Ht. 16in., total height 20in. **$12,925**

A-ME James D. Julia, Inc.
10 Gebruder Heubach Character Doll w/fully jointed pink body, head mkd. Germany I w/sunburst mark. Wearing a newer blond mohair wig & dress w/oil cloth shoes, ht. 11in. **$1,437**

A-ME James D. Julia, Inc.
29 Chad Valley Snow White Set, ca.1930s doll group w/felt bodies & velvet clothing from Snow White movie, together w/1994 limited edition Making of Snow White. Snow White ht. 16, dwarfs average 10in. **$920**

A-PA Conestoga Auction Company, Inc.
150 Papier-mâché Belsnickle in mica covered lavender coat & feather tree in crook of arm, ht. 7½in. **$715**
151 Papier-mâché Belsnickle in mica covered seafoam green coat & holding feather tree, ht. 10in. **$1,210**
152 Papier-mâché Belsnickle in gold coat w/feather tree in crook of arm, ht. 11¼in. **$825**

A-ME James D. Julia, Inc.
6 **Early German Doll,** unmkd., wearing orig. mohair wig, cotton gauze undergarments & dress w/blue ribbon inserts, ht. 6in. **$747**

A-ME
James D. Julia, Inc.
45 **Kley & Hahn Character Doll,** mkd. w/fully jointed body & wears her orig. mohair wig and antique dress frail in spots, ht. 15½in. **$3,680**

A-ME James D. Julia, Inc.
29 **Tête Jumeau Bébé** w/fully articulated body stamped Jumeau Médaille D'or Paris, w/orig. arm band on costume, orig. blond mohair wig, bonnet, orig. costume w/ slight deterioration to shoes & one panel on skirt, ht. 18½in. **$7,475**

A-ME James D. Julia, Inc.
35 **Jules Steiner Bébé** mkd. w/red stamp & Bte S.G.D.G. Bourgoin, fully jointed body w/straight wrists & dressed in a 2 piece blue wool sailor costume & hat, blond wig & brown leather shoes, ht. 22½in. **$6,325**

A-ME James D. Julia, Inc.
11 **French Bébé** w/bisque head incised 9 over EJ & torso mkd. Jumeau Médaille D'OR Paris. Body has 8 separate ball joints & large oversized hand, & wearing her orig. mohair wig, ht. 24in. **$2,880**

A-ME   James D. Julia, Inc.
9A Simon & Halbig 719 Character Doll on an 8-ball jointed comp. body w/straight wrists, blue paperweight eyes, one cracked, wearing German shoes & socks, repl. wig., ht. 19in. $2,750

A-ME   James D. Julia, Inc.
37 Early Jumeau Bébé w/incised mark 2 Paris, w/antique mohair wig, early 8 ball joint body w/straight wrist & orig. finish & wearing a period outfit, ht. 18in. $18,400

A-ME   James D. Julia, Inc.
62 Three American Cloth Dolls by Johnny Gruelle, incl. Raggedy Ann & Andy, w/painted facial features, shoe button eyes, yarn hair & orig. clothing att. to Volland, ht. 15in., together w/Beloved Belindy w/painted facial features, button eyes & orig. clothing, ht. 15in. $2,530

A-ME James D. Julia, Inc.
7 **Simon & Halbig Asian Doll,** mkd., on a five-piece papier-mâché body wearing an elaborate silk period costume w/platform shoes & orig. wig, ht. 15½in. **$2,990**

A-ME James D. Julia, Inc.
103 **Kestner Doll,** all original w/head mkd. Made in Germany w/orig. fully jointed body & wearing the orig. factory chemise w/pink ribbons & white silk shoes, ht. 12¼in. **$1,035**

A-ME James D. Julia, Inc.
26 **Bru Jne Bébé,** mkd. on right shoulder, w/swivel neck & bisque head on the shoulder plate mounted on Chevrot style body w/wooden lower legs, kid leather over metal upper arms & wears orig. underwear & stockings. Wearing antique dress & bonnet w/Bru leather shoes. ht. 24in. **$29,325**

The furnishings of America's past had a particular flair... functionalism that was the natural design expression of a country where practicality meant survival. The bulk of the early furniture was utilitarian and commonplace, made to serve a useful purpose. The earliest cabinetmakers were generally itinerant craftsmen who borrowed their ideas from several periods, oftentimes adding a bit of individuality of their own. Therefore, furniture produced in America was a combination of Yankee ingenuity in adopting revered Old World styling to New World materials, resulting in furniture having a timeless appeal in uniqueness that is purely American, with simplicity of line being its most characteristic feature.

As our population increases and collectors become more knowledgeable, no other field has attracted more attention than furniture from all periods. This chapter includes a variety of case pieces... that is furniture that encloses a space such as cabinets, chests of drawers, cupboards, desks, sideboards and the linen press. In addition, a variety of many other furnishings are included. Each illustrated entry describes the object, its condition and provides historical background information when available. Surprisingly, even restoration and repairs have become more acceptable these days. However, when the original finish or decoration has been removed from a period – or just an elderly – piece of furniture, it reduces the value substantially.

Because of the quality of much mass-produced furniture today, combined with the demand for and unavailability of quality, there has become an increased demand for custom-made furniture from all periods by well recognized cabinetmakers. Many of these pieces will become the sought-after antiques of tomorrow.

A-PA   Pook & Pook, Inc.
90 Federal Canopy Bed, MA, ca.1815, mah. The reeded post w/central foliate carving, ht. 76in. **$1,404**

A-PA   Freeman's
136 Daybed, PA, first third of 18th C., w/adjustable back, double curved crestrail & spindles w/rectangular rush seat, ht. 20½, lg. 80½in. **$14,340**

A-PA   Alderfer's
1495 William & Mary Daybed w/crown cresting above a loose-cushion on cane seat, walnut frame, ca.1720-1740, ht. 33, lg. 71, wd. 21in. **$4,887**

A-PA   Freeman's
222 Classical Bedstead & Tester, ca.1825, mah., w/spiral turned & acanthus leaf carved posts, shaped & paneled headboard & engine turned brass collars on ornamented feet, ht. 97in. **$6,500**

A-NH
Northeast Auctions
1045 N. Eng. Sheraton Canopy Bed, birch w/canopy frame. The posts terminating in urn & vase form feet, ht. 93½in. **$812**
1046 Salem Sheraton Carved Canopy Bed, all in black paint w/gilt highlights, ring & vase turned swelled post w/pineapple finials, ht. 66in. **$2,320**

A-SC   **Charlton Hall**
664 Burl Walnut Highlander Tall Post Bed w/tester, side rails, 20th C. by M. Craig, king size, ht. 97½, wd. 92, lg. 97in. **$7,000**

A-NH   **Northeast Auctions**
1520 Am. Federal Carved Four Post Bed, mah. w/fluted posts, urn finials & blocked supports on Marlborough legs, ht. 46in. **$464**

A-PA   **Freeman's**
82 Windsor Cradle, PA 1780-1810 w/oval finials, tapering spindles & bamboo turned legs joined by swelled stretchers, ht. 24, wd. 11½, lg. 33in. **$2,000**

FURNITURE

A-NH   Northeast Auctions
215 N. Eng. Stepdown Windsor Side
Chairs, painted & decorated
w/flower heads above seven faux
bamboo spindles, bamboo box
stretcher & each chair dec. w/brick
red accents. $4,500

A-NH Northeast Auctions
756 English Bow-back
Windsor Arm Chairs,
yew & elm, an
assembled set.
$9,000

A-PA   Freeman's
1023 Low Back Windsor Settees, pair,
PA, late 18th C. w/incised plank
seat, ht. 27, lg. 83in. $8,962

A-NH   **Northeast Auctions**
345 **Sheraton Tiger Maple Chairs,** each w/concave swept back, ball splats, & plank seat. **$4,700**

A-PA   **Pook & Pook, Inc.**
163 **Pair of Chester Co., PA Ladderback Chairs,** 18th C., retaining a 19th C. black surface w/yellow pinstriping. **$6,435**

A-PA   **Freeman's**
94 **Sack-back Windsor High Chair,** brand of Joseph Burden, Phil., active 1793-1827, w/bamboo turnings & dated 1775, ht. 38in. **$1,300**

A-NH   **Northeast Auctions**
604 **Philadelphia High-back Windsor Armchair** in dark green paint, ca.1775. The D form seat fitted for a commode, ht. 43½in. **$5,220**

A-PA   **Freeman's**
79 **Sack-back Windsor Writing Arm Chair,** CT, late 18th C., w/drawer, old black painted surface, ht. 34in. **$550**

80 **Writing Arm Windsor Chair** w/brown paint, 19th C. **$250**
81 **Two Windsor Chairs,** the first a Lancaster Co., fan-back, the second a rod-back bamboo burned chair. **$2,500**

83 **Two Sack-back Windsor Armchairs,** Phil. late 18th C. **$1,500**
84 **Fan-back Windsor Armchair,** 19th C., w/black paint., ht. 42in. **$600**
85 **Comb-back Windsor Armchair** w/arm supports, ht. 42½in. **$650**

A-PA Pook & Pook, Inc.
110 **Philadelphia Comb-back Windsor Armchair**, ca.1765, retaining early brown surface over the orig. green. **$9,945**

A-ME James D. Julia, Inc.
790 **Fan-back Brace-back Windsor Side Chair**, Wallace Nutting, unsgn. but branded. **$977**

A-NH Northeast Auctions
235 **Q.A. Wing Chair**, Philadelphia, ca.1700s, walnut. **$45,000**

A-ME James D. Julia, Inc.
792 **Colonial Style Side Chairs**, maple, att. to Wallace Nutting, second qtr. of 20th C. **$402**

A-PA Pook & Pook, Inc.
186 **Rod-back Windsor Dining Chairs**, set of eight, N. Eng., early 19th C. & retaining their original black painted surface w/hand-painted oak leaf & acorn dec. **$11,700**

A-PA   Freeman's
54 **George I Dining Chairs,** set of seven, walnut w/solid splats, over drop-in seats, raised on cabriole legs ending in shell carved feet. **$21,510**

A-PA   Pook & Pook, Inc.
896 **Philadelphia Chippendale Dining Chairs,** set of four, mah., ca.1785, w/carved & serpentine crest over gothic splat, slip seat & squared beaded edge legs joined by H-stretchers. **$9,360**

A-NH

Northeast Auctions

827 Chippendale Dining Chairs, set of eight, mah., w/serpentine crest above a pierced vasiform splat. Set includes two armchairs. **$7,250**

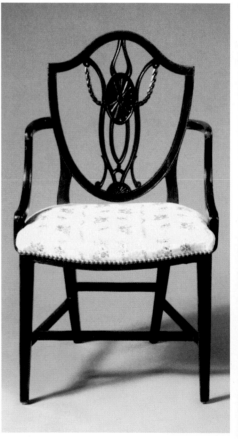

A-PA

Freeman's

210 Chippendale Side Chairs, walnut, pair, ca. 1765 w/serpentine crestrail w/plain flaring volutes & a centered shell, claw & ball feet. **$11,353**

A-NH

Northeast Auctions

1534 Hepplewhite Carved Shieldback Armchair w/arches crest rail above a pierced & molded splat w/bellflower design, centering a rayed patera. **$522**

A-NH   **Northeast Auctions**
694 Q.A. Balloon Seat Side Chairs,
MA, mah. Each w/yoked crest above
a vasiform stepped shoe joining a
balloon slip-seat & recessed box
stretcher terminating in pad feet, two
from a set of four. **$48,000**

A-NH   **Northeast Auctions**
**1535 Pair of Hepplewhite Carved Shieldback Dining
Chairs,** mah., each molded arched crest above a pierced
splayed splat carved w/sheaves of wheat & drapery, on
square tapered molded legs. **$580**

A-NH   **Northeast Auctions**
342 Set of Six Federal Dining Chairs,
New Hampshire, mah., each
w/modified yoke crest above a
vasiform splat joined to a trapezoidal
slip seat raised on square chamfered
legs. **$2,750**

A-ME   **James D. Julia, Inc.**
700 Windsor Painted Settee branded G&R Gaw for Gilbert & Robert Gaw. The partnership lasted between 1793-1798. The old black paint in parts shows an earlier reddish paint, ht. 38, lg. 57½in.
$23,000

A-PA   **Pook & Pook, Inc.**
353 Child's Birdcage Windsor Settee, PA, ca.1820, retaining an old red surface surrounding a salmon seat, seat ht. 26½, lg. 36½in. **$19,890**

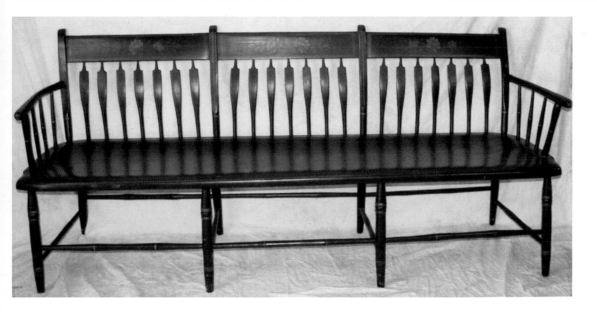

A-PA   Alderfer's
1455 Philadelphia Windsor Settee, ca.1810-1825 w/bent arrow-back of poplar & hickory w/brown painted finish & hand-painted floral dec., repainted & reprs., lg. 76½in. **$2,587**

A-PA   Pook & Pook, Inc.
457 Small Windsor Settee, ca.1825 w/birdcage back & bamboo turned legs joined by stretchers, ht. 35, lg. 47in. **$5,290**

A-PA   Freeman's
1347 Low-back Windsor Settee, PA, early 19th C. w/plank seat raised on eight baluster turned stretchers, ht. 29, lg. 81in. **$3,226**

FURNITURE

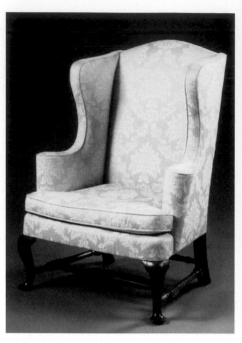

A-MA   Skinner, Inc.
113 Q.A. Carved Side Chairs, N. Eng., maple, ca. last half 18th C. w/yoked & spooned carved crest rails above vasiform splats, rush seats & block, vase & ring-turned front legs ending in carved Spanish feet, ref. & minor imp., ht. 42in.
$2,820

A-NH   Northeast Auctions
1904 Q.A. Wing Chair, MA, maple w/frontal cabriole legs, pad feet & turned stretcher, ht. of back 46in.
$2,900

A-NH
Northeast Auctions
1708 New Hampshire Chippendale Bonnet Top Chest On Chest w/molded full bonnet swan's neck crest w/pinwheel terminals, unusual winged pinwheel carved faux drawer, molded base & bracket feet w/scalloped returns, ht. 90, wd. 38½in.
$20,880

A-PA   Freeman's
42 Q.A. High Chest, walnut, PA, ca.1760, in two parts w/shaped skirt & cabriole legs ending in pad feet, ht. 78, wd. 41½in. **$11,000**

A-PA   Freeman's
27 **Q.A. High Chest**, PA, ca.1760, in two parts, walnut w/shaped skirt & cabriole legs carved at knees w/shell & trifid stockinged feet, ht. 69, wd. 40½in. $17,000

A-NH
   Northeast Auctions
471 **N. Eng. High Chest of Drawers**, QA. maple, ca.1770, in two parts, the apron is scalloped & has a large central shell, plain cabriole legs on pad feet. $47,800

A-NH
   Northeast Auctions
113 **N. Eng. William & Mary High Chest**, maple & pine, two parts w/valanced apron raised on six bell & baluster turned legs joined by cyma-curved box stretcher raised on ball feet, ht. 63, wd. 40in. $3,000

A-NH
   Northeast Auctions
206 **N. Eng. Chippendale Tall Chest**, maple, in two parts; the upper w/cove & dentil molded cornice above a central fan carved drawer; the lower part w/central drawer fan carved, raised on cabriole legs w/scrolled returns, on ball & claw feet, ht. 77½, wd. 42in. $7,500

A-PA   **Freeman's**
282 A Schwenkfelder Painted Blanket Chest, Montgomery Co., PA, dated 1847 and descended in the Wiegner family (name on chest misspelled) to the present owner, ht. 27, wd. 45in. **$8,365**

A-PA   **Freeman's**
1326 Paint & Stenciled Blanket Chest, poplar, PA, dated 1827, on bracket feet, hinged lid & till, ht. 25, wd. 53, dp. 24in. **$38,240**

A-PA   **Freeman's**
283 Painted & Decorated Blanket Chest, PA, dated 1788, fitted w/till cover, the ends grain-painted & molded base w/bracket feet & provenance. **$5,079**

A-NH   Northeast Auctions

617 N. Eng. Country Blanket Chest, red painted pine w/two faux-tiger maple grained drawers, ca.1820-1835, ht. 37, top 18x38in. **$4,930**

A-NH   Northeast Auctions

850 Massachusetts Chippendale Blanket Chest, pine w/dark red paint, first half 19th C. w/orig. brasses, the sides continuing to legs w/ogee arch cut-outs, ht. 38, top 18½x42½in. **$8,700**

A-PA   Pook & Pook, Inc.

748 N. Eng. Putty Grained Blanket Chest w/storage compartment & two long drawers below w/bootjack ends, ht. 39½, wd. 39in. **$2,500**

A-PA   Pook & Pook, Inc.

979 Lancaster Co., PA Chippendale Blanket Chest, walnut, dated 1799, the lift lid over a dov. case w/inlaid inscription & date, centering a star, two drawers & ogee bracket feet, ht. 27½, wd. 50½in. **$4,212**

A-PA   **Pook & Pook, Inc.**
478 **PA Painted Blanket Chest,** late 18th C., dov. case w/arched panels, each depicting black urns w/red & blue tulips & each inscribed Johanns Rank, w/central panel dated 1798, ht. 22½, wd. 51½in. **$19,890**

A-PA   **Pook & Pook, Inc.**
649 **N. Eng. William & Mary Chest,** maple, ca.1730 w/turned bun feet, ht. 40, wd., 35½in. **$6,325**

A-PA   **Pook & Pook, Inc.**
797 **Painted Diminutive Blanket Chest,** PA, 19th C., retaining a vibrant faux crotch mah. surface, ht. 21, wd. 37½in. **$2,340**
798 **Painted Pine Blanket Chest,** NY, 19th C. w/dov. case, turned three-quarter columns supported by turned feet. Retains a yellow & green sponge dec., ht. 21, wd. 41¾in. **$1,521**
799 **Painted Poplar Blanket Chest,** PA, early mid-19th C., w/raised panel case supported by turned feet & retains a yellow & red grain surface, ht. 27½, wd. 47½in. **$2,223**

FURNITURE

A-NC   **Brunk Auctions**
0707 **Punched Tin Hanging Bread Safe,** red-painted poplar & oak w/elaborately punched tins that include stags, squirrels & other animals & Bread Safe, dated 1894. Tins w/scattered rust, dents & corrosion, ht. 36, wd. 40, dp. 19½in. **$3,200**

A-PA   **Pook & Pook, Inc.**
81 **Chester Co. PA Q.A. Spice Chest,** ca. 1760, walnut & poplar w/fitted int. incl. 12 drawers & a long secret drawer, ht. 24½, wd. 17½in. **$11,115**

A-NC   **Brunk Auctions**
0046 **Southern Sugar Chest,** mah. throughout, 19th C., repl. drawer & reprs., w/old dry finish, possibly original, ht. 38, wd. 19½in. **$1,300**

A-NC   **Brunk Auctions**
0306 **North Carolina Chippendale High Chest,** walnut w/yellow pine secondary, fluted quarter columns, orig. brass pulls & feet, ht. 61, wd. 20¾in. **$5,000**

A-NH **Northeast Auctions**

695 **N. Eng. Chippendale Chest On Chest,** figured maple, in two parts: the upper w/projecting cornice above three short drawers, the center one w/fan carving, all drawers thumbmolded on base w/bracket feet, ht. 70, wd. 38in. **$21,000**

A-NH **Northeast Auctions**

1647 **Rhode Island Chippendale Chest of Drawers,** tiger maple w/central carved fan & supported by bracket feet, ht. 48½, wd. 36in. **$37,700**

A-OH **Garth's Arts & Antiques**

245 **Chippendale Tall Chest,** walnut w/dov. case, repl. brasses, old ref. & reprs. to feet, ht. 68½, wd. 43in. **$6,037**

A-PA Freeman's
10 **Chippendale Chest,** late 18th C. w/beaded drawers enclosed by fluted quarter columns & ogee feet, ht. 39, wd. 37¾in. **$2,000**

A-PA Freeman's
1206 **Chippendale Chest,** walnut, last qtr. 18th C., w/graduated beaded drawers, fluted columns & ogee feet, ht. 37, wd. 37½in. **$3,465**

A-PA Freeman's
184 **Chippendale Chest,** mah., Phil., ca.1770 w/applied lip molded top above lip molded drawers flanked by quarter-round reeded columns on ogival bracket feet, ht. 42½, wd. 37½in. **$8,963**

A-NH Northeast Auctions
114 **N. Eng. Chippendale Tall Chest of Drawers,** pine & maple w/scalloped bracket base, ht. 55½, wd. 35½in. **$3,000**

A-PA   **Freeman's**
1251 Federal Tall Chest, PA, ca.1780 w/flat cove molded top, cockbeaded drawers, chamfered corners & French bracket feet, ht. 68¼, wd. 42in. **$5,490**

A-PA   **Freeman's**
1063 Chippendale Chest on Chest, PA, 18th/19th C. w/lip molded drawers quarter round fluted corners on ogival bracket feet, ht. 73, wd. 40¼in. **$10,157**

A-NH   **Northeast Auctions**
291 New Hampshire Q.A. Chest On Frame, maple w/shaped apron joining bandy cabriole legs ending in pad feet, case wd. 36in. **$9,500**

A-PA

Pook & Pook, Inc.

146 **Hepplewhite Tall Chest**, PA, ca.1810, cherry w/cross inlaid band over three short doors & below graduated drawers, flanked by barber pole corners & glaring French feet. Retains an old crackled varnish surface, ht. 65½, wd. 42in. **$11,115**

A-NH   Northeast Auctions

842 **Maine Sheraton Chest** in old red, first-half 19th C., cherry & maple w/shaped splashboard w/brass rosettes, brass pulls, cylindrical legs, ringed cuffs & peg feet, ht. 43½, wd. 38¾in. **$3,712**

A-ME

James D. Julia, Inc.

505 **Sheraton Four Drawer Inlaid Chest**, rectangular top w/block shape corners, satin birch drawer fronts flanked by fluted columns, shaped apron, orig. period brass hardware & raised on high tapering legs, ht. 39, wd 44¾in. **$4,025**

A-NH   Northeast Auctions

795 **N. Eng. Sheraton Deck Top Chest**, figured mah. bowed case w/outsets rounded corners & ringed stiles continuing w/reeded & ringed legs tapering to ringed cuffs, ht. 53½, wd. 41in. **$1,800**

A-ME

James D. Julia, Inc.

812 **Late Sheraton Chest**, mah. w/deck top & backsplash over base, three qtr. spiral carved columns, wood knobs & portioned turned feet, ca.1815-1830, ht. 48½, wd. 42¾in. **$517**

A-SC   Charlton Hall
596 Hepplewhite Inlaid Bow Front Chest, Baltimore, mah., ca.1800, bowed top, scalloped skirt & splayed feet, ht. 37¼, wd. 40½in. **$8,000**

A-NH   Northeast Auctions
347 Chippendale-Style Bombé Chest, mah. w/graduated drawers, cabriole legs, ending in ball & claw feet, ht. 32, top 39x21in. **$4,750**

A-ME   James D. Julia, Inc.
794 Block Front Four Drawer Chest, mah. w/dov. drawers, ball & claw feet bracket base, unsgn. custom bench made, ht. 32, wd. 32, dp. 18in. **$1,150**

A-PA   Pook & Pook, Inc.
172 Pennsylvania Dutch Cupboard, walnut, ca.1790, two parts, w/rattail hinges, pie shelf & straight bracket feet, ht. 87, wd. 65in. **$17,550**

A-OH   Garth's Arts & Antiques
551 Decorated Chest att. to PA stylistically similar to Soap Hollow chests, poplar & chestnut, red paint w/yellow & brown graining which appears orig., dov. drawers & straight skirt w/repair & back feet are repl., ht. 54, wd. 39in. **$2,760**

A-PA
Pook & Pook, Inc.
352 Soap
Hollow Dutch
Cupboard, PA,
att. to Peter K.
Thomas, dated
1876, painted
poplar & pine
w/quarter turned
stiles, scalloped
skirt & bracket
feet. Retains the
orig. overall red
& black paint
w/stenciled gold
floral & bird
motifs, ht. 80¼,
wd. 56½in.
$39,780

FURNITURE

A-PA
Conestoga Auction Company, Inc.
323 Dutch Cupboard, two-part, softwood w/old red painted surface & blue int., sunken panel doors & bracket feet. Some rest., ht. 84½in. **$6,600**

A-PA   Freeman's
1459 Pine Corner Cupboard, early 19th C. w/painted int. & bracket feet, ht. 84, wd. 37in. **$1,792**

A-OH   Garth's Arts & Antiques
672 Two-piece Wall Cupboard, cherry & poplar w/crown molding, three shelves w/plate rail & grooves, reeded center panel & corners w/applied half columns, knobs not orig. & minor repair, ht. 87, wd. 61in. **$4,312**
673 Carved Wooden Canadian Goose standing on iron legs & preening, lg. 32in. **$690**

NH   Northeast Auctions
1781 Chippendale Stepback Cupboard, PA, walnut w/H hinges, fluted quarter columns, stepped back lower case & bracket feet, ht. 88, wd. 68in. **$29,000**

A-PA

Pook & Pook, Inc.

477 Q.A. Corner Cupboard, walnut, ca.1860, PA, two parts w/rattail hinges & paneled doors, ht. 85, wd. 43in. **$4,680**

A-PA Alderfer's
1482 George III Welsh Oak Dresser, English, ca. late 18th C., sitting on block feet, ht. 73, lg. 69in. **$8,050**

A-PA Pook & Pook, Inc.
275 George II Welsh Cupboard, oak, mid 18th C. **$5,616**

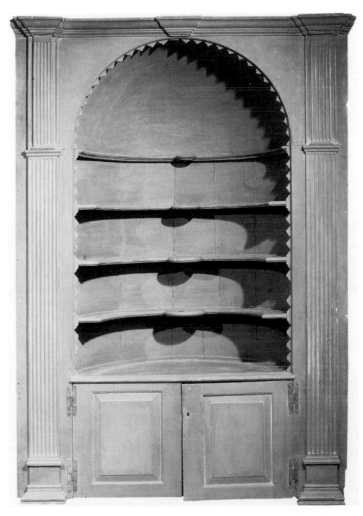

A-OH Garth's Arts & Antiques
708 Architectural Barrel Back Corner Cupboard, 18th C., orig. built in, pine w/plastered interior & old blue paint, graduated shelves & a center projection, H hinges, repairs & rest., ht. 86, wd. 59in. **$5,290**

A-NH　　　　　　　　　　　　**Northeast Auctions**
858 **N. Eng. Stepback Cupboard**, red painted,
pine w/drawers, each w/brass knob, ht. 72,
wd. 36in. **$9,000**
859 **Continental Tin-glazed Blue & White Drug
Jar**, titled Carpion, ht. 8¼in. **$400**

A-NH　　　　　　　　　　　　**Northeast Auctions**
619 **Cupboard**, MA, early 19th C. in old red
paint w/twin recessed panel doors & cut-out feet,
ht. 72, wd. 60in. **$4,930**

A-NH　　　　　　　　　　　　**Northeast Auctions**
823 **Federal Jelly Cupboard**, painted & faux-
grained pine & poplar, 19th C., on cut-out legs,
ht. 48¾, wd. 41in. **$1,044**

A-PA   Freeman's
1050 Walnut Corner Cupboard, PA, ca.1800, w/architectural cresting, block band inlay above dentil inlay, pencil line & fan corner inlays & bracket feet, ht. 95½, wd. 44in. $3,885

A-MA Skinner, Inc.
633 N. Eng. Painted Corner Cupboard, last half 18th C. w/molded case, canted corners flanking divided door & H-hinges, ht. 86, wd. 40in. $4,700

A-PA   Conestoga Auction Co., Inc.
475 Painted Softwood Canning Cupboard w/old green paint over red surface, w/sunken door panels & turned feet. Shelved int., ht. 49¾, wd. 44½in. $15,950

A-PA   Conestoga Auction Co., Inc.
486 Softwood Canning Cupboard in old yellow alligatored paint having single door w/divided sunken panels & cut-out feet, ht. 45, wd. 38in. $3,190

A-PA   Pook & Pook, Inc.
164 Pewter Cupboard, two-part, early 19th C. w/scalloped sides, two drawers & straight bracket feet, retaining old red surface, ht. 80, wd. 49in. **$4,680**

A-MA   Skinner, Inc.
21 Corner Cupboard, paint dec. w/glazed hinged door, PA ca.1820-40 w/orig. surface, ht. 85½, wd. 40in. **$28,200**

A-OH   Garth's Arts & Antiques
125 Corner Cupboard, pine w/bold graining in red & ochre, att. to Lancaster Co. PA, w/minor age wear, ht. 84½, wd. 37in. **$6,325**

A-PA Freeman's
159 **George III Inlaid Secretaire Breakfront Bookcase**, mah., 18th C. w/fallfront opening to reveal a fitted int., over two pairs of paneled doors, ht. 99, wd. 80½in. **$17,925**

A-OH Garth's Arts & Antiques
35 **Chippendale Secretary**, two-part, walnut & poplar w/ maple int. drawer fronts, fitted int., dov. drawers & a secret drawer, ref. & reprs., ht. 83, wd. 40in. **$27,000**

A-OH Garth's Arts & Antiques
501 **Mahogany Extra Grade Wooton Desk** w/bird's-eye maple & ebonized veneer, brass hardware including a Letters slot & mkd. Manufactured by the Wooton Desk Co., Indianapolis, Ind. Pat. Oct. 6, 1874. The dov. drawers have orig. cardboard boxes w/repl. marbelized paper fronts & fold down writing surface with orig. green fabric. ht. 68, wd. 36¼in. **$23,000**

FURNITURE

A-NH   Northeast Auctions
146 Chippendale Oxbow Slant Lid Desk, MA, mah., dov. case w/hinged lid opening to an int. of valanced cubbyholes, centering a fan carved prospect door, on boldly carved ball & claw feet, ht. 44¼, wd. 40in. **$3,500**

A-PA   Pook & Pook, Inc.
117 George II Burled walnut Secretary Desk, early 18th C., in two parts, w/double domed top, blocked amphitheatered int. Straight bracket feet, ht. 82½, wd. 36½in. **$12,600**

A-PA   Conestoga Auction Co., Inc.
481 Chippendale Block Front Desk, walnut w/shaped top over conforming case, & recessed center door w/scrolled shell carving, resting on ball & claw feet w/carved shell knees, ht. 32¼, wd. 40½in. **$9,350**

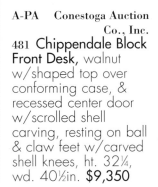

A-PA   Freeman's
72 George II Tilt Top Writing Desk, mah., ca.1750, w/hinged rectangular top opening to reveal a fitted int. w/hinged baize lined writing surface & recessed glass inkpots, resting on cabriole legs & pad feet, ht. 29, wd. 32¾in. **$2,629**

A-OH   Garth's Arts & Antiques
414 Cherry Slant Front Desk w/detailed int., old ref. & cabriole legs w/pad feet, ht. 45, wd. 41in. **$8,050**

A-OH   Garth's Arts & Antiques
664 Chippendale Slant Front Desk, Philadelphia area, mah., w/pigeonholes that pull out to reveal three hidden drawers, thumbnail molding, orig. pulls & dov. case. Repl. locks, bracket feet & base molding, ht. 46¼in. **$3,450**

A-SC   Charlton Hall Auctions
064 Q.A. Chinoiserie & Red Lacquered Slant Front Desk/Bureau w/bun feet. Dec. overall w/gilt-and-green animals & figures. Relacquered in England within past ten years, ht. 89½, wd. 43in. **$40,000**

A-PA   Pook & Pook, Inc.
652 Chippendale Secretary, late 18th C., PA, cherry, two-part w/fall front supported by ogee bracket feet, ht. 86½, wd. 41in. **$4,446**

FURNITURE

A-PA   Freeman's
247 **Classical Breakfront Bookcase,** Phil., ca.1825, mah. w/tombstone-shaped paneled doors & lion paw feet, ht. 94, wd. 84in. $30,000

A-NH   **Northeast Auctions**
824 **George III Bureau/Bookcase**
w/swan's neck pediment & leaftip terminals, mah., ht. 9ft.2½in., wd. 56in. $22,000

A-NH   **Northeast Auctions**
840 **Regency Breakfront Bookcase,** mah., w/molded cornice, astragal-glazed doors, adjustable shelves & raised on molded plinth, ht. 79in., lg. 8ft.11in. $5,000

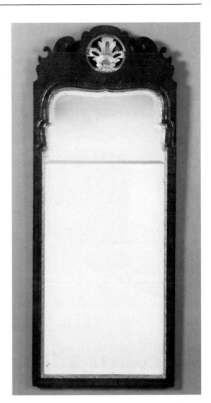

A-PA   Pook & Pook, Inc.
96 Federal Giltwood Convex Mirror,
ca.1790 w/foliate crest & three griffin
head over mirror & serpent-form
girandole arms, ht. 52in. $11,700

A-NH   Northeast Auctions
268 Q.A. Walnut Veneer Two-
part Mirror w/solid shaped
crest, the upper section beveled
to fit into lower glass, within
molded frame, ht. 34½, wd.
14in. $5,000

A-NH   Northeast Auctions
686 Q.A. Walnut & Parcel Gilt
Wall Mirror w/scrolled
crest,carved & gilded shell
above a two-part beveled plate
w/molded frame & carved gilt
slip, ht. 48, wd. 18½in.
$3,500

A-NH   Northeast Auctions
273 Inlaid Mirror w/gilded trumpet
lily, mah., & stringing over a shaped
pendant apron, ht. 34½, wd. 17¾in.
$1,500

A-MA   Skinner, Inc.
15 Walnut Veneer & Gilt-gesso Mirror, late 18th C., w/scrolled cresting above a
molded frame & gilt incised liner, w/imper., ht. 18, wd. 11in. $529
16 Federal Eglomisé Mirror, N. Eng., early 19th C., mah. w/tablet of sea battle
of *Frolic & Wasp*, mirror below, imper., ht. 26¾, wd. 12½in. $940

FURNITURE

A-NH   Northeast Auctions
292 Federal Giltwood Constitution Mirror, MA, w/stepped gilt cornice w/spherules over an eglomisé panel depicting a woman w/white drape above a rectangular plate flanked by concave stiles, ht. 31, wd. 18½in. **$1,400**

A-PA   Pook & Pook, Inc.
384 Philadelphia Chippendale Shaving Mirror, mah., late 18th C., mkd. Wayne & Biddle, w/a revolving mirror above three drawers supported by ogee feet. **$5,616**

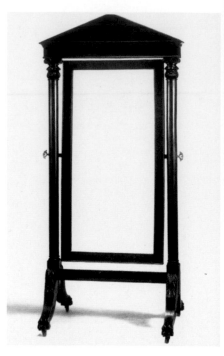

A-PA   Freeman's
221 Philadelphia Mirror, ca.1825. The molded pediment above carved & turned posts supporting the pivoting mirror on acanthus carved legs w/paw feet on casters, ht. 77, wd. 52in. **$2,400**

A-PA   Freeman's
154 Carved & Gilded Girandole Mirror dec. w/an eagle w/outstretched wings & a chain on plinth flanked by foliage above molded frame, reeded liner mirror plate & foliate pendant, lg. 30in. **$4,500**

A-NH   Northeast Auctions
Miniature Mirrors
613 Am. Q.A. Pine Wall Mirror w/ogee arch crest, ca.1790 w/brown stain & hanging ring, 6⅞x3⅛in. **$3,364**
614 Pine Wall Mirror w/peaked crest & orig. pumpkin paint, early 19th C.,5⅝x3⅛in. **$3,712**
615 Small Chip-carved Mirror w/arched crest & Indian red paint, 19th C. w/fluted arch ending in starflower rosettes above frame & a border row of crosses ending in diamond-form starflower rosettes, 5¼x3½in. **$1,508**
616 Chip-carved Walnut Mirror w/incised concentric hearts on raised crest, mid-19th C. The reverse w/paper covering & inscription This is George...1848, 4½x2in. **$1,624**

FURNITURE

A-NC   **Brunk Auctions**
0733 **Chippendale Mirror,** mah. w/pierced frets, scroll base & gilt phoenix imp. w/fine detailing, 18th C., w/old dry surface & small repr. to scrolled ear, ht. 31½, wd. 16¼in. **$1,200**

A-PA   **Pook & Pook, Inc.**
233 **George III Mirror,** walnut veneer & parcel gilt, 18th C., ht. 62in. **$3,660**

A-PA   **Pook & Pook, Inc.**
212 **New York Classical Cheval Mirror,** mah., ca.1825, the rectangular swiveling mirror w/turned supports & ormolu capitals on formed feet, ht. 71½, wd. 36in. **$1,380**

A-PA   **Pook & Pook, Inc.**
885 **N. Eng. Q.A. Dressing Table,** maple, ca.1760 w/cabriole legs terminating in pad feet, ht. 28½, wd. 32½in. **$14,040**

A-MA   **Northeast Auctions**
313 **Q.A. Dressing Table,** cherry, possible western MA, ca.1740-60, w/cabriole legs ending in pad feet on platforms, old ref., impr. & reprs., ht. 32, wd. 25½in. **$14,100**

A-NH   Northeast Auctions
1736 N. Eng. Sheraton Sideboard
of diminutive proportion, mah.,
case w/swelled front & molded
panelled ends fitted w/a central
bowed drawer, all w/mah.
crossbanding. Raised on tapering
reeded & ring turned legs, ht. 39½,
wd. 61in. **$5,800**

A-PA   Freeman's
158 Federal Sideboard, Phil., late
18th/early 19th C., mah.
w/concave center flanked by a
door on left side & a drawer to the
right side, w/square tapering legs,
ht. 37in. **$6,500**

A-PA   Pook & Pook, Inc.
**778 George III Hepplewhite
Sideboard**, mah., ca.1790
w/bowfront top w/inlay, two bottle
drawers & tapering legs terminating
in spade feet, ht. 36, wd. 65½in.
$5,859

A-SC   Charlton Hall
591 **Linen Press**, mah., att. to the circle of William
Marlen, in the late Neo-classical style, exhibiting
finely figured veneers, crossbanded doors & a
bookmatched veneer frieze, typical of Charleston
work, ca.1800-1815, ht. 105, wd. 48in. **$23,000**

A-PA   Freeman's
1267 **Federal Inlaid Linen Press**, cherrywood,
ca.1800, panel doors inlaid w/flower-filled urns &
bracket base, ht. 79, wd. 48¼in. **$5,079**

A-SC   Charlton Hall
535 **Piedmont North Carolina Clothes Press**, early
19th C., painted in faded blue & embellished
w/stylized floral-and-heart motifs. Paint scrubbed &
old reprs., ht. 94, wd. 50in. **$12,000**

A-PA   Pook & Pook, Inc.
742 New Jersey Kas, late 18th C., gumwood w/boldly molded cornice, case w/two panel doors flanked by recessed walnut stiles & diamond panels, supported by straight bracket feet, ht. 71, wd.59½in. **$6,435**

A-PA   Pook & Pook, Inc.
111 New Jersey Kas, late 18th C., three-part, gumwood w/panel cupboard doors, & supported by turned bun feet, ht. 70¾, wd. 60½in. **$15,210**

A-PA   Pook & Pook, Inc.
68 Southern Federal Hunt Board, mah., early 19th C., w/central cupboard door & flanked by four drawers, supported by square tapering legs, ht.39½, lg. 47½in. **$5,382**

A-PA   Pook & Pook, Inc.
173 Delaware Valley Q.A. Dressing Table, walnut, ca.1765 w/scalloped skirt w/heart cut-out, supported by cabriole legs & trifid feet, ht. 30¼, wd. 32½in. **$19,550**

A-NC   Brunk Auctions
0303 North Carolina Federal Sideboard, figured walnut veneers w/yellow pine secondary, old finish & brasses, att. to Wake Co., NC, early 19th C., w/scattered stains, abrasions & wear, ht. 42, lg. 63in. **$9,000**

A-PA   Alderfer's
1471 William & Mary Oval Gate-leg Table
w/two drawers, scalloped apron, vase & ring turned legs ending in ball feet, PA, ca.1725, no defects, ht. 29¼, lg. 56, dia. 48in.
$14,950

A-NH   Northeast Auctions
999 Pine Trestle Table, PA, w/rectangular plank top, rounded corners raised on a carved, stepped trestle shoefoot base w/medial stretcher, ht. 30, lg. 83, wd. 36in. **$6,960**

A-PA   Pook & Pook, Inc.
659 N. Eng. Sawbuck Table, pine, early 19th C. w/rectangular top over X-supports, retaining an old red wash surface, ht. 28, lg. 94, wd. 36in.
$7,020

A-NH   Northeast Auctions
1506 Chippendale Carved Tilt-top Tea Table
w/birdcage, mah. w/single board dish-top hinged on a swiveling ring-turned standard w/flattened ball, raised on a tripod base w/ball & claw feet, ht. 29, dia. 33½in. **$23,200**

A-PA   Pook & Pook, Inc.
740 N. Eng/ William & Mary Gate-leg Table, tiger maple, ca.1730, w/single drawer, turned legs & stretchers w/orig. surface, ht. 28¼, wd. 19, dia. 43in. **$14,040**

A-PA Freeman's
1272 Side Table, PA, walnut, ca. 1770, rectangular three-plank top, two lip molded apron drawers on plain cabriole legs w/claw feet, top 66½, wd. 32¾in. **$3,585**

A-PA Freeman's
276 Soap Hollow Painted & Stencil-decorated Work Stand, Somerset Co., PA. w/square oversized top, dated 1875 w/brown overall finish, top 22x21⅞in. **$7,170**

A-SC Charlton Hall Auctions
592 Charleston, SC Gaming Table, ca. 1770-1785, mah. w/rectangular folding top on chamfered & beaded Marlborough legs, ht. 29, wd. 36in. **$13,000**

A-SC Charlton Hall Auctions
595 Hepplewhite Pembroke Table, NY, ca. 1795, mah. w/inlay, tapered legs & ankle banding, ht. 28½in. **$7,000**

A-NH Northeast Auctions
1509 Chippendale Tilt-top Birdcage Candlestand, Phil. w/circular dish-top hinged on a birdcage support, tripod base terminating in bulbous ridged platform pad feet, ht. 28, dia. 22in. **$6,380**

A-NH Northeast Auctions
839 Regency Style Triple Pedestal Dining Table, mah. w/reeded downswept legs ending in brass capped pawfoot casters & w/two additional 12in. leaves. Ht. 29, wd. 46, lg. extended 118in. **$3,500**

FURNITURE

A-PA Freeman's
118 Chippendale Dressing Table, Phil., walnut, mid-18th C., w/lip molded drawers, fishtail & scalloped apron on cabriole legs w/ball & claw feet. Ht. 31, wd. 33¼in. **$17,925**

A-PA Pook & Pook, Inc.
776 George III Card Table, mah., ca.1760 w/serpentine top overhanging skirt w/egg & dart border supported by cabriole legs, ball & claw feet, ht. 28½, wd. 34¾in. **$5,148**

A-OH Garth's Arts & Antiques
553 Hepplewhite Drop-leaf Table w/single board tiger maple top & leaves, legs swing to support leaves w/screws replaced, ht. 28½, wd. 42in. **$1,255**
554 Decorated Bible Box, PA, pine w/square nails, orig. black paint w/yellow & bittersweet sponging, 17x13½x10½in. **$1,552**

A-NH Northeast Auctions
330 Boston Sheraton Work Table, mah. w/figured maple & satinwood, rounded corners, center oval medallion & banded border w/ebony inlaid corner spandrels & reeded legs. Retains orig. brasses, ht. 29, top 16½x21in. **$5,000**

A-MA Skinner, Inc.
647 Classical Tiger Maple Tilt-top Candlestand, ca.1820-1825, w/ring-turned post continuing to scrolled legs ending in ball feet, w/minor rest. & imper., ht. 28in. **$2,115**
648 Federal Tiger Maple & Maple Stand Table, N. Eng., ca.1825, w/ring turned legs, repl. brasses, ref. & minor imper., ht.28¾in. **$3,055**
649 Federal Tiger Maple Candlestand, first qtr. 19th C. w/rectangular top on vase & ring-turned support, tripod base & shaped tapering legs, w/minor repairs, ht. 28¾, top 15x7½in. **$2,115**

A-PA   Pook & Pook, Inc.
741 **New Jersey Work Stand,** walnut, late 18th C. w/cut-corner top, scalloped skirt & turned legs joined by H-stretcher, ht. 28½, wd. 26in.
$6,435

A-NH   Northeast Auctions
1846 **Hepplewhite Three-part Dining Table,** NY, mah. w/swing legs w/crossbanded cuffs, joined to two demilune tables w/conforming aprons, ht. 28, wd. 48in. Length closed 58, open 109in. **$4,640**

A-PA   Pook & Pook, Inc.
316 **Sheraton Three-part Dining Table,** cherry, ca.1820, w/ring & rope turned legs, ht. 30, wd. 48, open 118in. **$3,510**

A-PA   Freeman's
1035 **Chippendale Drop-leaf Dining Table,** PA, ca.1770, walnut w/arched carved apron on cabriole legs, claw & ball feet, ht. 28, lg. 55, wd. 48in. **$13,145**

A-NH   Northeast Auctions
1864 Two Matching Classical Astragal-end Work Tables, NY, each w/rectangular hinged lid & astragal ends opening to a baize-lined adjustable writing surface & adjustable recessed dressing mirror w/int. fittings w/acanthus-carved legs & brass-capped paw foot casters, ht. of tallest 29, wd. 26, dp 13½in. One table w/label of John T. Dolan, a contemporary of Duncan Phyfe from 1808-1813. **$25,520**

A-NH   Northeast Auctions
1492 Sheraton Two-drawer Work Table, MA, inlaid-mah. w/cross-banded top w/canted corners, string-inlaid panels & lower drawer w/pleated bag, ht. 29, wd. 22in. **$3,770**

A-NH   Northeast Auctions
344 N. Eng. Tray Top Tea Table, cherry w/straight skirt, slender cabriole legs & pad feet, ht. 28, top 21¼x26½in. **$8,500**

A-PA   Freeman's
1235 Chippendale Drop-leaf Dining Table, last third 18th C., mah. w/slightly curved ends, D-shaped drop-

leaves, carved apron w/ball & claw feet, top lg. 60¾, wd. 52½in. **$2,390**
1236 Classical Center or Loo Table, Phil., ca.1830, mah. & mah. flame

veneer, w/urn form support, reeded downswept legs ending in brass caps on casters, ht. 28¾, dia. 48in.
$32,000

FURNITURE

A-NH   Northeast Auctions
466 N. Eng. Empire Work Table, mah. w/rolled molded feet, ht. 32in. **$200**
467 Diminutive Vermont Empire Dressing Table, cherry w/bird's-eye maple. **$550**
468 Empire Work Table w/lyre form pedestal, inside top drawer stamped Springer's Furniture, Wil. Del., ht. 30, wd. 20½in. **$300**

A-MA   Skinner, Inc.
69 Federal Inlaid Card Table, MA or NH, mah. ca.1810, ref. ht. 26, wd. 35½in. **$5,581**
70 MA Federal Card Table w/inlay, ca.1795-1805 w/inlaid panel & string inlaid double-tapering legs w/cuffs, ref. & minor imper., ht. 29½, wd. 36in. **$4,113**

A-NH   Northeast Auctions
717 William & Mary Tavern Table, Taunton, MA area, maple & pine w/rectangular top, breadboard ends, baluster turned legs & box stretcher ending in ball feet, ht. 27, top 37x25in. **$4,000**

A-NH   Northeast Auctions
337 N. Eng. Federal Stand Table, inlaid cherry w/stringing & square tapering legs. **$5,000**

A-NH   Northeast Auctions
1043 N. Eng. Butterfly Table, tiger maple w/hinged demi-lune leaves above a straight apron on turned baluster splayed legs w/winged supports, joined by a rectangular stretcher on ball feet, ht. 27, lg. 37, wd. 16in. **$3,480**

A-NH **Northeast Auctions**

444 NY Classical Carved Card Table, mah. w/rectangular cross-banded hinged top, canted corners, ring & urn turned acanthus leaf carved pedestal, & acanthus carved feet w/brass casters, ht. 29½, wd.36in. **$1,100**

445 NY Classical Empire Center Table w/carrara marble top, mah., att. to Joseph Meeks, w/urn form pedestal & stepped plinth on a shaped platform base raised on rolled feet w/brass casters, ht. 29, top 36sq.in. **$2,900**

A-NH **Northeast Auctions**

708 N. Eng. Q.A. Drop-leaf Table, cherry & maple w/hinged leaves, & legs headed w/rings on pad feet w/disks, ht. 28, top 41¾x51¼ open. **$5,220**

A-PA **Freeman's**

71 George III Architect's Table, ca.1770, w/ratchet adjustable caddy molded top over one compartmented frieze drawer & two lateral candle slides, w/chamfered square legs, ht. 30½, wd. 38½in. **$2,629**

A-NH **Northeast Auctions**

664 N. Eng. Country Scrubbed Tea Table, pine & maple, last quarter 18th C., retaining original red paint & square molded legs joined by X-stretcher, ht. 29, top 26½x49in. **$22,040**

FURNITURE

A-SC   **Charlton Hall Auctions**
678 Eastlake Bedroom Suite, walnut, 3 pcs., ca.1875, incl. a carved &

paneled bed, ht. 86½in.; marble-topped washstand, ht. 43in.; & a marble-topped dresser centered w/tall

mirror, ht.94in., w/chips & scuffs consistent w/age. **$2,199**

A-IA   **Jackson's International Auctioneers**
872 Eastlake Cylinder Secretary, walnut w/burl veneer, ht. 95in. **$1,527**

A-IA   **Jackson's International Auctioneers**
873 Victorian Pier Mirror w/carved crest & marble shelf, ht. 95in. **$646**

A-IA   **Jackson's International Auctioneers**
1003 Walnut Renaissance Revival Dresser w/center well, marble tops & burl veneer on drawer fronts, ht. 86in. **$1,175**

1736   1735   1734

A-PA   Freeman's

1734 **Two Rococo-revival Upholstered Side Chairs,** NY, mid-19th C., crestrail carved w/spray of roses, cabriole legs ending in scrolls, on casters, ht. 37¼in. **$896**

1735 **Victorian Armchair,** walnut, mid-19th C. w/rose & scroll-carved crestrail, molded arms & leaf carved cabriole legs & scroll feet on casters. **$1,434**

1736 **Rococo-revival Carved Chair,** rosewood, mid 19th C. w/oval back & floral carved cresting to upholstered arms & carved seat rail, ht. 40in. **$239**

1737 **Rococo-revival Chaise Longue,** mid-19th C. w/asymmetrical back carved w/floral spray & scrolls, cabriole legs & scrolled feet w/casters. **$5,377**

1737

A-OH   Garth's Arts & Antiques

74 **Diminutive Empire Style Sofa,** mah. w/scrolled arms, splayed & reeded legs ending in brass paw feet, old finish & repr. lg. 62in. **$230**

FURNITURE

A-OH   **Garth's Arts & Antiques**
567 Empire Sofa, flame grain mah. veneer over pine w/scrolled back crest w/carved eagle heads, floral arms & hair paw front feet w/carved cornucopias & replaced upholstery, ht. 33½, wd. 79½in. **$1,150**

A-NH   **Northeast Auctions**
1845 Sheraton Sofa w/ring turned tapering reeded legs, lg. 72in. **$1,044**

A-OH   **Garth's Arts & Antiques**
566 Empire Sofa, mah. flame grain veneer on a paneled & scrolled back & arms. Hairy paw feet w/gilt feathers & oak leaves. Repl. upholstery. ht. 31½, lg. 82½in. **$1,150**

A-NH   **Northeast Auctions**
1737 Federal Carved & Inlaid Settee, mah., w/inlaid bird's eye maple panels centering an upholstered seat, reeded tapering legs, ringed cuffs & brass casters, lg. 72in. **$5,220**

A-NH Northeast Auctions
1070 Chippendale Camelback Sofa
w/arched serpentine crest rail
continuing to roll arms, seat raised on
square molded legs & joined by
recessed box stretchers. **$5,510**

A-NH Northeast Auctions
**1503 Am. Chippendale Camelback
Sofa,** mah. w/upholstered back
above out-scrolled rolled arms
centering upholstered seat w/cushion
& raised on square molded legs
joined by box stretcher, lg. 86in.
$7,540

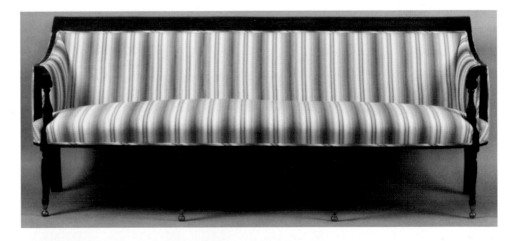

A-PA Pook & Pook, Inc.
100 New York Federal Sofa, mah.,
ca.1810 w/repl. upholstery, lg.
81in. **$7,020**

A-NH Northeast Auctions
328 Federal Sofa, mah.,
w/rectangular rail & tablet crest inlaid
w/an oval patera depicting a moth,
on square tapered legs w/stone
inlays & banded cuffs, ht., repl.
upholstery, ht. 32, lg. 85in. **$10,000**

A-PA Pook & Pook, Inc.
686 George III Sofa, ca.1790, mah. frame w/tapering legs terminating in brass casters, repl. upholstery. **$3,042**

A-MA Skinner, Inc.
198 Classical Carved Sofa, mah. frame, ca.1820, att. to Samuel F. McIntire, Salem, MA. The crest of flanking spiral & acanthus-carved scrolls ending in floral rosettes w/grapevines below on star-punched background, centering a basket of fruit, ref. & repl. upholstery w/minor imper., ht. 38, lg. 80in. **$9,400**

Below, left. A-PA Freeman's
376 Carved Walnut Sideboard, Phil., late 19th C., in two parts w/mirrored panels. **$7,170**

A-PA Alderfer Auction Co., Inc.
1531 Eastlake Wardrobe, walnut & burl veneer w/center beveled mirror, two side sections w/burled blind doors, dov. drawers & orig. hdw. ht. 88, wd. 78in. **$1,380**

1667   1668   1669   1670

1516   1517   1518   1519

1702   1703   1704   1705

A-IA   **Jackson's International Auctioneers**

1667 Victorian Walnut Chest w/applied racetrack molding, ht. 38in. **$146**

1668 Victorian Dresser w/carved pulls, ht. 84in. **$587**

1669 Kitchen Cupboard, oak, w/white enameled top, ht. 69, wd. 41in. **$205**

1670 Victorian Dresser, walnut w/raised burled panels, ht. 82, wd. 39in. **$1,057**

1516 Corner Cupboard, walnut, ca.1850-1860 w/paneled doors & pegged. **$881**

1517 Seller's Oak Kitchen Cupboard, ca.1800 w/tambor front & enameled top, ht. 68, wd. 43in. **$499**

1518 Stacking Oak Bookcase, early 20th C. w/five sections & glazed door fronts, ht. 77, wd. 34in. **$587**

1519 Triple Curved Glass China Cabinet, oak w/mirrors & panel carved crest, ht. 63, wd. 35in. **$646**

1702 English Oak Hall Chair, late 19th C. w/carved mask, ht. 39in. **$176**

1703 Victorian Parlor Arm Chair w/upholstered back & seat, ht. 39in. **$176**

1704 Louis XVI Parlor Chair, late 19th C. w/carved back crest. **$105**

1705 Victorian Walnut Parlor Table, late 19th C., ht. 29, dia. 23in. **$35**

FURNITURE

1401

1402

1403

1404

1405

1406

A-IA   Jackson's International Auctioneers
1401 English Bow Front Chest, ca.1800, mah. w/inlay, brass pulls & ivory escutcheons, ht. 43, wd. 42in. **$881**
1402 Sheraton Style Game Table, mah., early 20th C. w/inlaid design

& fluted legs, ht. 30, wd. 36in. **$264**
1403 Burlwood Breakfast Table, walnut, early 19th C., drop-leaf oval top & gate-legs, ht. 29, wd. 39in. **$440**
1404 Regency Server, ca.1800 w/drop-leaves on 4-legged base w/brass claw

feet, ht. 28, wd. 28, lg. 59in. **$881**
1405 Early Windsor Settee, 19th C., maple w/spindle back, lg. 72in. **$94**
1406 Cherry Drop-leaf Table, ca.1845 w/turned legs, ht. 28in. **$381**

1687   1688   1689   1690

1691   1692   1693   1694

1695   1696   1697   1698

1699   1700   1701

A-IA   Jackson's International Auctioneers
1687 Victorian Bentwood Rocker
w/painted dec., ht. 40in. **$176**
1688 Victorian Maple Rocker
w/scrolled swan's head arms, caned
seat & back, ht. 42in. **$117**
1689 Lincoln Rocker, maple, 19th C.
w/fiddle back splat & spindle
supports, ht. 40in. **$117**
1690 Child's Press Back Oak Rocker
w/turned spindles, ht. 25in. **$94**
1691 Eastlake Walnut Rocker

w/caned seat & back, ht. 32in. **$47**
1692 Victorian Oak Rocker w/caned
back & seat, ht. 39in. **$117**
1693 Victorian Walnut Rocker,
upholstered, ht. 39in. **$176**
1694 Victorian Platform Rocker,
upholstered, ht. 38in. **$35**
1695 Windsor Style Rocker, early 20th
C., w/bow-back, ht. 35in. **$11**
1696 Twist Carved Rocker w/woven
seat & back, ht. 34in. **$47**
1697 Victorian Oak Pressback Rocker,

ca.1900 w/triple pressback panels,
ht. 40in. **$47**
**1698 Victorian Pressback Child's
Highchair,** oak, ht. 41in. **$47**
1699 Set of Six Victorian Side Chairs,
maple w/carved handle back &
lacking cane seats. **$58**
1700 Victorian Oak Settee/Lounge
w/reclining arm supports & carved
feet, ht. 37, lg. 54in. **$70**
1701 Victorian Settee w/brass dec. &
worn upholstery, ht. 39, wd. 46in. **$11**

A-ME   James D. Julia, Inc.

1048 Carved Oak Leaded Glass Sideboard, oak throughout in three sections. The upper section w/two concave leaded glass doors w/pink frosted & jewel glass flower panels & the int. fitted w/a mirror back. The front of this section is supported by two fully carved supports which have a large C-scroll with full seated winged lady figures, ht. 83, wd. 61in. **$11,212**

A-IA   Jackson's International Auctioneers
191 Walnut Dining Room Set incl. nine pieces, ca.1925, w/applied & intaglio carved panels, incl. a drop-leaf table, six chairs, china cabinet, silver chest & buffet. **$646**
192 Three Victorian Oak Pieces incl. a 6-drawer dresser, 4-drawer dresser & 3-drawer commode, all w/mirrors. **$1,634**
193 Walnut Drop-front Desk

w/pigeon hole compartments, ht. 44¼in. **$264**
194 Victorian Oak Sideboard w/beveled mirror & scroll carved w/claw feet below four beveled glass panels, ht. 66, wd. 50in. **$528**
195 Victorian Oak Sideboard w/beveled & scalloped mirror, round posts & carved dec., ht. 61, wd. 48in. **$264**
196 Pine Hutch, mid.-19th C.,

w/bracket feet & square nail construction, ht. 81, wd. 48in. **$440**
197 Continental Walnut Hutch w/pierced scrolled dec., ht. 82, wd. 50in. **$440**
198 Q.A. Dining Room Set, walnut, ca.1925, comprising an oval table, buffet & four chairs/not illus. **$117**
199 Pair of Victorian Side Chairs, walnut w/balloon backs, **$35**

191

192

193

194

195

196

197

198

199

223

224

225

226

227

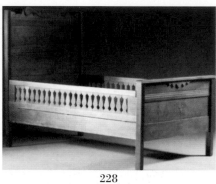

228

229

230

231

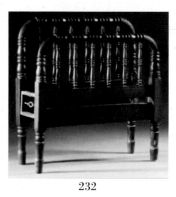

232

233

234

235

236

237

238

A-IA   Jackson's International Auctioneers
223 Oak Roll Top Desk w/eight drawers, ht. 50, wd. 54in. **$940**
224 Drop-leaf Table, walnut, ca.1850 w/ceramic knobs, ht. 29in. **$146**
225 Victorian Head/Foot Board, walnut w/side rails & carved top, ht. 62, wd. 49in. **$70**
226 Carved Lectern, oak, ca.1880, of pedestal form, ht. 41in. **$146**
227 Victorian Head/Foot Board w/side rails & carved top, ht. 41, wd. 56in. **$146**

228 Victorian Youth Bed w/fold-out fiddle back side panels, ht. 52, wd. 40in. **$265**
229 Country Pine Head/Foot Board w/dec. top, 19th C. **$176**
230 Pine Piano Stool w/turned legs & walnut finish, ht. 20in. **$47**
231 Pair of Victorian Beds, one walnut w/matching footboard, other is oak without matching footboard. **$94**
232 Pine Jenny Lind Youth Bed w/walnut finish & turned spindles, ht. 39, wd. 36in. **$23**

233 Victorian Sling Seat Bench w/turned legs, ht. 18in. **$58**
234 Pine Work Table, 19th C. ht. 28, top 24x18in. **$70**
235 Drop-leaf Table, walnut w/turned legs, ht. 29, dia. 52in. **$70**
236 Oak Drop-leaf Table w/some repair, ht. 28¼, dia. 54in. **$70**
237 Victorian Commode, oak, ht. 34, wd. 32in. **$117**
239 Iron & Wood School Desks, pr. **$235**

1604

1607

466

A-IA   Jackson's International Auctioneers
1604 **Victorian Stick & Ball Hat Rack,** ca. 1880, w/bent wire hooks &

mirror, ht. 16, lg. 32in. **$176**
1607 **Gout Stools,** pr., 19th C., walnut w/storage top, dia. 11in. **$205**

466 **Victorian Child's Sled** w/orig. painted finish & swan head iron finials, lg. 35in. **$264**

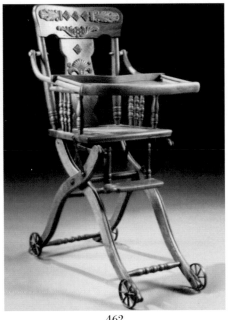

462

463

464

A-IA   Jackson's international Auctioneers
462 **Child's Oak High Chair & Stroller,** late 19th C. w/caned seat & applied

carvings, ht. 36in. **$205**
463 **Combination Child's High Chair & Stroller,** ca. 1900, ht. 41in. **$94**

464 **Victorian Child's High Chair & Stroller Rocker,** walnut w/caned seat & back, ht. 36in. **$235**

1411

1408

1410

A-IA   Jackson's International Auctioneers
1411 **French Style Vernis Martin Vitrine,** ormolu mounted, early 20th C. w/painted courting scene on gilt

ground, ht. 75, wd. 36in. **$1,057**
1408 **Sheraton Work Table,** mah. w/drop-leaf & twisted legs, ht. 30in. **$998**

1410 **George III Canterbury,** mah. w/twist carved spindles & brass caster feet, ht. 23in. **$881**

A-NJ Craftsman Arts & Crafts Auction
163 Gustav Stickley Knock-down Even-arm Settle, ref. & newly recovered brown leather cushions, lg. 84in. **$1,200**

A-NJ   **Craftsman Arts & Crafts Auction**
164 Gustav Stickley Hexagonal Library Table w/trumpeted cross-stretchers, ref. & one repl. key. Paper label under top, ht. 29½, wd. 48in. **$4,250**

A-NJ   **Craftsman Arts & Crafts Auction**
161 Gustav Stickley Chest of Drawers w/paneled sides & strap hardware. Ref., separation to top, & w/brand mark, ht. 47½, wd. 36in. **$11,000**

A-NJ   **Craftsman Arts & Crafts Auction**
162 Early Two-drawer Library Table by Gustav Stickley, w/faceted wooden knob pulls, orig. finish & unmkd, ht. 30, wd. 36in. **$8,500**

A-NH   **Northeast Auctions**

633 Am. Arts & Crafts Oak Dining Set, nine pieces, by Limbert, Grand Rapids & Holland, MI. Dia. of table 54in., wd. of each leaf 11in.; ht. of china cabinet 57, wd. 46in. **$4,300**

A-NJ   **Craftsman Arts & Crafts Auction**

240 Revolving Book Rack by Gustav Stickley, w/dov. joinery, orig. finish & mkd. w/red decal on inside, 9½x13in. sq. **$2,100**

A-NJ   **Craftsman Arts & Crafts Auction**

515 Schumann Upright Arts & Crafts Piano & Bench, quarter-sawn oak case & mkd. w/metal tag on back, ht. 55, wd. 62in. **$4,000**

516 Even-arm Settee in the style of Gustav Stickley w/tapering posts & drop-in spring cushion covered in brown leather, ref. & unmkd. lg. 59½in. **$2,800**

A-NJ   **Craftsman Arts & Crafts Auction**

615 L. & J.G. Stickley Leather-top Trestle Table w/orig. finish, repl. tacks & leather. Decal under top, 29x48x29¾in. **$1,200**

616 Gustav Stickley Cellarette w/pull-out copper surface, iron V-pulls & int. cubbies complete w/rotating bottle rack. Orig. finish, major veneer damage to both sides & mkd. w/red decal in drawer, 39x22x16in. **$2,200**

617 Morris Rocker w/drop-in spring cushion covered in light linen-weave upholstery by L.& J.G. Stickley, ref. & unmkd. **$1,700**

618 Drink Stand by L.& J.G. Stickley w/orig. finish & shadow of decal on leg, ht. 29, dia. 18in. **$950**

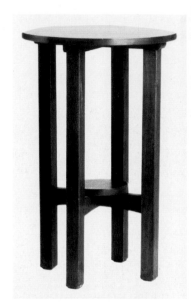

A-NJ   **Craftsman Arts & Crafts Auction**

759 Stickley Brothers Library Table w/ring pulls & good orig. finish & quaint decal, 30x48x30in. **$1,000**

A-NJ   **Craftsman Arts & Crafts Auction**

763 Arts & Crafts Trapezoidal China Cabinet w/overhanging top supported by corbels, eyed-through tenons on an arched apron. Orig. finish & stenciled No. 6012, ht. 61¼in. **$3,000**

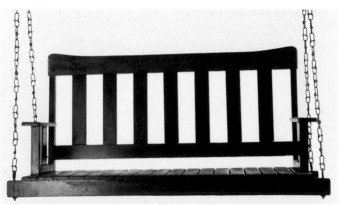

A-NJ   **Craftsman Arts & Crafts Auction**

771 Limbert Porch Swing w/evidence of orig. green stain under overcoat, orig. chains & branded under center slat, 59x29x20in. **$2,600**

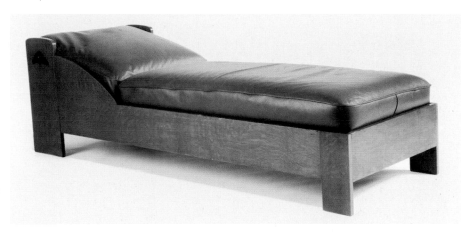

A-NJ   Craftsman Arts & Crafts Auction
337 **Limbert Daybed** w/spade shaped cut-outs to plank sides & drop-in spring cushions covered w/brown leather, orig. finish, edge nicks & wear, mkd. Lg. 75in. **$2,600**

A-NJ   Craftsman Arts & Crafts Auction
767 **Limbert Chest of Drawers** w/pivoting mirror, copper hdw., & orig. green finish w/overcoat, 66x35x20in. **$1,100**

A-NJ   Craftsman Arts & Crafts Auction
78A **L.& J.G. Stickley Side Chairs,** set of six w/one arm chair, ref. & seats covered w/leather. **$2,200**

A-NJ   Craftsman Arts & Crafts Auction
148 **Drop-arm Morris Chair** by Gustav Stickley w/drop-in seat cushion and loose back, newly recovered, ref., unmkd. **$4,500**

A-NJ   Craftsman Arts & Crafts Auction
72 **Spindled Library Table** by Gustav Stickley, w/orig. finish, minor warping to spindles & mkd. w/paper label under top, 26x36x24in. **$2,500**

A-NJ   **Craftsman Arts & Crafts Auction**
73 **Gustav Stickley Drop-front Desk** w/int. gallery, hammered iron pulls, orig. finish & missing inset escutcheon, mkd. ht. 43¼in. **$2,600**

A-NJ   **Craftsman Arts & Crafts Auction**
167 **Dresser** w/pivoting mirror, orig. finish & repl. period hardware. Handcraft decal inside top drawer, ht. 69¼, wd. 48in. **$3,250**

A-NJ   **Craftsman Arts & Crafts Auction**
899 **Roycroft Footstool** w/tapering legs & tacked-on brown leather, orig. finish & mkd. w/carved orb & cross mark. **$950**

A-NJ   **Craftsman Arts & Crafts Auction**
256 **Lifetime Puritan Line Console Table** w/single drawer w/bell-shaped pulls, orig. finish & mkd. w/decal in drawer, ht. 31¼, wd. 67in. **$8,000**

A-NJ   **Craftsman Arts & Crafts Auction**
897 **Gustav Stickley Gout Stool** w/orig. finish & recovered upholstery, unmkd. 5x11¾in. **$1,000**

A-NJ　　　　　　　　　Craftsman Arts & Crafts Auction
149 **Bookcase by Gustav Stickley,** w/eight panes per door, iron V-pulls, orig. finish & mkd. w/paper label on back, 56x48x13in. **$5,500**

A-NJ　　　　　　　　　Craftsman Arts & Crafts Auction
351 **Limbert Two-door China Cabinet** w/plate rail & adjustable shelves, ref. & branded on back, ht. 61½, wd. 46in. **$2,600**

A-NJ　　　　　　　　　Craftsman Arts & Crafts Auction
61 **Roycroft Vanity** w/matching chair, bird's-eye maple w/partially rest. finish, pivoting mirror & branded. **$12,000**

A-NJ　　　　　　　　　Craftsman Arts & Crafts Auction
62 **Roycroft Bookcase,** mah. w/fixed shelves, hammered copper escutcheon & knob-pull, w/orig. finish & mkd. w/carved orb & cross on door, ht. 56½, wd. 40in. **$7,500**

Agata Glass was patented by Joseph Locke of the New England Glass Company of Cambridge, Massachusetts, in 1877. The application of a metallic stain left a mottled design characteristic of agata, hence the name.

Amber Glass is the name of any glassware having a yellowish-brown color. It became popular during the last quarter of the 19th century.

Amberina Glass was patented by the New England Glass Company in 1833. It is generally recognized as a clear yellow glass shading to a deep red or fuchsia at the top. When the colors are opposite, it is known as reverse amberina. It was machine-pressed into molds, free blown, cut and pattern molded. Almost every glass factory here and in Europe produced this ware, but few pieces were ever marked.

Amethyst Glass – The term identifies any glassware made in the proper dark purple shade. It became popular after the Civil War.

Art Glass is a general term given to various types of ornamental glass made to be decorative rather than functional. It dates primarily from the late Victorian period to the present day and, during the span of time, glassmakers have achieved fantastic effects of shape, color, pattern, texture and decoration.

Aventurine Glass The Venetians are credited with the discovery of aventurine during the 1860s. It was produced by various mixes of copper in yellow glass. When the finished pieces were broken, ground or crushed, they were used as decorative material by glassblowers. Therefore, a piece of aventurine glass consists of many tiny glittering particles on the body of the object, suggestive of sprinkled gold crumbs or dust. Other colors in aventurine are known to exist.

Baccarat Glass was first made in France in 1756, by La Compagnie des Cristelleries de Baccarat – until the firm went bankrupt. Production began for the second time during the 1820s and the firm is still in operation, producing fine glassware and paperweights. Baccarat is famous for its earlier paperweights made during the last half of the 19th century.

Bohemian Glass is named for its country of origin. It is ornate, overlay, or flashed glassware, popular during the Victorian era.

Bristol Glass is a lightweight opaque glass, often having a light bluish tint, and decorated with enamels. The ware is a product of Bristol, England – a glass center since the 1700s.

Burmese – Frederick Shirley developed this shaded art glass at the now famous old Mt. Washington Glass Company in New Bedford, Massachusetts, and patented his discovery under the name of "Burmese" on December 15, 1885. The ware was also made in England by Thomas Webb & Sons. Burmese is a hand-blown glass with the exception of a few pieces that were pattern molded. The latter are either ribbed, hobnail or diamond quilted in design. This ware is found in two textures or finishes: the original glazed or shiny finish, and the dull, velvety, satin finish. It is a homogeneous single-layered glass that was never lined, cased, or plated. Although its color varies slightly, it always shades from a delicate yellow at the base to salmon-pink at the top. The blending of colors is so gradual that it is difficult to determine where a color ends and another begins.

Cambridge glasswares were produced by the Cambridge Glass Company in Ohio from 1901 until the firm closed in 1954.

Cameo Glass can be defined as any glass in which the surface has been cut away to leave a design in relief. Cutting is accomplished by the use of hand-cutting tools, wheel cutting and hydrofluoric acid. This ware can be clear or colored glass of a single layer, or glass with multiple layers of clear or colored glass.

Although cameo glass has been produced for centuries, the majority available today dates from the late 1800s. It has been produced in England, France and other parts of Europe, as well as the United States. The most famous of the French masters of cameo wares was Emile Gallé.

Carnival Glass was an inexpensive, pressed iridescent glassware made from about 1900 through the 1920s. It was made in quantities by Northwood Glass Company, Fenton Art Glass Company and others, to compete with the expensive art glass of the period. It was originally called "taffeta" glass during the 1920s, when carnivals gave examples as premiums or prizes.

Chocolate Glass, sometimes mistakenly called caramel slag because of its streaked appearance, was made by the Indiana Tumbler & Goblet Company of Greentown, IN, from 1900 to 1903. It was also made by the National Glass Company factories, and later by Fenton from 1907 to 1915.

Consolidated Lamp & Glass Co. of Coraopolis, PA, was founded in 1894 and closed in 1967. The company made lamps, art glass and tablewares. Items made after 1925 are of the greatest interest to collectors.

Coralene – The term coralene denotes a type of decoration rather than a kind of glass – consisting of many tiny beads, either of colored or transparent glass, decorating the surface. The most popular design used resembled coral or seaweed, hence the name.

Crackle Glass – This type of art glass was an invention of the Venetians which spread rapidly to other countries. It is made by plunging red-hot glass into cold water, then reheating and reblowing it, thus producing an unusual outer surface which appears to be covered with a multitude of tiny fractures, but is perfectly smooth to the touch.

Cranberry Glass – The term "cranberry glass" refers to color only, not to a particular type of glass. It is undoubtedly the most familiar colored glass known to collectors. This ware was blown or molded, and often decorated with enamels.

Crown Milano glass was made by Frederick Shirley at the Mt. Washington Glass Company, New Bedford, Massachusetts, from 1886-1888. It is ivory in color with a satin finish, and was embellished with floral sprays, scrolls and gold enamel.

Crown Tuscan glass has a pink-opaque body. It was originally produced in 1936 by A.J. Bennett, president of the Cambridge Glass Company of Cambridge, Ohio. The line was discontinued in 1954. Occasionally referred to as Royal Crown Tuscan, this ware was named for a scenic area in

Italy, and it has been said that its color was taken from the flash-colored sky at sunrise. When trans-illuminated, examples do have all of the blaze of a sunrise – a characteristic that is even applied to new examples of the ware reproduced by Mrs. Elizabeth Degenhart of Crystal Art Glass, and Harold D. Bennett, Guernsey Glass Company of Cambridge, Ohio.

Custard Glass was manufactured in the United States for a period of about 30 years (1885-1915). Although Harry Northwood was the first and largest manufacturer of custard glass, it was also produced by the Heisey Glass Company, Diamond Glass Company, Fenton Art Glass Company and a number of others.

The name custard glass is derived from its "custard yellow" color which may shade light yellow to ivory to light green glass that is opaque to opalescent. Most pieces have fiery opalescence when held to the light. Both the color and glow of this ware came from the use of uranium salts in the glass. It is generally a heavy type pressed glass made in a variety of different patterns.

Cut Overlay – The term identifies pieces of glassware usually having a milk-white exterior that have been cased with cranberry, blue or amber glass. Other examples are deep blue, amber or cranberry on crystal glass, and the majority of pieces have been decorated with dainty flowers. Although Bohemian glass manufacturers produced some very choice pieces during the 19th century, fine examples were also made in America, as well as in France and England.

Daum Nancy is the mark found on pieces of French cameo glass made by August and Jean Daum after 1875.

Durand Art Glass was made by Victor Durand from 1879 to 1935 at the Durand Art Glass Works in Vineland, New Jersey. The glass resembles Tiffany in quality. Drawn white feather designs and thinly drawn glass threading (quite brittle) applied around the main body of the ware, are striking examples of Durand creations on an iridescent surface.

Findlay or Onyx art glass was manufactured about 1890 for only a short time by the Dalzell Gilmore Leighton Company of Findlay, Ohio.

Flashed Wares were popular during the late 19th century. They were made by partially coating the inner surface of an object with a thin plating of glass of another, more dominant color – usually red. These pieces can readily be identified by holding the object to the light and examining the rim, as it will show more than one layer of glass. Many pieces of "rubina crystal" (cranberry to clear), "blue amberina" (blue to amber), and "rubina verde" (cranberry to green), were manufactured in this way.

Francisware is a hobnail glassware with frosted or clear glass hobs and stained amber rims and tops. It was produced during the late 1880s by Hobbs, Brockunier and Company.

Fry Glass was made by the H.C. Fry Company, Rochester, Pennsylvania, from 1901, when the firm was organized, until 1934, when operations ceased. The firm specialized in the manufacturing of cut glassware. The production of their famous "foval" glass did not begin until the 1920s. The firm also produced a variety of glass specialties, oven wares and etched glass.

Gallé glass was made in Nancy, France, by Emile Gallé at the Gallé Factory, founded in 1874. The firm produced both enameled and cameo glass, pottery, furniture and other art nouveau items. After Gallé's death in 1904, the factory continued operating until 1935.

Greentown glass was made in Greentown, Indiana, by the Indiana Tumbler and Goblet Company from 1894 until 1903. The firm produced a variety of pressed glasswares in addition to milk and chocolate glass.

Gunderson Peachblow is a more recent type of art glass produced in 1952 by the Gunderson-Pairpoint Glass Works of New Bedford, Massachusetts, successors to the Mt. Washington Glass Company. Gunderson pieces have a soft satin finish shading from white at the base to a deep rose at the top.

Hobnail – The term "hobnail" identifies any glassware having "bumps" – flattened, rounded or pointed – over the outer surface of the glass. A variety of patterns exists. Many of the fine early examples were produced by Hobbs, Brockunier and Company, Wheeling, West Virginia, and the New England Glass Company.

Holly Amber, originally known as "golden agate," is a pressed glass pattern which features holly berries and leaves over its glossy surface. Its color shades from golden brown tones to opalescent streaks. This ware was produced by the Indiana Tumbler and Goblet Company for only 6 months, from January 1 to June 13, 1903. Examples are rare and expensive.

Imperial Glass – The Imperial Glass Company of Bellaire, Ohio, was organized in 1901 by a group of prominent citizens of Wheeling, West Virginia. A variety of fine art glass, in addition to carnival glass, was produced by the firm. The two trademarks which identified the ware were issued in June 1914. One consisted of the firm's name, "Imperial," by double-pointed arrows.

Latticino is the name given to articles of glass in which a network of tiny milk-white lines appear, crisscrossing between two walls of glass. It is a type of filigree glassware developed during the 16th century by the Venetians.

Legras Glass – Cameo, acid cut and enameled glasswares were made by August J.F. Legras at Saint-Denis, France, from 1864-1914.

Loetz Glass was made in Austria just before the turn of the century. As Loetz worked in the Tiffany factory before returning to Austria, much of his glass is similar in appearance to Tiffany wares. Loetz glass is often marked "Loetz" or "Loetz-Austria".

Lutz Glass was made by Nicholas Lutz, a Frenchman, who worked at the Boston and Sandwich Glass Company from 1870 to 1888, when it closed. He also produced fine glass at the Mt. Washington Glass Company. Lutz is noted for two different types of glass – striped and threaded wares. Other glass houses also produced similar glass, and these wares were known as Lutz-type.

Mary Gregory was an artist for the Boston and Sandwich Glass Company during the last quarter of the 19th century. She decorated glassware with white enamel figures of young children engaged in playing, collecting butterflies, etc., in white on transparent glass, both clear and colored. Today the term "Mary Gregory" glass applies to any glassware that remotely resembles her work.

Mercury Glass is a double-walled glass that dates from the 1850s to about 1910. It was made in England as well as the United States during this period. Its interior, usually in the form of vases, is lined with flashing mercury, giving the items an all over silvery appearance. The entrance hole in the base of each piece was sealed over. Many pieces were decorated.

Milk Glass is an opaque pressed glassware usually of milk-white color, although green, amethyst, black, and shades of blue were made. Milk glass was produced in quantity in the United States during the 1880s, in a variety of patterns.

Millefiori – This decorative glassware is considered to be a specialty of the Venetians. It is sometimes called "glass of a thousand flowers" and has been made for centuries. Very thin colored glass rods are arranged in bundles, then fused together with heat. When the piece of glass is sliced across, it has a design like that of many small flowers. These tiny wafer-thin slices are then embedded in larger masses of glass, enlarged and shaped.

Moser Glass was made by Ludwig Moser at Karlsbad. The ware is considered to be another type of art nouveau glass, as it was produced during its heyday – during the early 1900s. Principal colors included amethyst, cranberry, green and blue, with fancy enameled decoration.

Mother-of-Pearl, often abbreviated in descriptions as M.O.P., is a glass composed of two or more layers, with a pattern showing through to the other surface. The pattern, caused by internal air traps, is created by expanding the inside layer of molten glass into molds with varying designs. When another layer of glass is applied, this brings out the design. The final layer of glass is then acid dipped, and the result is mother-of-pearl satin ware. Patterns are numerous. The most frequently found are the diamond quilted, raindrop and

herringbone. This ware can be one solid color, a single color shading light to dark, two colors blended or a variety of colors which include the rainbow effect. In addition, many pieces are decorated with colorful enamels, coralene beading, and other applied glass decorations.

Nailsea Glass was first produced in England from 1788 to 1873. The characteristics that identify this ware are the "pulled" loopings and swirls of colored glass over the body of the object.

New England Peachblow was patented in 1886 by the New England Glass Company. It is a single-layered glass shading from opaque white at the base to deep rose-red or raspberry at the top. Some pieces have a glossy surface, but most were given an acid bath to produce a soft, matte finish.

New Martinsville Peachblow Glass was produced from 1901-1907 at New Martinsville, Pennsylvania.

Opalescent Glass – The term refers to glasswares which have a milky white effect in the glass, usually on a colored ground. There are three basic types of this ware. Presently, the most popular includes pressed glass patterns found in table settings. Here the opalescence appears at the top rim, the base, or a combination of both. On blown or mold-blown glass, the pattern itself consists of this milky effect – such as Spanish lace. Another example is the opalescent points on some pieces of hobnail glass. These wares are lighter weight. The third group includes opalescent novelties, primarily of the pressed variety.

Peking Glass is a type of Chinese cameo glass produced from the 1700s well into the 19th century.

Phoenix Glass – The firm was established in Beaver County, Pennsylvania, during the late 1800s, and produced a variety of commercial glasswares. During the 1930s the factory made a desirable sculptured gift-type glassware which has become very collectible in recent years. Vases, lamps, bowls, ginger jars, candlesticks, etc., were made until the 1950s in various colors with a satin finish.

Pigeon Blood is a bright reddish-orange glassware dating from the early 1900s.

Pomona Glass was invented in 1884 by Joseph Locke at the New England Glass Company.

Pressed Glass was the inexpensive glassware produced in quantity to fill the increasing demand for tablewares when Americans moved away from the simple table utensils of pioneer times. During the 1820s, ingenious Yankees invented and perfected machinery for successfully pressing glass. About 1865, manufacturers began to color their products. Literally hundreds of different patterns were produced.

Quezal is a very fine quality blown iridescent glassware produced by Martin Bach, in his factory in Brooklyn, New York, from 1901-1920. Named after the Central American bird, quezal glassware has an iridescent finish, featuring contrasting colored glass threads. Green, white and gold colors are most often found.

Rosaline Glass is a product of the Steuben Glass Works of Corning, New York. The firm was founded by Frederick Carter and T.C. Hawkes, Sr. Rosaline is a rose-colored jade glass or colored alabaster. The firm is now owned by the Corning Glass Company, which is presently producing fine glass of exceptional quality.

Royal Flemish Art Glass was made by the Mt. Washington Glass Works during the 1880s. It has an acid finish which may consist of one or more colors, decorated with raised gold enameled lines separating into sections. Fanciful painted enamel designs also decorate this ware. Royal Flemish glass is marked "RF," with the letter "R" reversed and backed to the letter "F," within a four-sided orange-red diamond mark.

Rubina Glass is a transparent blown glassware that shades from clear to red. One of the first to produce this crystal during the late 1800s was Hobbs, Brockunier and Company of Wheeling, West Virginia.

Rubina Verde is a blown art glass made by Hobbs, Brockunier and Company, during the late 1800s. It is a transparent glassware that shades from red to yellow-green.

Sabino Glass originated in Paris, France, in the 1920s. The company was founded by Marius-Ernest Sabino, and was noted for art deco figures, vases, nudes and animals in clear, opalescent and colored glass.

Sandwich Glass – One of the most interesting and enduring pages from America's past is Sandwich glass produced by the famous Boston and Sandwich Glass Company at Sandwich, Massachusetts. The firm began operations in 1825, and the glass flourished until 1888, when the factory closed. Despite the popularity of Sandwich Glass, little is known about its founder, Deming Jarvis. The Sandwich Glass house turned out hundreds of designs in both plain and figured patterns in colors and crystal, so that no one type could be considered entirely typical – but the best known is the "lacy" glass produced there. The variety and multitude of designs and patterns produced by the company over the years is a tribute to its greatness.

Silver Deposit Glass was made during the late 19th and early 20th centuries. Silver was deposited on the glass surface by a chemical process so that a pattern appeared against a clear or colored ground. This ware is sometimes referred to as "silver overlay."

Slag Glass was originally known as "mosaic" and "marble glass" because of its streaked appearance. Production in the United States began about 1880. The largest producer of this ware was Challinor, Taylor and Company.

Spanish Lace is a Victorian glass pattern that is easily identified by its distinct opalescent flower and leaf pattern. It belongs to the shaded opalescent glass family.

Steuben – The Steuben Glass Works was founded in 1904, by Frederick Carder, an Englishman, and T.G. Hawkes, Sr., at Corning, New York. In 1918, the firm was purchased by the Corning Glass Company. However, Carder remained with the firm, designing a bounty of fine art glass of exceptional quality.

Stevens & Williams of Stourbridge, England, made many fine art glass pieces covering the full range of late Victorian ware between the 1830s and 1930s. Many forms were decorated with applied glass flowers, leaves

and fruit. After World War I, the firm began producing lead crystal and new glass colors.

Stiegel-Type Glass – Henry William Stiegel founded America's first flint glass factory during the 1760s at Manheim, Pennsylvania. Stiegel glass is flint or crystal glass; it is thin and clear, and has a bell-like ring when tapped. The ware is quite brittle and fragile. Designs were painted free-hand on the glass – birds, animals and architectural motifs, surrounded by leaves and flowers. The engraved glass resulted from craftsmen etching the glass surface with a copper wheel, then cutting the desired patterns.

It is extremely difficult to identify, with certainty, a piece of original Stiegel glass. Part of the problem resulted from the lack of an identifying mark on the products. Additionally, many of the craftsmen moved to other areas after the Stiegel plant closed, producing a similar glass product. Therefore, when one is uncertain about the origin of this type of ware, it is referred to as "Stiegel type" glass.

Tiffany Glass was made by Louis Comfort Tiffany, one of America's outstanding glass designers of the art nouveau period, from about 1870 to the 1930s. Tiffany's designs included a variety of lamps, bronze work, silver, pottery and stained glass windows. Practically all items made were marked "L.C. Tiffany" or "L.C.T." in addition to the word "Favrile".

Tortoiseshell Glass – As its name indicates, this type of glassware resembles the color of tortoiseshell, and has deep, rich brown tones combined with amber and cream colored shades. Tortoiseshell glass was originally produced in 1880 by Francis Poh, a German chemist. It was also made in the United States by the Sandwich Glass Works and other glass houses during the late 1800s.

Val St. Lambert Cristalleries – The firm is located in Belgium, and was founded in 1825. It is still in operation.

Vasa Murrhina glassware was produced in quantity at the Vasa Murrhina Art Glass Company of Sandwich, Massachusetts, during the late 1800s. John C. Devoy, assignor to the firm, registered a patent on July 1, 1884, for the process of decorating

glassware with particles of mica flakes coated with copper, gold, nickel or silver, sandwiched between an inner layer of clear or transparent colored glass. The ware was also produced by other American glass firms and in England.

Vaseline Glass – The term "vaseline" refers to color only, as it resembles the greenish-yellow color typical of the oily petroleum jelly known as Vaseline. This ware has been produced in a variety of patterns both here and in Europe – from the late 1800s. It has been made in both clear and opaque yellow, vaseline combined with clear glass, and occasionally the two colors are combined in one piece.

Verlys Glass is a type of art glass produced in France after 1931. The Heisey Glass Company, Newark, Ohio, produced identical glass for a short time, after having obtained the rights and formula from the French factory. French produced ware can be identified from the American product by the signature. The French is mold marked, whereas the American glass is etched script signed.

Wavecrest Glass is an opaque white glassware made from the late 1890s by French factories and the Pairpoint Manufacturing Company at New Bedford, Massachusetts. Items were decorated by the C.F. Monroe Company of Meriden, Connecticut, with painted pastel enamels. The name wavecrest was used after 1898 with the initials for the company "C.F.M. Co." Operations ceased during World War II.

Webb Glass was made by Thomas Webb & Sons of Stourbridge, England, during the late Victorian period. The firm produced a variety of different types of art and cameo glass.

Wheeling Peachblow – With its simple lines and delicate shadings, Wheeling Peachblow was produced soon after 1883 by J.H. Hobbs, Brockunier and Company at Wheeling, West Virginia. It is a two-layered glass, lined or cased inside with an opaque, milk-white type of plated glassware. The outer layer shades from a bright yellow at the base to a mahogany red at the top. The majority of pieces produced are in the glossy finish.

A-OH   Early Auction Company, LLC
571 **Webb Fairy Lamp**, three-part w/acid finish & dec. w/oak leaves in various shades of green & w/a clear mkd. Clarke cricklite holder & paper sleeve mkd. Clarke's Pyramid, ht. 6½in. **$2,150**

A-ME   James D. Julia, Inc.
22 **Burmese Syrup** dec. w/yellow & white flowers topped w/a silverplated rim and lid. The applied handle is trimmed in gold, ht. 6¼in. **$4,600**

A-OH   Early Auction Company, LLC
Burmese
573 **Webb Vase** w/Prunus design w/acid finish & footed, ht. 7½in. **$525**
577 **Crimped & Ruffled Rim Vase by Webb** w/acid finish, ht. 2½in. **$75**
570 **Squatty Rose Bowl by Webb** & dec. w/acorns & leaves on branches,

Prunus design, ht. 3in. **$300**
572 **Footed Ovoid Bowl** w/scalloped rim & three applied feet, ht. 7½in. **$325**
575 **Webb Perfume** dec. w/colorful butterfly surrounded by gold leafy branches & red flowers, w/silver mounted lid, ht. 5½in. **$800**

574 **Melon Ribbed Vase by Webb** & dec. w/pine cones on needle filled branches, ht. 4½in. **$275**
576 **Webb Vase** w/star-shaped everted rim & dec. w/acorns & oak leaves, sgn. w/Thomas Webb & Son's Queen's Burmese acid stamp, ht. 6½in. **$600**

Opposite:
A-IA   Jackson's International Auctioneers
Burmese
1 **Webb Epergne**, ca.1890 w/mirrored plateau, dec. glass center post, three posy vases & a central flower form vase w/blossoms. Two vases have minor chips on mounting ring, ht. 10in. **$822**
2 **Mt. Washington Cruet**, ca.1890, w/melon ribbed body & matching tear drop stoppers, ht. 6¼in. **$205**
3 **Mt. Washington Condiment Set**, ca.1890 w/a pair of melon ribbed

shakers & matching mustard, ht. 4in. **$170**
4 **Webb Fairy Lamp** w/domed shape & dec. w/branched oak leaves & crystal base mkd. S. Clarke, ht. 4in. **$411**
5 **Bohemian Gilt Footed MOP coralene glass vase**, 19th C., w/butterscotch shading to yellow in the diamond quilted patt., & dec. w/red seaweed coralene, ht. 10¼in. **$558**
6 **Webb Fairy Lamp**, ca.1890, domed shape & set in a mkd. S. Clarke base, ht. 4in. **$146**

7 **Stevens & Williams Ruffled Rim Vases**, pair, ca.1880, deep pink MOP glass dec. w/peppermint stripe & set in a footed metal holder, ht. 6in. **$411**
8 **Mt. Washington Sugar Shaker**, ca.1890, egg shape, blue shading to white & dec. pink dogwood blossoms, ht. 4½in. **$235**
9 **English Satin Glass Rose Bowl**, late 19th C., shaded, ht. 3¼in. **$176**
10 **Four Satin Glass Bobeches**, late 19th C., lime colored glass w/scalloped rim, dia. 3¼in. **$235**

A-OH   Early Auction Company, LLC
76 **Smith Brother's Biscuit Jar,** melon shaped & dec. w/flowers, sgn. w/lion trademark, wd. 7½in. **$325**
75 **Pairpoint Biscuit Jar** w/dec. white medallions, sgn. wd. 7½in. **$350**
79 **Mt. Washington Crown Milano**

Vase, mkd. w/CM & crown, wd. 7in. **$450**
78 **Mt. Washington Crown Milano Biscuit Jar** w/pastel dec. & lid stamped MW, ht. 7½in. **$350**
77 **Mt. Washington Cracker Jar** w/blue flowers & rope handle, wd.

6in. **$150**
73 **Crown Milano Biscuit Jar** dec. w/ oak leaves & acorns & orig. lid. **$250**
81 **Mt. Washington Crown Milano Stick Vase,** dec. & sgn., ht. 10in., reduced & rim scalloped. **$200**

GLASS

A-IA   Jackson's International Auctioneers

11 Ewer, late 19th C., MOP in the herringbone patt. w/camphor handle, ht. 12in. **$176**

12 Vase, late 19th C., MOP in the diamond quilted patt., shouldered, ht. 9¾in. **$70**

13 Bulbous Stick Vase, MOP in the diamond quilted patt., ht. 10¼in. **$70**

14 Water Pitcher, ca.1890, MOP in the diamond quilted patt., ht. 8in. **$293**

15 Three Pink Tumblers, ca.1890, MOP in the diamond quilted patt. **$117**

16 Blue Celery Vase, melon ribbed, MOP. in the herringbone patt., ht. 7in. **$235**

17 Bride's Bowl w/trifold ruffled rim, MOP in the diamond quilted patt., dia. 9¼in. **$381**

18 Two Fairy Lamps, the first pink satin w/an S. Clarke base, together w/ a MOP diamond quilted lamp in an Eden base, ht. 3¾in. **$146**

19 Trumpet Form Vase, MOP w/ruffled rim in the herringbone patt. Minor bruise to the body at foot, ht. 7in. **$117**

20 Four Pink MOP Tumblers, two in a diamond quilted patt., & two peacock eye patt., one cracked. **$117**

21 Two Diminutive MOP Vases in the diamond quilted patt. & dec. w/yellow coralene. One w/an open bubble. **$265**

A-OH   Early Auction Company, LLC
441 Webb Alexandrite Finger Bowl, ovoid form w/pie crust ruffled rim, wd. 5in. **$900**

439 Libbey Amberina Compote, coinspot patt. w/footed knopped stem in amber extending to amethyst blue. Mkd. w/acid stamp signature –

Libbey, ht. 4, wd. 6in. **$850**
440 Webb Alexandrite Vase w/ruffled top, ht. 2½in. **$950**

A-OH   Early Auction Company, LLC
New England Plated Amberina
435 Syrup Pitcher, cased clear to rose ribbed body & fitted w/an emb. flip lid w/James W. Tufts silver plate caddy, ht. 6in. **$8,000**
436 Tumbler w/amber foot graduating to a rose rim, ht. 3¾in. **$1,800**
437 Lily Vase shading from fuchsia to custard yellow on tapering standard w/amber disc, ht. 8in. **$3,000**

Opposite:
A-OH   Early Auction Company, LLC
Amberina
185 Harrach Vase, bulbous urn-form w/ diagonally swirled patt. accented w/an amber rigaree rim, ht. 10in. **$150**
190 New England Amberina Finger Bowl w/ruffled rim, wd. 5in. **$175**
182 Hobbs Brockunier Water Pitcher

in coin spot patt. w/applied reeded handle, ht. 8in. **$175**
187 Hobbs Brockunier Hobnail Water Pitcher w/applied amber handle, **$350**
184 Water Pitcher, coinspot patt. w/ applied reeded handle, ht. 6½in. **$175**
189 New England Amberina Footed Vase w/trifold rim in the diamond quilted patt. & reeded feet, ht. 6in. **$550**

191 Vase, coinspot patt., diminutive bulbous form w/amber rigaree collar, ht. 3¼in. **$450**
183 Three Tumblers, one in the diamond quilted patt, two in coinspot. **$50**
186 Lily Vase, footed form w/tri-fold rim, ht. 8¼in. **$150**
188 Two Pitchers in the coinspot patt. w/reeded handles, tallest 5½in. **$175**

GLASS

449

450

451

452

453

454

455

456

457

458

459

460

461

462

463

A-IA

Jackson's International Auctioneers, Inc.
Carnival Glass

449 Two Green Glass Bowls incl. a Fenton Autumn Acorn & a Cambridge Intaglio Strawberry mkd. Nearcut. **$146**

450 Northwood Amethyst Bowl in the Three Fruits patt. **$58**

451 Two Blue Glass items incl. a Fruits & Flowers double handled nappy, & a compote in the Wreath of Roses patt. **$70**

452 Three Pieces incl. a marigold bowl in the Arch patt., together w/a green bowl & an tray in the Scroll Embossed patt. **$105**

453 Blue Fenton Carnival Bowl in the Thistle patt. **$94**

466 Imperial Glass Water Set, 8 pcs. in the Grape patt. **$176**

455 Dugan Amethyst Plate in Grape Vine Lattice patt., dia. 7in. **$146**

456 Three Piece Group incl. a Northwood Grape & Cable nappy together w/a Dugan rose bowl in Grape Delight patt., & a Fenton nappy in Butterflies patt. **$105**

457 Two Northwood Items, ca.1920, incl. a clear vase in Basketweave patt. ht. 11in., together w/a bowl in the Wishbone patt. **$176**

458 Two Bowls, Fenton glass, one in

Captive Rose, the second in the Coin Dot patt. **$94**

459 Imperial Glass Bowl in the 'Pansy' patt. **$70**

460 Pair of George Dugan Glass Tumblers in the Stork & Rushes patt. Chip on one foot. **$176**

461 Five-piece group of Dugan glass in the Grape Delight patt. **$105**

462 Four-piece group incl. a Northwood bowl in Three Fruits patt., together w/a marigold vase, an amethyst bowl & a Fenton goblet in Iris patt. **$105**

463 Fenton Covered Jar in Orange Tree patt., and a European pitcher. **$58**

73   74   75

76   77   78

79   80   81

82   83   84

85   86   87

A-IA

Jackson's International Auctioneers, Inc.

73 Satin Glass Group incl. a blue vase, two pink ewers & two vases w/painted dec. **$105**

74 Grouping of vintage glass incl. a Vasa Murrhina rose bowl, spangled glass, a cased & footed yellow vase and two pink vases. **$117**

75 Victorian Handled Baskets, both w/applied thorny handles. **$146**

76 Collection of vintage glass, nine pcs., including a pair of MOP shakers by New Martinsville Glass Co. **$176**

77 Rose Bowls, four incl. a

Northwood pull up, a French amethyst mottled & two custard type bowls. **$1,057**

78 Eight Bowls incl. two yellow by Webb, four optic ribbed, & two blue satin glass bowls. **$470**

79 Six Bowls incl. a peppermint stripe, two opalescent, a Vasa Murrhina, and two green dec. bowls. **$293**

80 Five Rose Bowls incl. a cranberry acid etched & four satin glass. **$82**

81 Eight Rose Bowls, one cranberry ribbed and seven satin glass. **$199**

82 Six Decorated Bowls & one satin glass. **$125**

83 Five Bowls incl. a yellow dec. Webb, a pink spangled, one footed & two w/satin finish. **$205**

84 Three Bowls inc. one w/MOP in Herringbone patt, a pink MOP in quilted patt., & a small yellow bowl. **$205**

85 Six Bowls w/floral or satin finish. **$176**

86 Eight Rose Bowls incl. two pink & one yellow w/dec. **$293**

87 Six Rose Bowls incl. two yellow and one blue satin glass w/shell moulding, tallest ht. 5in. **$205**

GLASS

545

547

550

549

A-OH   Early Auction Company, LLC
English Cameo Glass
545 Three-color Rose Bowl w/fully developed dec. of leaves & pods by Thomas Webb & Sons, ht. 3½in. **$3,100**

547 Three-color Shoulder Vase w/cascading branch of leaves & large flowers, ht. 9in. **$4,500**
550 Stevens & Williams Vase w/opaque cutting of branches & ripe fruit w/ three camphor applied

supports & berry pontil, ht. 5½in. **$3,500**
549 Thomas Webb & Sons Vase dec. w/opaque dahlia dec. & sgn. w/banner, ht. 8in. **$3,250**

A-OH   Early Auction Company, LLC
Cologne/Perfume Bottles
498 Steuben Cranberry Swirl Bottle
sgn. Steuben fleur-de-lis, ht. 4in. $200
499 Steuben Ruby Melon-shaped
Perfume w/matching teardrop
stopper, ht. 4½in. $350
500 Perfume w/melon ribbed body,
ribbed green tear drop stopper & mkd.
w/ Steuben fleur-de-lis, ht. 4½in. $250
501 Steuben Bottle w/crystal oval body
& dec. w/random black threading &
black stopper, ht. 3in. $375
502 Melon Ribbed Perfume sgn. Verre-
de-Soie w/topaz teardrop stopper, ht.
4½in. $375

503 Steuben Verre-de-Soie Perfume
w/melon ribbed body & ruby Cintra
stopper, ht. 4¼in. $450
504 Blue Jade Perfume w/alabaster
stopper, bell-shaped & sgn.
w/Steuben's fleur-de-lis &
professionally repr. pontil. $225

A-OH   Early Auction Company, LLC
203 Two Thomas Webb & Sons Lay Down
Perfumes incl. a blue bottle w/emb. flip lid on
one end & twist emb. lid on the other, lg. 5in.,
along w/a red perfume having both ends
w/emb. flip lids, lg. 4in. $225
200 English Cameo Perfume w/yellow teardrop
form dec. w/stemmed flowering branches & a
butterfly in reverse w/emb. twist silver cap., ht.
4in. $1,000
201 Webb English Cameo Perfume, tricolor
w/teardrop form dec. w/white over red
stemmed leaves & metal hallmark lid w/orig.
clear stopper, ht. 3½in. $1,300
202 Webb Peachblow Perfume w/silver hallmark
lid & dec. w/raised gold ginkgo flowers, lg. 4in.
$650

A-OH   Early Auction Company, LLC
505 Steuben Blue Aurene Atomizer w/emb. metal lid, ht. 7¼in. $350
506 Steuben Gold Aurene Perfume w/teardrop stopper, sgn., ht. 7½in. $450
507 Melon Ribbed Gold Aurene Perfume w/teardrop stopper, sgn. Aurene, ht.
5¼in. $1,000
508 Blue Aurene Cologne Bottle w/ball stopper, sgn. Steuben, ht. 5¼in. $1,250
509 Steuben Aurene Cologne Bottle w/ball stopper, ht. 5¼in. $1,300

A-ME

James D. Julia, Inc.
682 Green Ribbed
& Opalescent
Scent Bottle
w/leaf dec. sgn.
on the side in
cameo Gallé,
w/orig. matching
stopper, ht. 6½in.
$1,322

GLASS

A-PA   Green Valley Auctions, Inc.
Glass Rolling Pins
1597 **Free-Blown Marbrie Loop Pin,** colorless w/opaque white & red loopings, knob handles, one end open & other w/rough pontil mark, ca.mid-19th C, lg. 17in. **$143**
1598 **Two Marbrie Loop Rolling Pins,** first w/opaque white & blue loopings, the second w/white & rose loopings, each w/knob handles, one open end & the other w/rough pontil. **$143**
1599 **Colorless Rolling Pin** w/wide deep rose stripes, knob handles, on open & one w/pontil mark, 19th C., lg. 16½in. **$121**

A-VA   Green Valley Auctions
1600 **Deep Sapphire Blue Rolling Pin** w/knob handles, one open & one w/pontil mark, mid 19th C., lg. 12in. **$99**
1601 **Sapphire Blue Rolling Pin** w/painted inscription, knob handles, one open & one w/pontil mark, light wear, lg. 14in. **$121**
1602 **Peacock Green Rolling Pin** w/traces of dec., knob handles, lg. 13½in. **$143**

A-OH   Early Auction Company, LLC
615 **Steuben French Blue Candlesticks** w/optic ribbing & applied prunts to connecting wafers, ht. 4in. **$350**

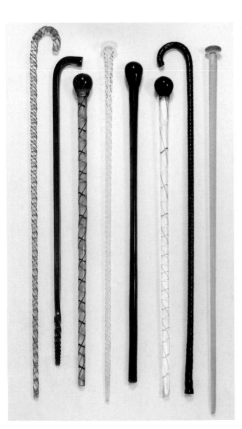

A-PA   Freeman's
Hand-blown Glass Walking Canes
523 **Two Canes,** the first pale green w/amber spiral overlay, together w/a Bristol blue example, lg. 43 & 40¾in. **$239**
524 **Two Canes,** late 19th C., a blue example w/red & pale green spiral & knob handle, together w/an amber square cane having a partial spiral twist stem & L handle, lg. 35½ & 36in. **$299**
522 **The Pale Green Cane** w/a spiral twist tapered shaft & a conforming pummel, the other w/a clear hollow Solomonic shaft & knob handle, lg. 42in. **$299**
519 **Two End of Day Glass Canes,** one w/clear tapered shaft w/white & red spiral inlay & Bristol blue knob handle, the other a similar green example w/blue knob handle, lg. 36¼ & 36¾in. **$269**

A-OH   Early Auction Company, LLC
447 **English Cameo Lay Down Perfume** w/flowering branch of leaves on front & back & flip lid mkd. Tiffany & Co., sterling, ht. 5¾in. **$900**
448 **Webb Cameo Perfume in Prussian** blue & dec. w/stemmed flowers mkd. flip lid, ht. 4in. **$1,150**

509 510 511 512 513
514 515 516
517 518 519
520, 521 522 523
524 525 526

A-IA   Jackson's International Auctioneers
Cut Glass
509 **Water Pitcher** w/intaglio cut stemmed flowers, ht. 10in. **$35**
510 **Brilliant Cut Water Pitcher** w/stars, ht. 8in. **$70**
511 **Cut Glass Basket** w/cut floral dec., ht. 12in. **$35**
512 **Water Pitcher** w/pinwheel cut dec., ht. 12in. **$82**
513 **Pair of Victorian Crystal Mantle Lustres,** each w/22 cut drop prisms, ht. 18in. **$117**
514 **Crystal,** six pcs., incl. a sgn. Hawks floral cut mayonnaise & two

sterling footed compotes. **$82**
515 **Console Bowl** of boat form w/minor loss, lg. 13in. **$47**
516 **Cut Glass** incl. 8 pcs. w/a sgn. Fry relish dish. **$105**
517 **Two Compotes,** one w/tear drop stem, ht. 9 & 8½in. **$150**
518 **Cut & Pressed Glass** incl. 40 pcs. w/7 open salts & 4 covered marmalades. **$176**
519 **Water Pitcher & Bowl** w/intaglio cut, each w/birds & butterflies, ht. of pitcher 10in. **$117**
520 **Cut Glass** incl. bowls & a faceted stopper bottle. **$58**

521 **Cut Glass Bowl** w/pinwheel & fan cuttings, dia. 8in. **$58**
522 **Four pcs. of Crystal** incl. a Steuben compote & a bottle w/ stopper att. to Daum. **$105**
523 **11 pcs. of Heisey Glass** in the Orchid patt. **$117**
524 **Cut Crystal,** 4 pcs. in the Queen Ann Lace patt. **$146**
525 **Vintage Cut & Press Glass** incl. 3 opal cup plates. **$47**
526 **30 pcs. of Glass** incl. Wedgwood, Kosta & Saworski. **$82**

748   749   750   751

752   753   754   755

A-IA   Jackson's International Auctioneers
Glass Wedding Bells, 19th C. unless noted.
748 **Cranberry Glass Bell,** English w/swirled base & pendant clapper, ht. 14in. **$70**
749 **Large Cobalt Blue Bell,** ht. 14in. **$117**

750 **Deep Cobalt Blue Bell** w/clear handle, ht. 12in. **$70**
751 **Nailsea Glass Bell** w/white swirled glass & clear handle, ht. 12in. **$176**
752 **Glass Bell** in white w/applied ruby rim & clear handle, ht. 12in. **$205**
753 **Ruby Bell** w/clear handle, ht.

11in. **$110**
754 **Two Pairpoint Glass Bells** w/enamel dec. & sgn. w/Pairpoint monogram, ca.1975, ht. 12in. **$94**
755 **Two Pairpoint Bells** w/enamel dec. & sgn., ca.1975, ht.12in. **$264**

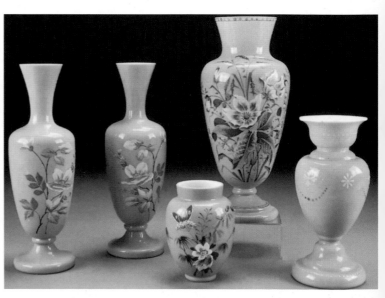

A-IA   Jackson's International Auctioneers
62 **Bohemian Mantle Set,** ca.1880 incl. a covered jar, ht. 19in., & two side vases, ht. 13in., each w/enameled dec. **$205**

63 **Pink Opalene Vases,** ca.1880 w/enameled dec. of dogwood blossoms, and a pink high shouldered urn, ht. 12in. **$205**

A-IA Jackson's International Auctioneers
502 Cranberry Hobnail Opalescent Glass, six pcs., cont. Fenton, 20th C.

$323
503 Five Pieces of Cranberry Hobnail Glass, cont. Fenton, 20th C. **$323**

504 Fenton Cranberry Hobnail Water Set, pitcher & six tumblers. **$440**

A-IA Jackson's International Auctioneers
49 Greentown Chocolate Glass Pitcher, early 20th C., in Feather patt., ht. 9in. **$1,410**

50 Slag Glass Compote, early 20th C., w/amethyst & white swirled mottling, ht. 9in. **$70**
51 Opalescent Compote w/pink

swirls & clear stem, ht. 5in. **$58**
52 Iridescent Class Vase by Dugan, early 20th C. w/pinched sides, ht. 5½in. **$35**

A-ME James D. Julia, Inc.
243 Mont Joye Vase, green shading to clear w/ enameled dec. of pansies & applied bumblebees, unsigned, ht. 14in. **$1,092**

A-IA Jackson's International Auctioneers
Chinese Peking Glass
1520 Pair of Vases, 20th C., in green & red glass over opal w/carved floral & bird designs, ht. 9 & 8¼in. **$300**
1521 Large Vase, 20th C., in red over

opal glass & carved w/goldfish, ht. 10in. **$146**
1522 Vases, 20th C., in mustard & blue over opal carved w/bird & floral dec., ht. 9 & 8¼in. **$235**

A-IA   Jackson's International Auctioneers
1344 **Pink Opalescent Smoke Bell,** early 20th C., optic ribbed w/a vaseline ring holder, dia. 10¼in. **$146**

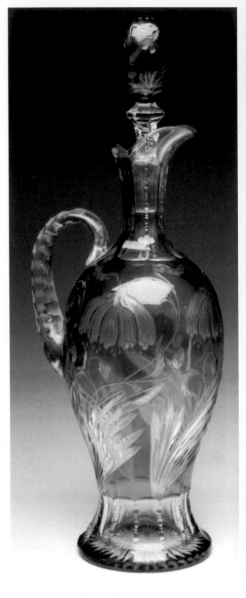

A-ME   James D. Julia, Inc.
260 **Durand Vase,** unsgn., iridescent gold w/heart & vine dec. w/int. iridescent gold finish, ht. 8¾in. **$920**

A-ME   James D. Julia, Inc.
210 **Loetz Silver Overlay Vase,** completely overlaid w/sterling silver leaves, flowers & stems w/silver trim on foot & lip, ht. 6½in. **$1,380**

A-ME   James D. Julia, Inc.
104 **Green Cut to Clear Overlay Decanter** w/matching stopper & applied cut handle, ht. 15in. **$2,300**

Opposite:
A-IA   Jackson's International Auctioneers
Pickle Casters, 19th C.
1314 **Prussian Blue Insert** w/an emb. flower Meriden holder & tongs, ht.10¼in. **$323**
1315 **Rubina Insert** dec. w/yellow daisies on green stems, orig. tongs &

set in a Wilcox gold washed holder, ht. 11in. **$499**
1316 **Large Victorian Caster** w/pressed glass insert w/raised birds set in an ornate pierced holder w/orig. tongs, sgn. Reed & Barton, ht. 14in. **$528**

1317 **Hobbs Brockunier Caster** w/blue insert in the Russian cut, set in a sgn. Pairpoint holder w/tongs. Chip to rim of insert, ht. 13in. **$381**
1318 **Cranberry Etched Insert** w/orig. tongs & plated silver holder, ht. 10¼in. **$411**

A-IA Jackson's International Auctioneers
1345 Wavecrest Dresser Tray & Mirror, early 20th C., dec. w/flowers & sgn. ht. 4¾in. **$264**
1346 Wavecrest Dresser Box together w/a metal footed cigarette holder, each dec. w/yellow flowers & a red banner mark. **$381**
1347 Wheeling Peachblow Water Pitcher w/glossy finish, together w/a

punch cup inscribed Claud 1887, both by Hobbs. **$949**
1348 Mt. Washington Condiment Set, ca.1890, ribbed pillar blue shakers & a mustard, dec. w/fall colored leaves set in an orig. Pairpoint caddy, ht. 8in. **$264**
1349 Webb Burmese Ruffled Rim Bowl, ca.1890 w/satin finish, dia. 9in. **$176**

1350 Mt. Washington Condiment Set, ca.1890 w/ribbed pillar Burmese shakers & a mustard, set in orig. mkd. Pairpoint caddy. **$411**
1351 Mt. Washington Condiment Set w/ribbed pillar mustard & shakers shading from cream to peach & dec. w/white flowers set in orig. Pairpoint holder, ht. 7¼in. **$381**

A-IA   Jackson's International Auctioneers
1328 Pink Satin Glass Pickle Caster, ca.1890 & dec. w/gold & blue flowers set in an emb. metal holder stamped Barbour Bros. Co. Quadruple, ht. 10in. **$352**
1329 Cranberry Caster, ca.1900, in the Coin Spot patt., set in an emb. frame w/pierced flower scrolling &

mkd. Aurora Quadruple Plate w/orig. matching tongs, ht. 12in. **$410**
1330 Victorian Cracker Jar, late 19th C., w/camphor body dec. w/purple lily accented w/an emb. stemmed flower, ht. 8in. **$235**
1331 Squatty Pickle Caster, ca.1900, in the Coinspot patt. & set in emb.

silver plate holder, ht. 12in. **$352**
1332 Cranberry Opalescent Syrup, ca.1900, conical form dec. w/vertical stripes & a spring loaded flip lid, ht. 7¼in. **$470**
1333 Cranberry Opalescent Syrup in the Rain Drop patt. w/reeded handle & spring loaded flip lid, ht. 7in. **$235**

A-ME   **James D. Julia, Inc.**
Wedgwood Fairyland Lustre
519 Punchbowl, Lahore patt. w/hanging lanterns, inside dec. w/elephants, a camel, war horse & flying goose, all figures done in black MOP & outlined in gold against a yellow lustre ground, ht. 5⅝, dia. 11in. **$8,625**

521 Octagon Bowl dec. on the outside in a pattern of Woodland Elves VI. The tree trunks are dark blue-green & all the elves are brown on a flame lustre background of orange over crimson. The inside patt. is a Ship & Mermaid w/flame lustre center. Pattern Z-5360, ht. 4, dia. 8½in. **$7,475**

A-IA   **Jackson's International Auctioneers**
1334 **Northwood Rubina,** Two Covered Jars & Syrup in
the Royal Ivy patt. **$411**

A-IA   **Jackson's International Auctioneers**
1319 **MOP Glass Vase** in the Herringbone patt.
w/applied camphor handles & leaves, ht. 14in. **$470**

A-IA   **Jackson's International Auctioneers**
1311 **Victorian Bride's Basket,** late 19th C. w/blue satin
glass bowl w/ruffled rim & yellow Coralene dec. set in a
fruit embossed silverplate holder, mkd. Middletown, ht.

12¼in. **$470**
1312 **Ruffled Rim Bride's Basket,** pink MOP in Diamond
Quilted patt. & dec. w/foliage. Set in Simpson silverplated
holder, ht. 12in. **$587**

KITCHENWARE

KITCHEN COLLECTIBLES

Of all the many types of kitchen collectibles, woodenware has the greatest appeal. It has been produced in America from the earliest times. From the Indians the colonists learned the art of making utilitarian objects such as trenchers, porringers, noggins and bowls. The completely hand-shaped pieces are prized by collectors, as no two were ever alike. Oftentimes cutting lines, copper, pewter and iron, left by the craftsman are clearly evident on the surface of an object. Even vessels may bear signs of crude decoration, having an incised geometric design, wiggle work, initials, a date or name… which, of course, enhances the value.

Although numerous kinds of wood were available to the colonists, it was the bulgy growth scar tissue found at the base of certain trees that was favored. This is known as "burl". Its grain, instead of running in the usual parallel lines, was twisted and coiled and produced an unusually attractive grain. In this field, it is the interesting early burl examples that fetch the highest prices when sold.

There are almost countless examples of many types of early kitchen utensils and gadgets… from the hearth to the cookstove… still available for a price, because "waste not, want not" was a favorite maxim. Recycling was simply a natural way of life for our ancestors. Objects were well made and designed to be functional. During the mid-1800s, when mass production was in full gallop, every imaginable device for the refinement of the culinary art was patented. Therefore, most of us have a few old or inherited items in our modern-day kitchens, and these old "classics" are treasured.

Because of the scarcity of early objects, many collectors have become interested in collecting not only gadgets but utensils dating from the second half of the 20th century, including appliances.

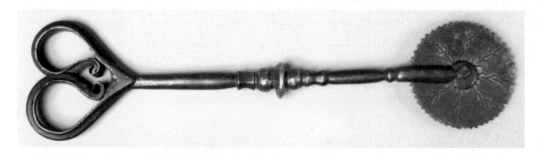

A-PA   Conestoga Auction Company, Inc.

551 Forged Iron Pie Wheel w/ball & ring turned shaft w/incised floral dec., lg. 9in. **$2,530**

A-PA   Conestoga Auction Company, Inc.
170 Cast Iron Enterprise Coffee Mill w/orig. paint & dov. walnut drawer, ht. 12½in. **$385**

A-PA   Conestoga Auction Company, Inc.
48 Butter Churn in old blue paint w/turned lid, tin bands & wood dasher, ht. 24¼in. **$660**
49 Wood Butter Churn in old red paint w/concave lid, tin bands & wood dasher, ht. 26in. **$357**

A-PA   Conestoga Auction Company, Inc.
542 Cherry & Tiger Maple Coffee Grinder w/dov. const., pewter bowl & dec. iron handle w/interior paper label, ca.1839. **$2,255**

A-PA Conestoga Auction Company, Inc.
550 **Forged Iron Dough Scraper** stamped M.F. 1835 on each side of blade w/punched work, ht. 3¼, wd. 4¼in. **$4,180**

A-PA Conestoga Auction Company, Inc.
45 **Walnut Slaw Board** w/double heart cut-out crest, ht. 16¾, wd 6in. **$220**
46 **Walnut Slaw Board** w/lollipop handle, lg. 22, wd. 7¼in. **$55**

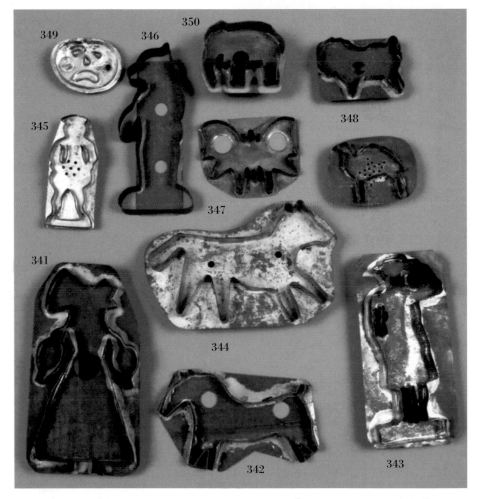

A-PA Conestoga Auction Company, Inc.
Tin Cookie Cutters
339 **Large Seated Squirrel** mounted to a flat plate w/double crossed strap handles, ht. 9¼, wd. 8in. **$440**
340 **Running Horse** on sloped base mounted to flat plate w/strap handles, ht. 9⅛, lg. 11½in. **$100**
341 **Cookie Cutter of Woman** in long dress w/puffy sleeves & bonnet mounted to flat plate w/strap handles,

ht. 9¼, wd 4⅞in. **$522**
342 **Horse** w/short legs & mounted to flat plate, missing handle, lg. 7in. **$49**
343 **Gentleman In Hat Saluting,** mounted to flat plate w/handle, ht. 8½in. **$165**
344 **Running Dog** mounted to flat plate w/handle, lg. 8¾in. **$44**
345 **Standing Gentleman** w/hands in his pockets w/strap handle, ht. 5¼in. **$5**

346 **Standing Bear** mounted to flat plate, ht. 8in. **$104**
347 **Flying Bat** mounted to flat plate & stamped H, wd. 4⅝in. **$60**
348 **Two Cutters, Lion & Camel,** ea. 4in. **$11**
349 **Jack-o-Lantern** w/frown mounted to flat plate & stamped HF, wd. 3in. **$71**
350 **Elephant** stamped 42 w/strap handle, lg. 4in. **$44**

A-PA   Conestoga Auction
            Company, Inc.
37 **Wood Bucket**
w/orig. painted surface,
tin bands, lid
w/notched handle &
wire bail, ht. 10in.
$110

A-PA   Conestoga Auction Company, Inc.
563 **Punched Tin Coffee Pot** dec. on either side w/a
large potted tulip & a peafowl on rim. Interior includes
receipt dated 6-17-45 for $15, ht. 11in. **$2,860**
564 **Tin Wrigglework Coffee Pot** w/stylized tulip dec.
& floral offshoots, lid w/offset brass mushroom finial,
ht. 11in. **$330**
565 **Embossed Tin Coffee Pot** having a tulip tree
centered by scalloped swag & sawtooth design, finial
missing, ht. 10¾in. **$770**

A-ME
 James D. Julia, Inc.
527 **Six Antique
Copper Long
Handled Pots,**
graduated sizes,
zinc lined, 9¾ x
5½ tapering to 5,
2½in. **$345**

A-PA   Conestoga Auction
              Company, Inc.
566 **Lard Tin** w/smoke
dec., loop side handles &
ring finial, ht. 8¾in. **$110**
567 **Miniature Tin Two Tube
Candle Mold,** ht. 3½in.
$297
568 **Tin Canister** w/painted
comma dec. on black
ground, ht. 9½in. **$110**
569 **Lard Tin** w/smoke dec.
on white background &
loop handles, ht. 6in. **$5**

A-PA   Conestoga Auction Company, Inc.
Butter Prints
73 **Rooster** w/foliate accents &
notched rim, dia.4½in. **$1,210**
74 **Two Prints,** a tulip w/notched rim,
dia. 3¾in; the other a hatch carved
flower, dia. 4¼in. **$302**
75 **Two Prints,** a flower w/foliate stem
& notch carved rim, dia. 4¼in; the
other w/foliate spray & carved rim,
dia. 3¾in. **$165**
76 **Three Prints,** a divided sheath of
wheat, dia. 4¼in; an acorn, dia.
1¾in. & a small foliate spray w/circle
rim, dia. 2in. not illus. **$110**

A-NH Northeast Auctions
579 **Native American Burl Bowl**, ht. 8¼, top 17 x 14¼in. **$3,500**

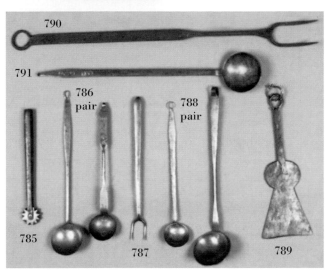

A-PA   Conestoga Auction Company, Inc.
790 **Wrought Iron Fork** stamped J.W. Snyder w/ring terminal, lg. 21in. **$44**
791 **Iron Ladle** w/slight hook terminal, stamped J. Schmidt, lg. 15in. **$363**
785 **Pie Crimper,** brass & wrought iron w/sawtooth wheel, lg. 7¾in. **$82**
786 **Two Wrought Iron Tasting Ladles** w/brass bowls. **$287**
787 **Wrought Iron Fork** w/brass inlay & stamped Koch, lg. 9¾in. **$352**
788 **Two Brass & Iron Ladles,** one w/iron handle, lg. 9¾; the second w/iron handle, rat-tail terminal & brass bowl, lg. 12in. **$209**
789 **Wrought Iron Dough Trimmer** in thistle form, rat tail terminal & attached twisted ram's horn ring, lg. 9¾in. **$104**

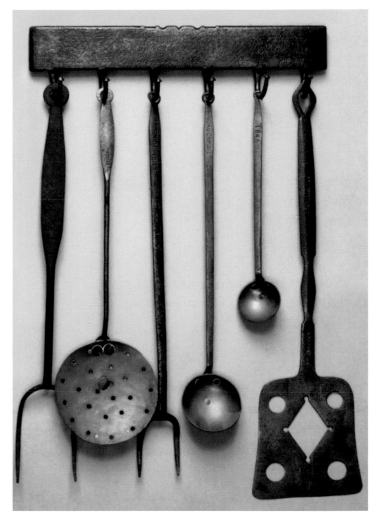

A-PA   Pook & Pook, Inc.
418 **Wrought Iron Utensil Rack w/Utensils,** Am., 19th C. incl. fork sgn. I. Dewald 1881; strainer sgn. W. Noble; fork sgn J. Schmidt 1843; a ladle w/brass bowl sgn. J. Schmidt w/a sgn. taster, mkd. 1846, and a spatula w/cutouts sgn. E.P. Sebastian. **$5,382**

A-PA   Conestoga Auction Company, Inc.
41 **Wood Firkin** w/orig. old yellow paint, wood finger joined bands & wood swing handle, ht. 9¼in. **$522**
38 **Wood Bucket** in old yellow paint

w/tin bands & washed interior, ht. 4, dia. 10in. **$165**
39 **Matching Dry Measures** w/old blue painted surface & tin bands, ht. 5½, dia. 7¼in. **$605**

40 **Wood Kerosene Bucket** in old green paint w/zinc cap, brass spigot & tin bands, ht. 11, dia. 9¾in. **$165**

KITCHENWARE

A-PA   Conestoga Auction Co., Inc.
80 **Large Turned Burl Bowl** w/molded rim, dia. 15¼in.
$9,350

A-OH   Garth's Arts & Antiques
376 **Knife Box** w/dov. canted sides., mah. w/heart cut-out handle & edge damage, ht. 6½, lg. 17in. $1,150

A-NH   Northeast Auctions
583 **Burl Bowl** w/carved handles & another w/everted rim & blue exterior, first illus. dia. 14in., second 10½in. $1,600
584 **Am. Bird's Eye Maple Burl Bowl** w/molded rim, dia. 16 ½in. $1,200
585 **Turned Footed Compote**, burlwood, ht. 6, dia. 8in. $7,500

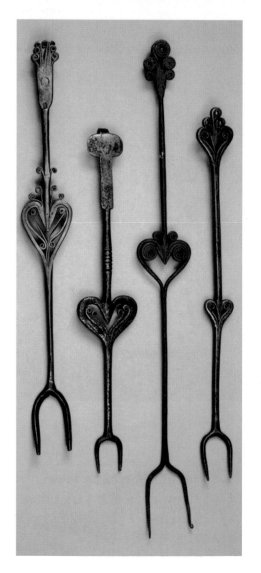

A-NH   Northeast Auctions
578 **Fifteen Treen Sanders** incl. an ink bottle in treen container & turned pen holder, together w/a painted burl bowl. $1,900

A-PA   Pook & Pook, Inc.
French Wrought Iron
436 **Flesh Fork**, ca.1800 w/elaborate scrolled heart & dec. handle, lg. 21in. $1,112
437 **Flesh Fork**, late 18th C. w/scrolled heart handle, lg. 17¾in. $793
438 **Flesh Fork**, ca.1800 w/heart dec. handle, lg. 25¾in. $936
439 **Fork**, ca.1800 w/scrolled dec., lg. 18in. $878

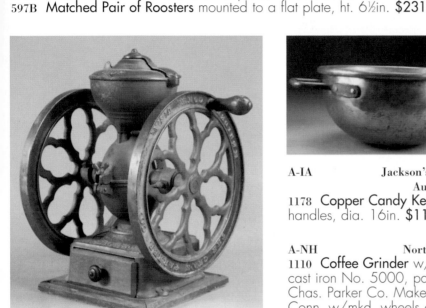

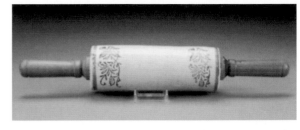

A-PA   Conestoga Auction Company, Inc.
Cookie Cutters
597A **Horse & Rider** mounted to a flat plate, ht. 8in. **$110**
597B **Matched Pair of Roosters** mounted to a flat plate, ht. 6½in. **$231**

A-IA   Jackson's International Auctioneers, Inc.
1197 **Blue Gray Stoneware Rolling Pin,** early 20th C. w/cornflower dec., lg. 16in. **$235**

A-IA   Jackson's International Auctioneers, Inc.
1178 **Copper Candy Kettle** w/iron handles, dia. 16in. **$117**

A-NH   Northeast Auctions
1110 **Coffee Grinder** w/drawer, cast iron No. 5000, pat. 1887 by Chas. Parker Co. Makers, Meriden, Conn. w/mkd. wheels on oak base, ht. 18in. **$900**

A-IA   Jackson's International Auctioneers, Inc.
1174 **Cast Iron Kettle** w/three feet & wrought iron bail handle, dia. 24in. **$146**

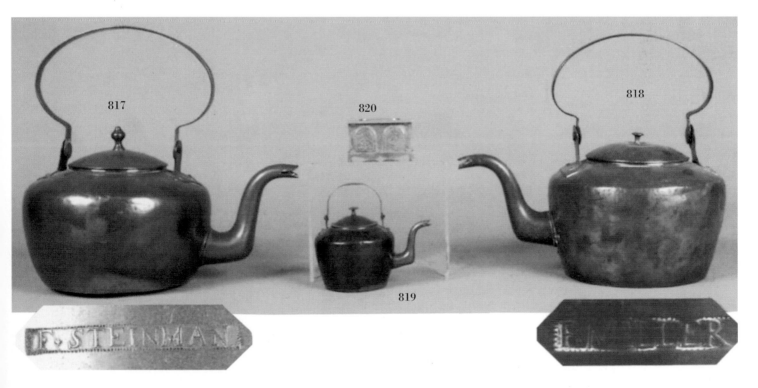

A-PA   Conestoga Auction Company, Inc.
817 **Copper Tea Kettle** w/gooseneck spout, swing handle & dov. const.,sgn. F. Steinman, ht. 8in. **$1,650**

818 **Copper Tea Kettle** sgn. E. Miller w/dov. const., gooseneck spout, swing handle & surface dents, ht. 7in. **$302**
819 **Miniature Copper Tea Kettle**

w/gooseneck spout, dov. const. & old repr. to swing handle, ht. 4in. **$660**
82C **Brass Bank** in form of dower chest, sgn. AB Fenster, w/heart dec. coin slot, ht. 2in. **$27**

LIGHTING

The commodities for producing light in colonial America were splints of wood, animal or vegetable oils, depending upon their availability. The oils were used for burning fluids in various forms of shallow flat grease lamps. Because domestic animals were not plentiful in America until the late 1600s, finding a substitute for beef tallow was a major difficulty. Substitutes included beeswax, found on stems of the bay shrub, and "spermaceti" from the head of the sperm whale.

An enormous variety of candlesticks were made of wood, tin and pewter. Candlemolds were made in quantity, as well as sconces with backplates of pewter and tin. Those made with bits of looking glass that reflected the candlelight are extremely desirable. Candlestands soon became fashionable which permitted height adjustments, but it was not until the 1700s that lanterns, portable and fixed, and fitted with candles became popular.

The availability of whale oil transformed lamp designs during the late 1700s, and remained the most important type of fuel for lamps well into the 1800s. Camphene lamps came into use during the second quarter of the 19th century. They resemble the whale oil lamps, but their wick tubes are set at opposing angles... "V" ... shape to compensate for the extreme combustibility of the fuel. From the 1830s until the 1860s the Argand whale oil burner dominated lamp designs. It was not until the 1860s that kerosene eventually replaced all fuels.

Between the rush light holders of the early settlers and the fancy kerosene lamps of the late Victorian era, to the very pricey colorful Art Deco creations, there still exists a seemingly endless variety of very fine lighting collectibles and accessories. Many are readily adaptable for modern decorative and functional usage.

A-ME   **James D. Julia, Inc.**
790 Pairpoint Enameled Chandelier w/heavily enameled leaves, scrolls & flying cherubs. Shade signed in black The Pairpoint Corp'n., dia. 14in. **$3,120**

A-IA   **Jackson's International Auctioneers, Inc.**
1257 French Gilt Bronze & Marble Floriform Table Lamp, ca.1900, 3-light w/acid finish shades, 1 cracked, ht. 20in. **$235**
1258 Silvered Bronze & Cut Glass Table Lamp, early 20th C., ht. 21in. **$382**

A-IA   Jackson's International Auctioneers, Inc.
1434 Victorian Hanging Hall Light, pink opalescent w/ruffled rim mounted on brass fittings, ht. 9in. **$264**

A-ME
James D. Julia, Inc.
763 Handel Table Lamp sgn. Handel R., base sgn. HA.., remainder of signature illegible, one chip to rim, ht. 27in. **$4,887**

A-ME
James D. Julia, Inc.
707 Pairpoint Jungle Bird Lamp w/reverse painted Carlisle shade depicts exotic birds against tropical foliage, sgn. Pairpoint Corp. on shade & base, ht. 21in. **$5,750**

A-IA
Jackson's International Auctioneers, Inc.
846 Puffy Pairpoint Lamp, ca.1907, dec. w/red roses & butterflies, base mkd., shade dia. 9, ht.14in. **$3,995**

847 Boudoir Lamp by Pairpoint, Rose Bonnet patt. set on tree trunk base mkd. Pairpoint, shade dia. 6¼, ht. 11in. **$3,525**

848 Boudoir Lamp w/puffy Stratford shade, ca.1907, dec. w/apple blossoms & roses, shade dia. 8¼, ht. 15in. **$3,995**

849 Balmoral Boudoir Lamp, ca.1907, dec. w/butterflies & white daisies, mkd. Pairpoint, ht. 10¼in. **$881**

850 Boudoir Lamp w/Stratford shade dec. w/orange & amethyst gladioli, mkd. Pairpoint Corp., ht. 15in. **$3,525**

851 Boudoir Lamp w/frosted puffy shade dec. w/yellow & red roses on blue lattice, ca.1907, in the Rose Bonnet patt. w/mkd. Pairpoint base & orig. paper label, ht. 11¼in. **$4,465**

852 Pairpoint Boudoir lamp w/Stratford shade dec. w/red & yellow roses, sgn., ht. 15in. **$4,935**

A-NJ

Craftsman Arts & Crafts Auction

93 **Period Lantern** w/leaded glass panels of stylized Glasgow roses in poly. slag glass, unmarked & without chain, 10 x 7½in. sq. **$1,700**

A-NJ

Craftsman Arts & Crafts Auction

95 **Handel Desk Lamp,** adjustable w/slag glass shade on single socket bronzed base, shade mkd. **$2,000**

A-VA   **Green Valley Auctions, Inc.**

2003 **Cut Overlay Quatrefoil & Punty Banquet Lamp,** kerosene period w/marble base & period Miller burner & chimney, Boston & Sandwich Glass Co. 1860-1875, ht. 20¼in. **$7,975**

2004 **Cut Overlay Banquet Lamp,** kerosene period, blue cut to colorless font w/matching Moorish windows stem, cast brass mounts & marble base, Boston & Sandwich Glass Co, ht. 15¼in. **$3,300**

A-VA   **Green Valley Auctions, Inc.**

2008 **Cut Overlay Moorish Windows Lamp,** kerosene, white cut to emerald green w/brass trim & etched Oregon shade, Boston & Sandwich Glass Co., minor imper., ht. 12½in. **$715**

2009 **Cut Overlay Stand Lamp,** kerosene, ruby cut to colorless font, applied peg, deep green cut overlay stem & opaque white glass foot w/brass connector, minor imper., N. Eng., ht. 10¼in. **$3,080**

2010 **Cut Overlay Moorish Windows Lamp,** kerosene w/brass mounts & double step marble base, Boston & Sandwich Glass Co., w/minor imper., ht. 14½in. **$770**

A-NJ   Craftsman Arts & Crafts Auction
358 Hammered Copper & Mica Table Lamp w/three panels on a three-socket base, w/new patina & mica. Stamped w/Windmill mark of Dirk Van Erp. $5,000

A-NJ
Craftsman Arts & Crafts Auction
239 Gustav Stickley Floor Lamp w/silk lined wicker shade, crossed base on shoe-feet & hammered copper arm w/single pivoting socket. Orig. finish & patina. Als-ik-kan die stamp, ht. 58in. $9,500

A-VA   Green Valley Auctions, Inc.
2001 Cut Overlay Banquet Lamp, kerosene w/finely cut & frosted 5in. Oregon shade, pat. dated 1859, probably Boston & Sandwich Glass Co., ht. 20¾in. $11,000
2002 Cut Overlay Banquet Lamp w/Moorish windows, kerosene, w/British collar, & marble base, Sandwich, ht. 28½in. $9,075

A-ME   James D. Julia, Inc.
100 Stevens & Williams Oil Lamp, amber gold satin glass features white & red swirls, eased w/white glass on interior in the Pompeian design. Sgn. w/spurious signature Thomas Webb & Son on underside of base, w/double wick burner & bronze feet stamped JD & 71, ht. 20in. $800

A-NJ Craftsman Arts & Crafts Auction
360 Prairie School Hanging Chandelier of amber & white slag glass in brass mounts. A couple breaks to glass & some pitting to metal, unmkd., 42 x 22in. sq. **$2,000**

A-NJ   Craftsman Arts & Crafts Auction
359 Gustav Stickley Table Lamp w/hammered copper three-socket base & silk lined wicker shade w/some tears to orig. silk, repatinated or new shade cap. Als-ik-kan stamp, ht. 21½in. **$5,500**

A-NJ   Craftsman Arts & Crafts Auction
87 Bean Pot Boudoir Lamp, hammered copper and mica w/flaring four–panel shade on a single socket base, by Dirk Van Erp w/open box mark, of D'Arcy Gaw, ht. 12¼in. **$7,000**

A-NJ   Craftsman Arts & Crafts Auction
97 Handel Table Lamp w/faceted slag-glass shade, brown & green cat-tails over a bronzed base, stamped Handel, ht. 28in. **$2,500**

A-NJ   Craftsman Arts & Crafts Auction
272 Quezal Brass Table Lamp w/eleven branches, topped by Quezal floriform shades, chips to fitters & two shades cracked. Shades etched Quezal, base unmarked, ht. 26½in. **$4,750**

A-IA
Jackson's International Auctioneers
1259 Argand Student/Library Table Lamp, late 19th C. w/later electric conversion, ht. 20in. **$352**

A-PA   Pook & Pook, Inc.
427 Wrought Iron Rush Light, 18th/19th C. w/candlecup counterweight, ht. 12in. **$1,952**
428 English Wrought Iron Wax Jack, 18th c. w/penny feet, ht. 5¼in. **$1,053**
429 Brass & Iron Gimbaled Lamp, early/mid-19th C., ht. 9in. **$1,404**
430 Wrought Iron Hanging Fat Lamp, 18th C. w/heart cut-out finial, ht. 9¾in. **$761**

A-PA   Freeman's
1474 Jade & Opaque White Whale Oil Lamps by Sandwich Glass Co., Sandwich, MA, 1835-1860. Each w/acanthus Leaf patt. font & standard square base, w/sanded surface, ht. 13in. **$2,031**
1477 Pressed Glass Oil Lamps attrib. to Boston & Sandwich Glass Co., the first of cobalt blue w/elongated loop patt.; the second an uncolored pressed & blown lamp, ht. 9¾ & 12in. **$1,792**
1475 Two Glass Oil Lamps, ca.1860, the first w/red cut-to-clear pyriform font w/brass waist ring & green cut-to-clear standard on milk glass base; the second w/uncolored spherical font w/brass waist ring & shaped green glass base w/gold highlights. **$1,015**
1476 Three Pressed & Mold-blown Lamps, ca.1865, the first w/clambroth font on marble base; the second w/uncolored spherical font on tapering standard & milk glass base & the third of teal color w/spherical font patt. w/grapevine & milk glass base. **$478**

LIGHTING

A-IA   Jackson's International Auctioneers
1212 Victorian Hanging Parlor Lamp w/emb. metal font & shade w/hobnail patt., ht. 32in. **$176**
1213 Victorian Shaded Glass & Brass

Pedestal Oil Lamp w/enameled dec., ht. 16in. **$70**
1214 Reverse Painted Boudoir Lamp w/gilt iron base, hat cap missing, ht. 14in. **$70**

1216 Moe Bridges Reverse Painted Boudoir Lamp w/textured finish, sgn., ht. 14in. **$176**

A-NH   **Northeast Auctions**

Student Lamps w/Milk Glass Shades
1039 Double Brass Lamp, ht. 20½in. **$400**
1040 German Brass Lamp, ht. 21½in. **$100**
1041 Am. Adjustable Lamp stamped The Miller Lamp, ht. 21½in. **$300**
1042 Brass Lamp, ht. 20½in. **$100**
1043 Single Brass Lamp, ht. 20¾in. **$100**

A-PA   **Freeman's**
304A Pair of Mirrored Tinware Candle Sconces, 19th C. w/oval backplates & single candle arm, lg. 14½in. **$1,200**

A-ME   James D. Julia, Inc.
784A Leaded Glass Floor Lamp
w/crocus floral border. Shade rests on
heavy five-socket ribbed floor base
w/sockets & pull chains. Mkd. Handel
in foot, ht. 65in. **$8,050**

A-ME   James D. Julia, Inc.
549 Tiffany Acorn Table Lamp,
shade sgn. Tiffany Studios, NY,
w/Tiffany bronze base w/some
minor wear to patina, also carries
the Tiffany Glass & Decorating
Co., logo, shade dia. 16in,
overall ht. 22in. **$18,400**

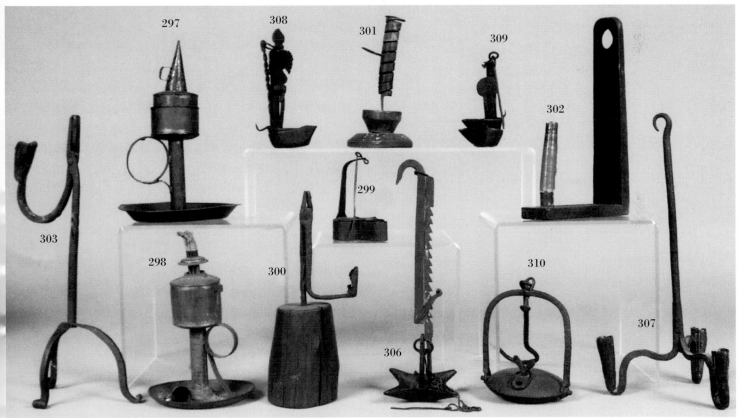

A-PA   Conestoga Auction Co., Inc.
First Row
297 Tin Grease Lamp w/lift out burner
& reservoir w/tin conical snuffer, ht.
7½in. **$121**
308 Iron Double Grease Lamp
w/scalloped crest & twisted iron pick,
ht. 7in. **$220**
301 Iron Helix Candlestick mounted to
flared wooden base, w/repr., ht.
7¾in. **$192**
309 Iron Double Grease Lamp w/
shaped crest & iron pick, ht. 5¼in. **$93**

302 Hanging Wooden Candle Holder,
dov. w/single candle socket, mkd. J.R.
on reverse, ht. 11½in. **$797**
Second Row
**303 Forged Iron Rush Light Candle
Holder** w/twisted shaft & scrolled feet,
ht. 15in. **$522**
298 Tin Grease Lamp w/double wick
burner & saucer base, ht. 8in. **$176**
300 Iron Rush Lamp Candle Holder
mounted to wood block & no candle
socket, ht. 10⅞in. **$220**
299 Iron Betty Lamp w/shaped

reservoir, wick channel & pick, ht.
4¼in. **$148**
**306 Forged Iron Four Spout Grease
Lamp** on ratchet hanger w/pick, ht.
18in. **$412**
310 Forged Iron Betty Lamp
w/circular flattened body & extended
iron hanging hook, ht. 18in. **$137**
**307 Forged Iron Three-Arm Hanging
Candle Holder** w/scrolled hook, ht.
14¾in. **$440**

A-ME James D. Julia, Inc.
785 Handel Parrot Globe Chandelier, sgn. on upper fitter rim w/orig. ceiling hdw., dia. of shade 10in., overall lg. 41in. **$3,600**

A-OH   Early Auction Company, LLC
68 Mt. Washington/Pairpoint Burmese Parlor Lamp w/diamond quilted ruffled Burmese shade & ovoid silverplate base emb. w/oriental motif, figural handles of Japanese men & four feet in form of mice, sgn. w/a "P" in Diamond, ht. 17in. **$800**

A-ME   James D. Julia, Inc.
557 Tiffany Candle Lamp, the candle is dec. w/green on white pulled feather dec. Hdw. stamped w/The Twilight, and the iridescent gold ruffled shade mkd. L.C.T., w/orig. amber chimney. Lamp has been electrified, ht. 15in. **$1,725**

A-PA   Conestoga Auction Co., Inc.

First Row

226 Brass Skater's Lantern w/swing handle, ht. 7in. **$143**

232 Tin Carry Lantern w/tapered glass shade & carry handle, no burner, ht. overall 15in. **$143**

224 Swing Handle Lantern w/wire cage & repainted black, ht. 10in. **$93**

221 Carry Lantern w/ring handle. Missing fluid reservoir & burner, ht. 13¾in. **$60**

225 Tin Carry Lantern w/wire cage pat. July 1870 & ruffled smoke shade, ht. 9½in. **$231**

222 Tin Nonpareil Lantern mkd. Archer & Pancoast, pat. 1864 w/square body, repainted body, ht. 10¼in. **$143**

229 Tin Carry Lantern w/wire cage surrounding punched tin conical top w/smoke shade, repl. burner, ht. 14½in. **$264**

Second Row

234 Candle Lantern w/square body having glass panes & wire cage & one glass pane missing, ht. 12in. **$231**

228 Onion Lantern w/bulbous glass shade, cylinder top & brass ruffled smoke shade & repl. burner, ht. 10in. **$550**

237 Small Christmas Lantern w/heavy tapered glass shade, ht. 12in. **$187**

227 Brass Skater's Lantern w/swing handle & shaped shade, ht. 7in. **$176**

219 Tin Onion Lantern w/bulbous glass shade & vent holes, ht. 16in. **$154**

233 Tin Candle Lantern w/flattened bulbous shade, emb. smoke ring & small carrying handle, ht. 12½in. **$412**

218 Onion Lantern w/wire cage & conical top w/vent holes, ht. 19½in. **$209**

230 Candle Lantern w/square body & glass panes, one w/crack, bulbous top & ring carry handle w/rust, ht. 10½in. **$132**

220 Carry Lantern w/paneled glass shade & crimped smoke shield. Missing burner, ht. 12½in. **$143**

236 Tin Carry Lantern w/heavy tapered glass shade, ht. 12in. **$187**

1192 **Large Tin Deep Dish Candleholder**, ht. 4¾, dia. 9½in. **$104**

1193 **Brass Spring-loaded Candlestick w/weighted Base**, ht. 8¾in. **$33**

1194 **Nickel Plated Student Lamp**, ht. 17in. **$302**

1195 **Pewter Lace Maker's Light**, ht. 15in. **$522**

1196 **Pewter Whale Oil Lamp** mkd. Morey & Ober, Boston, ht. 4in. **$253**

1197 **Spout Fat Lamp**, tin & iron basket-form, ht. 4¾in. **$687**

1188 **Wrought Iron Standing Candle & Splint Holder** w/trim scissors, ht. 49in. **$1,485**

1101 **Tin Candle Lantern** w/glass window & pierced top, ht. 14in. **$137**

1198 **Wrought Iron Splint/Rush Holder** on wood block, ht. 7½in. **$357**

1199 **Wrought Iron Splint/Rush Holder**, ht. 7in. **$275**

1100 **Brass Student Lamp** mkd. Stern Bros's, NY, ht. 20¾in. **$467**

1102 **Brass Candlesticks** on octagonal base, pr., ht. 12in. **$137**

1103 **Penny Match Dispenser** w/orig. finish, ht. 13½in. **$632**

1104 **Adjustable Wooden Tidy-top**, 18th C., w/strong turnings, ht. 9¾in. **$198**

1106 **Spring-loaded Pulpit Candleholder** for two candles, ht. 15in. **$82**

1156 Tin Tomlinson's Patent Lamp w/saucer base, ht. 6¼in. **$550**

1157 Wooden Taper Holder w/wax tapers still intact, w/some base damage, ht.12in. **$1,210**

1158 Tin Betty Lamp on stand, ht. 7¾in. **$1,045**

1159 Tension Splint/Rush Holder, iron & wood, ht. 8¼in. **$467**

1160 Small Pair of Pricket Candleholders, ht. 6¼in. **$55**

1161 Twelve-hole Circular Candle Mold w/crimped top & bottom ht. 12½in. **$198**

1163 Four-hole Tin Candle Mold, ht. 10¼in. **$49**

1162 Candle Dripping Ladder, mortised & pinned, orig., 10¼ x 25¼in. **$605**

1164 Four-hole Candle Mold, ht. 3½in. **$93**

1165 Wooden Candle Dipping Rack for thirty-six candles, orig., 10½ x 17in. **$880**

1166 Nickel Plated Brass Lamp w/circular wick mkd. Argand Diamond Light, complete, ht. 20¼in. **$132**

1168 Tin Candle Lantern w/pierced top, three glass windows & removable crimped candleholder, ht. 12¾in. **$154**

1167 Wrought Iron Standing Candleholder, tri-leg w/penny feet & two crimped candle cups, ht. 56½in. **$1,925**

1169 Brass Hooded Wall Sconce w/attached cone snuffer, ht. 14in. **$121**

1170 Brass & Cast Iron Candleholder, spring-loaded w/bulbous chimney, ht.14½in. **$451**

1171 Toleware Candle Food Warmer, ht. 8¼in. **n/s**

1172 Wrought Iron Sliding Trammel-type Candle w/splint holder, lg. 32½in. **$907**

1173 Tin Ring Form Candelabra w/twelve candle sockets, ca.1828, ht. 1¾, dia. 24in. **$1,705**

1174 Brass Taper Holder w/cut-out heart motif in base, ht. 5¾in. **$357**

1175 Flintlock Iron & Wood Tinder Pistol, mkd. Wooll, lg. 7½in. **$1,375**

1176 Wooden Betty Lamp Stand, 18th C., ht. 10in. **$1,705**

A-OH   Early Auction Company, LLC

229 Steuben Cintra Lamp, bulbous stick form base in yellow Cintra, cut w/deco flower & leaf design, stalacite & stalagmite borders w/floral emb. metal base, ht. 27in. **$660**

A-ME   James D. Julia, Inc.

821 Daum French Cameo Lamp w/acid-etched red flowers, green & white leaves, on frosted background. sgn. w/engraved signature on shade & base, ht. 27¾in. **$8,625**

A- OH

Early Auction Company, LLC

233 Steuben Lamp, bulbous stick form in celadon glass cut in the Grape patt., overall ht. 28in. **$600**

1164

1165

1166

1167

1168

1169

1170

1171

1172

A-NY   Hesse Galleries

1164 Christmas Candleholders, three, blown in mold diamond patt., ht. 3¼in. **$60**

1165 Amber Glass Christmas Candleholders, two, ht. 2½in. **$71**

1166 Eight-sided Multi-colored Glass & Tin Christmas Candleholder, ht. 3¼in. **$71**

1167 Hand Painted Fabric Candle Shield w/spring clip, 4½ x 5in. **$11**

1168 Saratoga Lard Oil Sconces w/aqua glass fonts & tin holders, ht. 5¼in. **$319**

1169 Miniature GWTW Milk Glass Kerosene Lamp w/tin pedestal base, ht. 8in. **$44**

1171 Vapo-Cresolene Lamp in orig. box, ht. 6¼in. **$44**

1172 Kerosene Signal Lantern mkd. VV&B w/traces of old finish, ht. 8½in. **$55**

1170 Miniature Kerosene Lamp w/cobalt blue glass font & shade, ht. 7¾in. **$143**

A-MA   Skinner, Inc.
First Row
384 **Tin & Glass Whale Oil Lanterns,**
Am., early mid-19th C., one w/wire-
work guard, whale oil burners &
vestiges of black paint, ht. 13 &
12½in. **$529**
385 **Brass Candlesticks,** four, French,
mid-18th C. w/hexagon fluted candle
cups, ht. 10⅜in. **$1,058**
386 **Push-up Hogscraper
Candlesticks,** Am., early 19th C.,

sheet iron w/brass ring at center &
lower shaft, ht. 10¼in. **$764**
Second Row
387 **Tin Candle Lantern** w/ring
handle, together w/an onion lamp
w/ring handle & whale oil burners,
both w/vestiges of black paint, the
first lacking a portion of the wire
guard, ht. 15½ & 11¾in. **$764**
388 **Tin Student Lamp** w/conical
shade, pierced rim, removable snuffer

& brass ring finial on weighted dish
base, ht. 19in. **$1,410**
389 **Pair of Diminutive Brass Oil
Lamps,** early 19th C., w/whale oil
burners, ht. 5⅛in. **$470**
390 **Two Tin & Glass Lanterns,** Am.,
mid-19th C., both w/ovoid globes,
ring handles & whale oil burners. One
mkd. New England Glass Co.,
Cambridge, MA, Pat. Oct. 24,
1854, ht. 16¼ & 18in. **$940**

The number of small objects made of metal and used in American households that were treated in such a way to attract collectors in this field is enormous. The pleasure of pewter lies not only in its softly rounded forms, but in its glowing surface. Copper has been used essentially for utilitarian articles since the 18th century. Pots, pans, molds and kettles for example are difficult to identify as American, because few were marked and American styles closely resemble European styles. Iron was the most commonly used metal because it was low in cost and high in strength. Early brass pieces, especially candlesticks, are very decorative and are becoming scarcer and more expensive with each passing year. Because tin-plate was a cheap and flexible medium, a tremendous variety of objects were produced. It is the early custom-made objects produced by tinsmiths that are sought after by collectors... such as decorative little cookie cutters and unusual candlemolds and sconces. It is the gaily decorated tinware known as "toleware" that is so popular among collectors. Although it dates from the 19th century, a great number of decorated pieces were produced by talented artists.

A century after America was settled, every center of population had a number of silversmiths to supply the needs of the wealthier colonist. Therefore, early American silver is understandably very rare, but on occasion a fine piece will surface. The majority of objects included in this chapter include silver plate, sterling and English old Sheffield plate. Silver plate is not solid silver, but a ware made of metal such as copper or nickel. The objects are simply covered with a thin coating of silver, whereas the term "sterling" refers to an object of solid silver, conforming to the highest standard. The term "Sheffield" refers to fused plate (a thin sheet of silver fused by heat to a thicker copper ingot), a process discovered by a Sheffield (England) man. Sheffield plate was, however, also produced in Birmingham (England), France and Russia. Lastly, it should be included that between 1836 and 1838 the English firm of G.R. & H. Elkington, of Birmingham, are credited with the invention of electroplating. By the 1840s, the first successful plating techniques were achieved in America.

Jackson's International Auctioneers

A-IA
1188 **Repoussé Sterling Flatware Set** by S. Kirk & Son, 81 pieces. **$1,880**
1190 **Sterling Flatware Set** by Gorham, 62 pieces. **$881**

A-IA   Jackson's
International
Auctioneers
1153 **Victorian Silver Ink Stand,** Sheffield, ca.1848 by Henry Wilkinson, lg. 11¼in.
$1,997

A-IA

1154 **Sheffield Silver Basket,** ca.1930, mkd. R&D w/scrollwork, lg. 8¼in. **$382**
1155 **Two Silver Salt Cellars,** London, ca.1848, mkd. W.M. together w/silver mustard pot, London, 1926 by Fold & Silver Co. **$441**

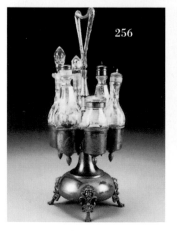

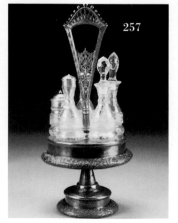

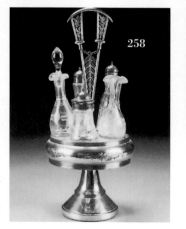

A-PA   **Pook & Pook, Inc.**

403 **Philadelphia Silver Snuff Box**, ca.1795 bearing the touch of John Myers, ht. 2½, wd. 1¾in. **$3,744**

404 **Continental Silver Nutmeg Grater**, late 17th C. w/touch TK, lg. 2¾in. **$1,830**

405 **Sterling Silver Nutmeg Grater** of cylindrical form, mkd. Tiffany & Co., ht. 1⅝in. **$410**

406 **Thermometer Case**, 19th C. w/engraved floral dec., 14K gold, lg. 4⅜in. together w/sterling silver traveling candleholder & match safe, ht. 4in. **$556**

407 **Birmingham Silver Vinaigrette/Perfume**, ca.1884 by D & L.S., lg. 3½in., together w/Gorham silver tea bag holder. **$556**

408 **Silver Birmingham Spectacles**, 1831-1832 by T.M.; a corkscrew mkd. JW, magnifying glass dated 1789, an unmkd. stamp & a Russian enamelwork spoon. **$1,342**

A-PA   **Pook & Pook, Inc.**

434 **Two Birmingham Silver Nutmeg Graters**, 1814-1825, bearing touches of Thomas Whitmore & Thomas Shaw, together w/a London silver nutmeg grater ca.1841 by Rawlins & Summer. **$1,872**

435 **Two Acorn Form Graters**, 19th C., together w/two egg form examples, all unmkd. **$936**

436 **Three Birmingham Silver Nutmeg Graters**, one 1792 & two 1801 mkd. S. Pemberton, Jos. Taylor, & John Turner, ht. 1¼in. **$1,586**

437 **Birmingham Silver Melon Form Nutmeg Grater**, ca.1860 by George Unite w/repoussé foliate dec. together w/another melon grater initialed TJ, ht. 1½ & 2⅛in. **$1,638**

438 **London Silver Nutmeg Grater**, 1824, bearing the touch CR, together w/an urn form example, 2½ & 3½in. **$4,914**

439 **Two English Silver Barrel Form Nutmeg Graters**, 1801, 1835, bearing touches of T.W. Matthews & S.M., ht. 1½ & 2in. **$1,872**

A-PA   **Conestoga Auction Company, Inc.**

146 **Pewter Porringer** w/pierced handle & old repr., unmkd., dia. 5¼in. **$55**

147 **Three Love Pewter Plates**, hallmarked London over love birds & crown, dia. 7¾in. **$990**

Opposite

A-IA   **Jackson's International Auctioneers**

247 **Victorian Silver Chatelaine**, Birmingham ca.1897, mkd. CM, each piece w/matching floral repoussé, lg. 12in. **$1,292**

249 **Ten Sterling Table Articles**, 20th C., incl. bowl, two compotes, 4 candle holders, shakers & napkin ring. **$146**

250 **Towle Sterling Flatware**, Candlewick patt., ca.1934, 43 pcs., service for eight w/silver chest. **$323**

252 **Sterling Flatware** by Lunt, 92 pieces, Modern Victorian patt., ca.1941, service for twelve. **$822**

253 **Victorian Cut Glass Basket** w/silvered Basket, lg. 10in. **$235**

254 **Victorian Figural Toothpick Caddy** by Poole & inscr. Have a Pick. **$235**

255 **Two Victorian Napkin Ring Holders** w/salt dip & pepper shakers by Aurora & Rogers. **$264**

256 **Caster Set** w/bearded man foot mounts & non-matching containers, silvered, ht. 18in. **$176**

257 **Victorian Caster Set** w/floral repoussé frame holding five matching bottles, silvered, ht. 17in. **$94**

258 **Caster Set**, w/five non-matching bottles & silvered frame, ht. 17in. **$58**

259 **Victorian Silvered Spoon Holder** w/bird finial, together w/pitcher & Cromwell mug. **$105**

A-PA   Pook & Pook, Inc.
204 **Two Boston Silver Spoons,** late 18th C. bearing touch of Paul Revere II, 1735-1818, lg. 8¾in. **$14,040**

A-ME   James D. Julia, Inc.
489 **Brass Candlestick** mkd. King of Diamonds, English w/push ups, ht. 12¼in. **$460**

A-PA   Pook & Pook, Inc.
186 **Birmingham Silver Egg-form Nutmeg Grater,** ca.1803 w/touch of Joseph Taylor & inscribed Semper Victor, ht. 1¾in. **$793**
187 **Birmingham Silver Barrel-form Nutmeg Grater,** ca.1803 w/touch of J. Whitmore, ht. 1¾in. **$819**
188 **Four Silver Nutmeg Graters** w/touches of R.G., H.B., E & Co.& Nathaniel Mills, lg. 1½ & 2½in. **$2,808**

A-PA   Pook & Pook, Inc.
410 **Three New York Silver Boxes,** one bearing touch of Albert Coles & two by Wood & Hughes w/engraved dec.& inscriptions, ht. 2½ & 3¼n. **$995**
411 **Scottish Silver Vinaigrette,** ca.1870, bearing the touch of Edmond Johnson Jr. The lid has elaborate cast floral dec, ht. 3½, wd. 1⅜in. **$995**
412 **Silver & Tortoiseshell Snuff Box,** early 19th C., wd. 2⅜in., together w/another unmkd. silver example & a silver plate snuff box. **$644**

A-PA   Conestoga Auction Company, Inc.
144 **Bulbous Pewter Mug** w/illegible hallmarks, ht. 3⅜in. **$209**
143 **Pewter Pitcher** w/incised lines around body, shaped handle & bulbous form by F. Porter, Westbrook, CT, ht. 6in. **$357**
145 **Pewter Mug** mkd. w/a crown over the initials V.A. ht. 4½in. **$275**

A-PA   Conestoga Auction Company, Inc.
139 **Coffee Pot,** mkd. F. Porter, Westbrook, CT, ht. 10½in. **$176**
141 **Two Pewter Whale Oil Lamps,** unmkd. w/double wick screw cap & saucer base, ht. 9in. **$187**
142 **Sugar Bowl** mkd. Sellew & Co., Cincinnati, w/scroll handles. **$385**
140 **Teapot,** mkd. Putnam w/shaped handle painted black, ht. 8½in. **$247**

A-PA   **Pook & Pook, Inc.**
221 Nine Wrought Iron Buttonhole Cutters, 19th C., two w/turned wooden handles & one w/bone handle, 3¼-8½in. long. Together w/a wrought iron hammer. **$936**

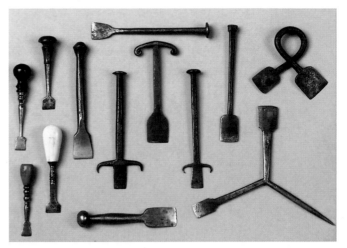

A-PA   **Pook & Pook, Inc.**
223 Four English Buttonhole Cutters, 19th C., one w/agate handle, one w/ivory & two w/turned wooden handles, lg. 2¾-3½in. **$702**
224 Seven Wrought Iron Buttonhole Cutters, 19th C., one mkd. SM 1846, lg. 4-4¾in. **$1,287**
225 Four 2-Prong Cutters, 19th C., one initialed DSB, together w/an iron hook, two thread pullers & two cutters. **$3,276**

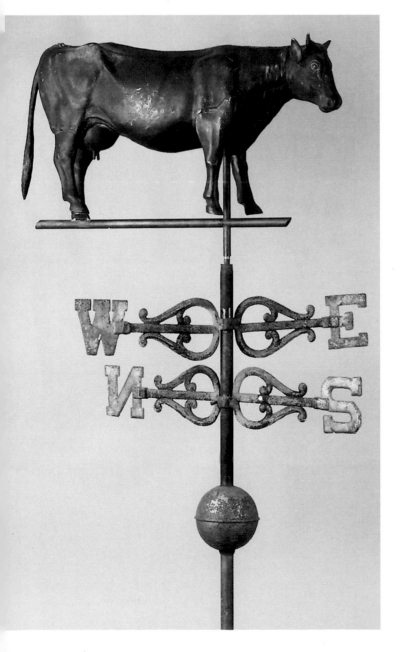

A-MA   **Skinner, Inc.**
114 Sheet & Wrought Iron Peacock Weather Vane, ca.1800, cut-out sheet iron body w/wrought iron comb & tail ornaments & strap reinforcements mounted to an iron shaft, w/rusty surface, ht. 27½in. **$12,925**
115 Molded Sheet Copper Gamecock Weather Vane, early 19th C., flattened full figure w/zinc legs, embossed sheet copper tail & mounted on copper rods, w/minor dents. ht. 22¾in. **$5,581**

A-PA   **Pook & Pook, Inc.**
447 Copper Full Body Cow Weathervane, Am., ca.1900 w/solid brass head & orig. directionals, ht. 17½, lg. 29in. **$10,925**

A-NH

Northeast Auctions

706 **Large Cast-iron Fireback** depicting two men at well, 36x26in. **$400**

707 **Fireback** w/portrait medallion & crossed flags & cannons, 25½ x 23in. **$1,000**

Opposite

A-PA   Pook & Pook, Inc.

1104 **Oak Welsh Cupboard,** George II, two parts, ca.1740, ht. 74½, wd.74in. **$2,990**

1091 **Three Pewter Coffee Pots,** 19th C., largest ht. 8½in., together w/a small tankard. **$230**

1092 **Nine Pieces of Tableware** incl. two funnels, two small boxes, two covered sugars & three food molds. **$431**

1093 **Three Chargers,** 19th C., largest 22in dia., together w/a pewter punch dec. trivet. **$978**

1094 **Nine Food Molds** including Uncle Sam & Abe Lincoln ice cream molds. **$489**

1095 **Seven Pewter Measures,** 19th C., largest ht. 5⅝in, smallest 2¼in. **$230**

1096 **Group of Pewter Utensils,** 19th C., including three pap boats, 3 infant feeding spoons, a taster & ladle. **$575**

1097 **Pair of English Pewter Candlesticks,** early 19th C. mkd. B & P, London on bases ht. 9¼in., together w/two unmkd. prs. of candlesticks. **$1,265**

1098 **Two English Pewter Chargers,** 19th C., dia. 16½ & 18in., & a covered tureen ht. 8½in. **$575**

1099 **Harbeson Plate,** dia. 6in., three measures & three tasters. **$288**

1100 **James Dixon & Sons Coffee Pot,** 19th C., ht. 11in., together w/a teapot. **$540**

1101 **Coffee Pot by R. Gleason,** ht. 12in., together w/one by B. Ward & Son, ht. 11in., & one by Quilkin, ht.

9½in. **$460**

1102 **Five Porringers,** late 18th/early 19th C., one w/eagle touchmark on handle & one w/incised initials A.B. **$518**

1103 **Two Coffee Pots,** one w/dog mask spout, together w/a hot water urn, ht. 16in. **$201**

1105 **Set of Four Push-up Candlesticks,** early 19th C., ht. 9in., together w/ another pr. ht. 9in. **$460**

1106 **Whale Oil Lamp,** 19th C., mkd. Capen & Molineaux, NY, ht. 14in., together w/a hanging gimbaled lamp, ht. 5½in., a single candlestick, ht. 8in., & a pr. of candlesticks, ht. 9in. **$431**

1107 **Inkstand** w/two drawers, dated 1790 & mkd. Coutts, Banking House, ht. 4in., together w/a double-flapped inkstand & two others. **$748**

1108 **Four Pewter Measures** mkd. James Yates & a miniature teapot mkd. E. Whitehouse. **$144**

1109 **Seven Pewter Measures,** 19th C., one mkd. E. Hall, largest 5in. **$300**

1110 **Six English Pewter Chargers,** 19th C., largest 18¼in. dia. **$1,150**

1111 **Five Measures,** 19th C., all of baluster form, largest 6¼in. **$316**

1112 **Five Lamps,** 19th C., two hour lamps, ht. 12¾in., a bull's-eye lamp & two oil lamps **$1,093**

1113 **Six Lamps,** two hour lamps, ht. 14in., & four oil lamps. **$840**

1114 **Seventeen German Pewter Plates,** 19th C., w/scalloped edges, largest 9½ dia., smallest 7¼in. **$518**

1115 **Four English Basins,** 19th C.,

largest, ht. 3, dia. 13¼in., together w/three shallow bowls. **$403**

1116 **English Lidded Pitcher,** one gal., 19th C., ht. 12½in., together w/an English coffee pot, ht. 10½in., & a flagon, ht. 10in. **$1,495**

1117 **Five English Tankards,** one incised Thorley Church, tallest 9in. **$3,450**

1118 **Bowl** w/eight shakers & three cup salts. **$633**

1119 **Four English Flagons,** tallest 13½in. **$345**

1120 **Four English Flagons,** tallest 10¾in. **$748**

1121 **Teapot** bearing touch of Josiah Danforth, Middletown, CT., ht. 6½in., together w/ shallow bowl w/touch of Ashbil Griswold, Meriden, CT. dia. 11½in. **$633**

1122 **Eight Plates,** 19th C., together w/two chargers, dia. of largest 14¾in. **$805**

1123 **Three Pieces of Pewter** by James Dixon & Son incl. a large flagon, ht. 12in., footed compote & lidded sugar. **$230**

1124 **Three Chalices,** 19th C., tallest 11in., together w/two footed salts. **$186**

1125 **Five Flagons,** largest 9¼in., together w/a pewter counterweight. **$431**

1126 **Tray, footed Plate & Warmer,** lg. 13in. **$201**

1127 **Massive English Double-handled Meat & Warming Platter,** ca.1790 bearing mark of Henry Richard Joseph, ht. 4½, wd. 27¼in. **$374**

A-NH   **Northeast Auctions**
708 Arched Fireback w/British coat-of-arms, together w/a brass & wire fire screen & ember pan, lg. of screen 47in. **$1,600**

A-NH   **Northeast Auctions**
709 Fireback w/ornate floral urn & inscription below, 30½x19½in. **$700**

1076

1079

1085

1088

1089

1055

1067

1016

1017

1020

1022

1027

A-IA   Jackson's International Auctioneers

1076 Ten Rocker & Roller Fluting Irons, incl. Geneva's Am. Machine. **$117**

1079 Eleven Sleeve Irons, 19th C. incl. Union T. Sensible iron. **$70**

1085 J.M.B. Davidson Stove Top Heater, 19th C. **$293**

1088 Five Gas Irons, 20th C., incl. The Rhythm & The Diamond. **$58**

1089 Five Gas Irons, 20th C., incl. an Aladdin Kerosene w/orig. box, a Green Fairy Prince & three English gas irons. **$528**

1055 Eight Charcoal Irons, 19th C., incl. a G&S Belgian brass iron. **$94**

1067 Four Goffering Irons, 19th C. w/all brass tops & one tripod base. **$646**

1016 Four Streeters Magic Combination Fluter & Polisher Slug Irons, late 19th C. **$352**

1017 Three Double Point Box Irons, 19th C., together w/a Jubilee & two handled sad irons. **$205**

1020 A Geneva Improved Hand Fluter, late 19th C., together w/a five-piece fluter & a Sundry base. **$70**

1022 An English Crimping Machine, late 19th C. w/four brass rollers mounted on later board. **$499**

1027 Knox Crimping Machine, late 19th C., w/6in. brass rollers, together w/an unmkd. Tripod Crimping Machine w/brass rollers. **$352**

Interest in American Indian crafts has attracted collectors from the late 19th century, but it has only been within the latter half of the 20th century that the demand reached the present fever pitch. The major areas of Indian collectibles are rugs, blankets, pottery, beadwork, basketry, wood carvings, leather work and jewelry. Each tribe has its own distinctive designs.

Blankets and rugs have had a great attraction for collectors. The Hopi and Zuni tribes have produced some very appealing examples. However, many collectors search for examples made by Navajo weavers. They worked on an upright loom of their own invention, using natural dyes and wool from their sheep. Today, examples of their early creations are considered art forms.

Perhaps the best known pottery is the black-on-black pieces that were made at the San Ildefonso pueblo, near Santa Fe, New Mexico, by the Martinez family. Julian and Maria signed pieces are especially sought by collectors. Other fine examples of pottery were made at the pueblos of Santo Domingo, Santa Clara and Acoma in New Mexico. And the Hopi Indians in Arizona made fine pottery.

The finest baskets, and the ones most sought by collectors, are those of the Southwest. Their light and durable Indian baskets were made in large quantities, for both personal use and as something to be sold to tourists.

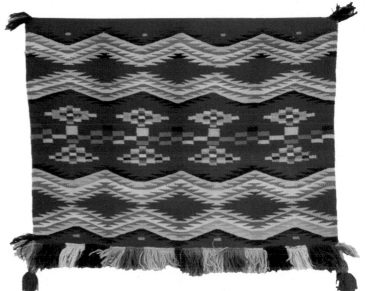

A-MA   Skinner, Inc.
547 Germantown Weaving, Navajo, late 19th C., a single saddle blanket w/ fringe on one side, 30½x24in. **$1,880**

A-MA   Skinner, Inc.
568 Southwest Figure Yei Weaving, Navajo, ca. early 20th C. w/stains, 84½x67½in. **$24,675**

A-MA   Skinner, Inc.
548 Navajo Woman's Shoulder Blanket, late 19th C. w/natural & commercial dyed wool in a fourth phase variation, 51x37½in. **$9,988**

A-MA　　　　　　　　　　　　　　　　　Skinner, Inc.
563　Navajo Woman's Wearing Blanket, last qtr. 19th C. w/natural & aniline dyed homespun wool, w/stains & wool loss, 52x45½in. **$9,400**

A-MA　　　　　　　　　　　　　　　　　Skinner, Inc.
559　Southwest Pictorial Germantown Weaving, Navajo, late 19th C. w/insect damage, 72x57in. **$2,938**

A-MA　　　　　　　　　　　　　　　　　Skinner, Inc.
565　Southwest Late Classic Wearing Blanket, late 19th C. w/natural & aniline dyed homespun wool in a second phase chief's patt., w/wool loss, reprs. and stains, 55x42in. **$11,750**

A-MA　　　　　　　　　　　　　　　　　Skinner, Inc.
539　Southwest Weaving, Navajo, Two Gray Hills, ca. second qtr. 20th C., w/minor wool losses & stains, 122x63in. **$5,228**

A-MA Skinner, Inc.
99 Northern Plains Cloth, Hide & Wood Rattles, Crow, ca. late 19th C. The wood handles wrapped w/cloth & hide w/three haw bell attachments, lg. 10½in. **$999**

A-MA Skinner, Inc.
100 Plains Wood & Rawhide Drum, late 19th C. w/commercial wood drum body, some damage to hide, dia. 24, wd. 12in. **$2,350**

A-MA Skinner, Inc.
101 Plains Wood Courting Flute, ca. late 19th C. w/two pieces of hollow cedar lashed together w/buffalo hide wrappings. The flute block in the form of an elk w/incised detail and six fingerholes, lg. 25in. **$2,820**
102 Southern Plains Wood & Hide Courting Flute. The two pieces of hollowed out wood are tied w/rawhide strips & the flute block is carved into form of a bird. An attached paper label reads in part Comanche Indian Love Flute, Oklahoma, lg. 21in. **$411**

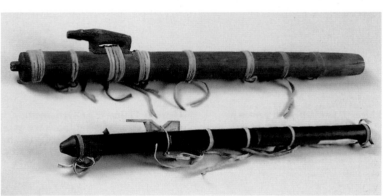

A-MA Skinner, Inc.
573 Classic Southwest Moki Serape, Navajo, ca. third qtr. 19th C., w/minor stains, 72x 47in. **$32,900**

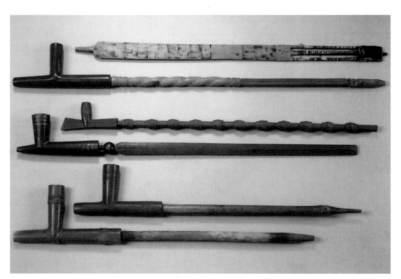

A-MA Skinner, Inc.
89 Great Lakes Quilled Wood Pipe Stem, ca. mid.-19th C., file branded w/cut-outs having remnant multicolored bird quill wrappings, damage, lg.26½in. **$1,528**
90 Plains Wood & Stone Pipe, ca. late 19th C. w/traces of red pigment & a red pipestone T-bowl, lg. 31in. **$499**
91 Plains Wood & Stone Pipe, 19th C. w/red pipestone bowl of canoe prow form & ash stem w/barrel-shaped forms. Patina of use, lg. 26in. **$2,233**
92 Plains Wood & Stone Pipe, ca. 19th C, w/tapered ash stem & red pipestone head w/locomotive bowl & six lead ring inlays, lg. 28in. **$2,115**
93 Two Central Plains Pipes, ca. late 19th C., both w/carved red pipestone ribbed T-bowls & round stems. lg. 24in. **$1,293**

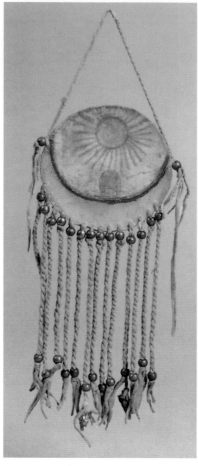

A-MA   Skinner, Inc.
213 Southwest Cloth, Hide & Wood Doll,
Apache, ca. last third 19th C. w/thread-wrapped head dec. w/brass pinheads, leather hair bow at back of head & an elaborate two-piece dress w/long fringe. The moccasins & dress are made of commercial leather, ht. 14in. $14,100

A-MA   Skinner, Inc.
154 Northern Plains Beaded & Tacked Hide Knife Sheath, Crow, ca. late 19th C., buffalo rawhide w/buffalo hide panel & dec. w/multi-colored devices on pink ground using seed & pony beads, lg. 10¾in. $14,100

A-MA   Skinner, Inc.
146 Southern Plains or Ute Painted Amulet, rawhide w/sun, moon & human face likeness on one side, a multi. elk on reverse. Twisted yellow fringe w/shells & brass beads hang from bottom, disc dia. 3¾in. $4,700

A-MA   Skinner, Inc.
144 Southern Plains Belt Set, Comanche, ca. late 19th C., both w/German silver buttons & large trade beads on straps, commercial leather & drop w/commercial nickel plated brass conchas & roller buckle. Beaded ornament lg. 6in. $2,703

A-MA   Skinner, Inc.
326 Southwest Katchina Dance Board w/poly. dec., ca. late 19th/early 20th C. w/cloth waist ties. This object, known as a moisture tablet, is part of a costume for Hopi katsinam, ht. 19, wd., 15½in. $15,275

A-MA   Skinner, Inc.
223 Plateau Beaded Hide &
Cloth Pouch, ca.1900 w/hide
edging & strap on a crystal
background, 12½x10½in. $588

A-MA   Skinner, Inc.
225 Plateau Beaded Flat Cloth Bag,
ca. early 20th C. dec. w/Am. eagle
& flags, insect damage to cloth,
14x13in. $1,880

A-MA   Skinner, Inc.
122 Northern Plains
Beaded Hide & Cloth
Martingale, Crow,
ca.1900, w/cloth loss,
lg. 33in. $5,288

A-MA   Skinner, Inc.
123 Northern Plains
Hide & Cloth
Martingale, Crow, late
19th C. w/bead &
cloth loss, lg. 31in.
$6,463

A-MA   Skinner, Inc.
127 Northern Plains Beaded Hide Mirror
Bag, Crow, ca. late 19th C. w/classic
Crow designs on both sides & strap, bead
loss, lg. 14in. $3,055
128 Northern Plains Beaded Hide & Cloth
Mirror Bag, Crow, first qtr. 20th C.
w/hawk bells along bottom, with fringe lg.
18in. $1,998

A-MA   Skinner, Inc.
166 Southern Plains Beaded Hide Bow & Quiver,
Mescalero Apache, ca.1870s w/orig. sinew-back
bow & ten arrow shafts w/metal & stone points, hide
loss & small tears, lg. 42in. $8,225

A-MA   Skinner, Inc.
168 Southern Plains Horse Hide Bow Case & Quiver, probably
Comanche, ca. mid-19th C., dec. w/white seed beads &
containing a bone-handled awl w/a wood & buffalo hide
arrow extractor. The orig. Osage orange wood bow w/sinew
string & an inscription on strap reads Paint Creek Texas,
March 7, 1868, w/old reprs., lg. 52, bow 47in. $9,988

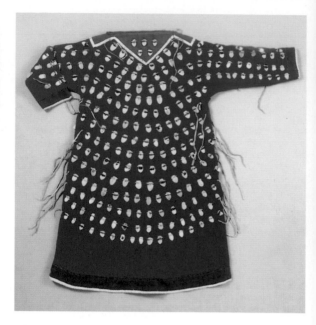

A-MA   Skinner, Inc.
177 Plains/Prairie Missouri War Axe, ca. mid-19th C., possibly Osage orange wood handle w/heart cut-out in blade & five-point metal star inlay on one side, patina of use, handle lg. 21, head 7¾in. **$5,875**

A-MA   Skinner, Inc.
196 Northern Plains Cloth Elk Tooth Child's Dress, ca. first qtr. 20th C. Red trade cloth w/multiple rows of carved bone simulated elk teeth on both sides & hide fringe, lg. 35in. **$4,406**

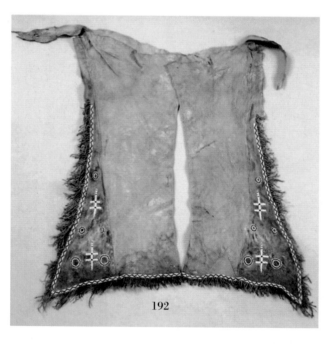

192

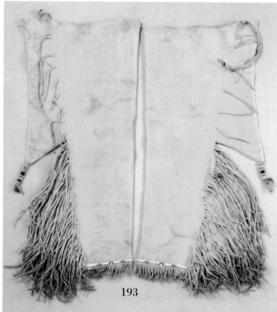

193

A-MA Skinner, Inc.
192 Southern Plains Beaded Hide Man's Leggings, Cheyenne, ca. late 19th C., beaded on both sides, lg. 32in. **$3,525**

A-MA Skinner, Inc.
193 Southern Plains Hide Boy's Leggings, Kiowa, ca.1900 w/hawk bells hanging from tab ends, lg. 26in. **$1,880**

A-MA   Skinner, Inc.
199 Southern Plains Beaded Hide Girl's Dress, Kiowa, ca. late 19th C. & dec. w/mescal beans & tubular trade bead attachments, w/bead loss, lg. 31in. **$1,293**

A-MA   Skinner, Inc.
195 Woman's Dress, Beaded Hide, Cheyenne, late 19th C. & fringed in various lengths, lg. 56in. **$47,000**

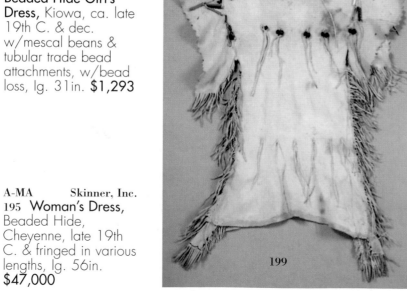

199

195

A-MA Skinner, Inc.
372 **Acoma Pottery Olla,** ca. second qtr. 20th C. w/four Acoma parrots patt., w/inscription on base Acoma Indian Pottery, Acomita, N.M., ht. 10½, dia. 13in. **$1,645**

A-MA Skinner, Inc.
378 **Southwest Pottery Olla,** Zuni, ca. last qtr. 19th C. w/geometric patt. & heart-line deer, ht. 12, dia. 14½in. **$17,625**
379 **Zuni Pottery Bowl,** late 19th C., w/geometric & avian devices, ht. 7, dia. 9in. **$6,463**

360   361   362   363   364

365   366   367

A-MA Skinner, Inc.
360 **Southwest Pottery Olla** w/poly. dec., Acoma, ca. 1920s, w/rim crack, ht. 8½, dia. 10½in. **$2,115**
361 **Acoma Pottery Olla,** early 20th C., w/Zuni-like dec. incl. small birds, large medallions & cross-hatched detail, ht. 10, dia. 11in. **$1,998**
362 **Painted Pottery Jar,** Acoma,

second qtr. 20th C. w/prehistoric designs, ht. 10½in. **$646**
363 **Acoma Pottery Olla,** ca.1920s w/black Zuni-like designs, ht.9, dia. 11in. **$2,585**
364 **Southwest Pottery Olla,** Acoma, w/overall prehistoric pattern, ht. 8, dia. 8in. **$1,175**
365 **Zia Pottery Olla,** late 19th C.

w/geometric pattern, ht. 11¼, dia. 12in. **$11,163**
366 **Zia Pottery Olla,** last qtr. 19th C., w/abstract foliate design & four large birds, chip on rim, ht. 12, dia. 12½in. **$1,527**
367 **Southwest Pottery Olla,** Acoma, ca. late 19th C. w/repeat patt., ht. 10, dia. 10½in. **n/s**

A-MA   Skinner, Inc.
263 **Northeast Painted Wood Splint Basket,** ca. 19th C., drum-form, ht. 9½, dia. 13½in. **$353**
264 **Northeast Painted Wood Splint Basket** w/stamped & painted dec., & round lid, ht. 9, dia. 12½in. **$470**

A-MA   Skinner, Inc.
258 **Northeast Birch Bark Lidded Storage Box,** Eastern Algonquin, late 19th C. & dec. w/avian & foliate devices & w/ minor damage, ht. 9½, wd.13½in. **$353**

A-MA   Skinner, Inc.
526 **Northwest Twined & Lidded Rattle-top Basket** w/poly. dec., Attu, ca.1900 w/snowflake devices w/split at lid's edge, ht. 7, dia. 6½in. **$4,700**
527 **Northwest Poly. Twined Lidded Basket,** Artu, ca.1900 & dec. w/colored yarn hourglass devices & wool loss, ht. 8, dia. 5½in. **$1,410**

A-MA   Skinner, Inc.
257 **Northeast Birch Bark Lidded Storage Box,** Eastern Algonquin, late 19th C. & dec. w/curvilinear foliate devices. Crack in lid, ht. 10, dia. 13½in. **$764**

A-MA   Skinner, Inc.
467 **California Poly. Coiled Basketry Bowl,** Mission, ca.1900 w/flaring sides & dec. w/two-color honeycomb patt., ht. 14, dia. 22in. **$8,813**

A-MA   Skinner, Inc.
259 **Northeast Pictorial Birch Bark & Wood Log Caddy,** Penobscot, ca. early 20th C. & dec. w/animal images. Handle broken in one place, damage, ht. 20, wd. 14½, lg. 22in. **$7,638**

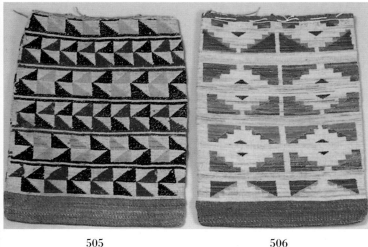

505   506   507   511

A-MA   **Skinner, Inc.**
505 **Plateau Cornhusk Bag,** ca.19th C., dec. on both sides w/poly. geometric designs using commercial yarns w/calico lining & wood loss, lg. 18in. **$411**

506 **Cornhusk Bag,** Plateau, ca. late 19th C., each side dec. w/different geometric devices, lg. 19in. **$823**
507 **Plateau Cornhusk Bag,** ca.1900 w/each side dec. w/different poly. geometric designs using commercial

yarn, minor fading, lg. 20in. **$646**
511 **Umatilla Plateau Cornhusk Bag,** ca. late 19th C., both sides dec. w/poly. geometric designs using commercial worsted wools, wool loss, 18½ x 14in. **$764**

346   347   348   349   350

A-MA   **Skinner, Inc.**
346 **Southwest Polished Black-ware Pottery Bowl,** Santa Clara, ca. mid-20th C, deeply carved & sgn. Tafoya, w/scratches, ht. 7½in. **$1,175**
347 **Blackware Lidded Jar sgn. Gutierrez,** Santa Clara Pueblo, in faceted melon style, ht. 5½in. **$323**
348 **Black-on-Black Pottery Bowl,** Santa Clara, Nicolasa, w/minor surface scratches, ht. 6½in. **$176**
349 **Blue Corn Pottery Bowl,** 20th C., w/curvilinear dec., scratches, ht. 2in., dia. 6¾in. **$529**
350 **Black-on-Black deep carved pottery bowl,** ht. 3½in. **$264**

352   354   351   353

A-MA   **Skinner, Inc.**
351 **Southwest Pottery Seed Jar,** Hopa w/poly. three-color geometric design, w/small corn woman inset at rim, sgn. Dextra, mid-20th C., ht. 5, dia.11in. **$5,875**
352 **Pottery Plate,** sgn. Blue Corn, San Ildefonso, w/rim crack, dia. 14¾in. **$2,115**
353 **Southwest Redware Pottery Plate,** Marie & Julian, San Ildefonso, dia. 11in. **$3,408**
354 **Pottery Bowl,** Hopi by F. Nampeyo, seed jar form w/black & red geometric devices on cream-orange slip, ht. 5½, dia. 9in. **$2,585**

The market has remained strong and a remarkable number of exceptionally important original American artwork has sold. Although professional artists did flourish in the more populated areas, most of our early American paintings fall under the heading of amateur work, painted by itinerant artists during the 18th and 19th centuries. Their inability to create a cohesive composition, and their lack of skill in depicting a true likeness or correct perspective, resulted in many naïve paintings. No one speaks more eloquently for our heritage than the folk artist. Their portraits of sober-faced children – especially those with their favorite toy or dog – are very valuable these days because all serve as a surviving link to a vital and fascinating past. These paintings with juvenile quality are extremely appealing to collectors.

Today there are available to collectors many charming and beautiful paintings, drawings and prints, from all schools and periods of art. As with all fields of collecting, values vary greatly and many factors – quality, size, an artist's signature, and condition – determine value. But, in general, a beautiful original work of art can be found to fit almost every budget.

Many charming works of art are available, including portraits, still-life, historical, and religious paintings. However, folk art paintings and pictures are in a class all of their own. They include paper cuttings, tinsel pictures, theorems on velvet, cotton or paper, calligraphic drawings, needlework pictures and silhouettes.

Collectors should never overlook artwork by an unknown artist, or an unsigned work if it is good. It will not only bring the owner the aesthetic pleasure of owning something beautiful, but it also offers the practical quality of generally being a good investment. However, it is the signed and dated pieces that will fetch substantially high prices in the marketplace.

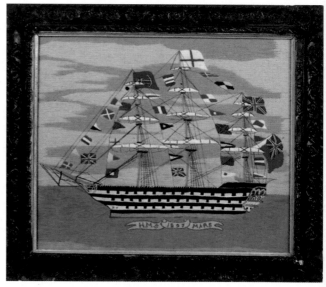

A-PA Pook & Pook, Inc.
428 English Woolwork Ship Portrait dated 1897 of the H.M.S. *Mars*, 19½x23¼in. **$995**

A-MA Skinner, Inc.
109 Pair of Portraits of Two Children, unsigned, watercolor on paper, ca.1840-45, depicting children in profile, attrib. to James Sanford Ellsworth, 1802/03-1874, sight size 3x1⅞in. **$27,000**
110 Portrait of Girl Holding a White Rose, unsigned, attrib. to Ellsworth, sight size 3⅜x2½in. **$6,463**

A-PA Freeman's Americana
336 Woolwork Picture by Eliza Seibert, PA, ca.1840. The inscription worked w/poly. wool yarns on linen & trimmed w/red ribbon, w/some discoloration. 26½x26in. **$500**

A-ME James D. Julia, Inc.

426 Portrait of Young Girl & Her Doll, oil on canvas, attrib. to Joseph Whiting Stock, Am. 1815-1855, housed in molded wood gilt frame, w/some rest. & old relining, 26¼x32in. **$6,900**

A-PA Conestoga Auction Co., Inc.

683 Theorem, Compote & Fruit by David Y. Ellinger, image 18¼x22in., in bird's-eye maple molded frame. **$5,500**

A-NH Northeast Auctions

281 Currier & Ives large-folio handcolored Lithograph Winter Morning Feeding The Chickens by George Henry Durrie, pub. 1863, in orig. frame, sight 17½x24in. **$1,500**

A-ME James D. Julia, Inc.

65 Oil on Canvas, Apples & Basket by Levi Wells Prentice, Am., 1851-1935, sgn. & housed in orig. gilt frame, 8x10in. **$15,525**

A-MA Skinner, Inc.

606 Lithograph The Road, Winter, ca.1853, Nathaniel Currier, publisher, hand coloring on paper, margins trimmed & on cardboard, 20⅛x25⅛in. **$2,585**

A-NH Northeast Auctions

900 **The Lost Scent,** oil on canvas sgn. J.F. Herring (British 1815-1907) 30x50in. **$27,840**

A-MA Skinner, Inc.

578 **The Celebrated Clipper Ship** *Dreadnought*, undated, published by Currier & Ives, small folio litho. w/hand coloring on paper, creases & mat stain, sheet size 9¾x13¾in. **$881**

616 **Maple Sugaring, Early Spring In The Woods,** by Currier & Ives, ca.1872, w/hand coloring, repr. tear & light mat stain, sheet size 9¾x13⅞in. **$1,410**

A-MA Skinner, Inc.

607 **American Homestead,** set of four small folio lithos, published by Currier & Ives, w/hand coloring on paper, identified in inscriptions in the matrix, each in possible orig. mah. frames w/imper. & toning. **$2,350**

A-MA   Skinner, Inc.
610 **The Old Farm House**, ca.1872, Currier & Ives, publishers, small folio litho. w/repr. tear & edge losses, 11¾x16in. **$1,058**

A-MA   Skinner, Inc.
617 **A Check. Keep Your Distance**, ca.1853, published by Nathaniel Currier, large folio litho. w/minor foxing & mat stain, sheet size 19¾x25⅝in. **$3,525**

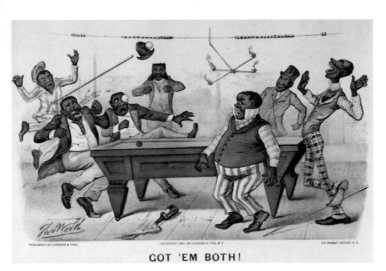

A-MA   Skinner, Inc.
601 **Got `Em Both!** ca.1882, small folio litho. w/hand-coloring on paper, old mat stains, tape repairs & creases, published by Currier & Ives, sheet size 13½x17½in. **$940**

A-MA   Skinner, Inc.
600 **Squirrel Shooting**, undated, small folio w/hand-coloring on paper, old mat stains & toning, sheet size 12x16in. **$1,059**

A-PA   Freeman's
365 **Oil Painting**, Rye Basket Filled With Fruit by Albert Francis King, 1854-1945, signed, sight 14x23¼in. **$7,500**

A-PA   Conestoga Auction Company, Inc.
684 **Theorem**, Strawberries by D. Ellinger, depicting a robin perched on a cherry branch, basket sits on a marble slab, image 15x23in. **$3,850**

PAINTINGS & PICTURES

A-PA Alderfer
Auction Company,
Inc.
897 Oil Painting
titled Yellow
House by Fern I.
Coppedge,
1888-1951,
12x12in.
$23,000

A-NJ Craftsman
Arts & Crafts
Auction
225 Tile dec. in
cuenca w/trees
in mountain
landscape,
unsigned by Van
Briggle, 6¼in.
square. **$2,200**

A-NJ Craftsman Arts & Crafts Auction
84A Color Woodblock Print titled In the Couyama
Country, pencil titled & sgn. by Frances H. Gearhart,
matted & framed, sight 12x9in. **$3,750**

A-NJ Craftsman Arts & Crafts Auction
87 Aspen Thicket, color woodblock print by Gustave
Baumann, pencil signed, titled & numbered, matted &
framed, image 10¾x9½in. **$6,000**

A-NJ Craftsman Arts & Crafts Auction
395 Plaque by Charles Volkmar, painted in barbotine
w/figure and cows, sgn. image 9½x8¼in. **$1,600**

A-PA   Conestoga Auction Company, Inc.
847 **Winter Landscape,** watercolor by Hattie K. Brunner, possibly a Christmas card, framed & matted, image size 5x6in. **$1,650**

A-PA   Freeman's
425 **Hand-colored Ambrotype,** ca.1850, 1/6 plate in a decorated leather case, lg. 3, wd. 2in. **$3,346**

A-NJ   Craftsman Arts & Crafts Auction
237 **Rookwood Scenic Vellum Plaque** by Fred Rothenbusch, ca.1912, winter landscape, image 6x8in. **$4,750**

A-PA   Alderfer Auction Company, Inc.
789 **Chinese Export Painting,** landscape w/figures, unsigned & relined. Framed wired & gold Chinese frame, 23x18in. **$8,050**

A-NJ   Craftsman Arts & Crafts Auction
156 **Woodblock Print** titled Windswept Eucalyptus by Gustave Baumann, pencil signed & mounted in new frame, image 9¼x11in. **$3,000**

A-PA   Conestoga Auction Company, Inc.
696 Theorem by D. Ellinger, depicting a bird w/cherry in its beak in an orig. dec. frame 9½x8in. **$2,530**

A-PA   Freeman's
118 The Deep Water Ship by Frank Vining Smith, 1879-1967, sgn. at bottom right, oil on canvas & inscribed w/title, 30x24in. **$15,535**

A-IA   Jackson's International Auctioneers
70 Gone Away, oil on canvas by Kenneth Wynn, British, b. 1922, sgn. & w/gallery label, 40x60in. **$5,875**
72 The Hunt, oil on canvas by Kenneth Wynn, British, sgn & w/gallery label, 20x30in. **$4,700**

A-PA   Freeman's
119 Oil Painting by Fern Isabel Coppedge titled Village In Winter, sgn. 25x30in. **$71,700**

ABC Plates – Alphabet plates were made especially for children as teaching aids. They date from the late 1700s and were made of various material including porcelain, pottery, glass, pewter, tin and ironstone.

Amphora Art Pottery was made at the Amphora Porcelain Works in the TeplitzTurn area of Bohemia during the late 19th and early 20th centuries. Numerous potteries were located there.

Anna Pottery – The Anna Pottery was established in Anna, IL, in 1859 by Cornwall and Wallace Kirkpatrick, and closed in 1894. The company produced utilitarian wares, gift wares and pig-shaped bottles and jugs with special inscriptions, which are the most collectible pieces.

Battersea Enamels – The name "Battersea" is a general term for those metal objects decorated with enamels, such as pill, patch, and snuff boxes, doorknobs, and such. The process of fusing enamel onto metal – usually copper – began about 1750 in the Battersea district of London. Today the name has become a generic term for similar objects – mistakenly called "Battersea".

Belleek porcelain was first made at Fermanagh, Ireland, in 1857. Today this ware is still being made in buildings within walking distance of the original clay pits, according to the skills and traditions of the original artisans. Irish Belleek is famous for its thinness and delicacy. Similar wares were also produced in other European countries, as well as in the United States.

Bennington Pottery – The first pottery works in Bennington, Vermont, was established by Captain John Norton in 1793, and for 101 years it was owned and operated by succeeding generations of Nortons. Today the term "Bennington" is synonymous with the finest in American ceramics because the town was the home of several pottery operations during the last century – each producing under different labels. Today items produced at Bennington are now conveniently, if inaccurately, dubbed "Bennington". One of the popular types of pottery produced there is known as "Rockingham". The term denotes the rich, solid brown glazed pottery from which many household items were made. The ware was first produced on the Marquis of Rockingham's estate in Swinton, England – hence the name.

Beswick – An earthenware produced in Staffordshire, England, by John Beswick in 1936. The company is now a part of Royal Doulton Tableware Ltd.

Bisque – The term applies to pieces of porcelain or pottery which have been fired but left in an unglazed state.

Bloor Derby – "Derby" porcelain dates from about 1755 when William Duesbury began the production of porcelain at Derby. In 1769 he purchased the famous Chelsea Works and operated both factories. During the Chelsea-Derby period, some of the finest examples of English porcelains were made. Because of their fine quality, in 1773 King George III gave Duesbury the patent to mark his porcelain wares "Crown Derby". Duesbury died in 1796. In 1810 the factory was purchased by Robert Bloor, a senior clerk. Bloor revived the Imari styles which had been so popular. After his death in 1845, former workmen continued to produce fine porcelains using the traditional Derby patterns. The firm was reorganized in 1876 and in 1878 a new factory was built. In 1890, Queen Victoria appointed the company "Manufacturers to Her Majesty" with the right to be known as Royal Crown Derby.

Buffalo Pottery – The Buffalo Pottery of Buffalo, New York, was organized in 1901. The firm was an adjunct of the Larkin Soap Company, which was established to produce china and pottery premiums for that company. Of the many different types produced, the Buffalo Pottery is most famous for its "Deldare" line, which was developed in 1905.

Canary Luster earthenware dates to the early 1800s, and was produced by potters in the Staffordshire district of England. The body of this ware is a golden yellow and decorated with transfer printing, usually in black.

Canton porcelain is a blue-and-white decorated ware produced near Canton, China, from the late 1700s through the 19th century and into the 20th. Its hand-decorated Chinese scenes have historical as well as mythological significance.

Capo-di-Monte, originally a soft paste porcelain, is Italian in origin. The first ware was made during the 1700s near Naples. Although numerous marks were used, the most familiar to us is the crown over the letter N. Mythological subjects, executed in either high or low relief and tinted in bright colors on a light ground, were a favorite decoration. The earlier wares had a peculiar grayish color as compared with the whiter bodies of later examples.

Carlsbad porcelain was made by several factories in the area from the 1800s and exported to the United States. When Carlsbad became a part of Czecho-slovakia after World War I, wares were frequently marked "Karlsbad". Items marked "Victoria" were made for Lazarus & Rosenfeldt, importers.

Castleford earthenware was produced in England from the late 1700s until around 1820. Its molded decoration is similar to Prattware.

Celadon – Chinese porcelain having a velvet-textured greenish-gray glaze. Japanese and other Oriental factories also made celadon glazed wares.

Chelsea – An early soft paste porcelain manufactured at Chelsea in London from around 1745 to 1769. Chelsea is considered to be one of the most famous of English porcelain factories.

Chelsea Keramic Art Works – The firm was established in 1872, in Chelsea, MA, by members of the Robertson family. The firm used the mark CKAW. The company closed in 1889, but was reorganized in 1891, as the Chelsea Pottery U.S. In 1895, the factory became the Dedham Pottery of Dedham, MA, and closed in 1943.

Chinese Export Porcelain was made in quantity in China during the 1700s and early 1800s. The term identifies a variety of porcelain wares made for export to Europe and the United States. Since many thought the product to be of joint Chinese and English manufacture, it has also been known as "Oriental" or "Chinese Lowestoft".

As much of this ware was made to order for the American and European market, it was frequently adorned with seals of states or the coat of arms of individuals, in addition to eagles, sailing scenes, flowers, religious and mythological scenes.

Clarice Cliff Pottery – Clarice Cliff (1889-1972) was a designer who worked at A.J. Wilkinson Ltd.'s Royal Staffordshire Pottery at Burslem, England. Cliff's earthenwares were bright and colorful Art Deco designs which included squares, circles, bands, conical shapes and simple landscapes incorporated with the designs. Cliff used several different printed marks, each of which incorporated a facsimile of her signature – and generally the name of the pattern.

Clews Pottery – (see also, Historical Staffordshire) was made by George Clews & Co., of Brownhill Pottery, Tunstall, England, from 1806-1861.

Clifton Pottery – William Long founded the Clifton Pottery in Clifton, NJ, in 1905.

Pottery was simply marked CLIFTON. Long worked until 1908, producing a line called Crystal Patina. The Chesapeake Pottery Company made majolica marked Clifton Ware, which oftentimes confuses collectors.

Coalport porcelain has been made by the Coalport Porcelain Works in England since 1795. The ware is still being produced at Stoke-on-Trent.

Coors Pottery – Coors ware was made in Golden, CO, by the Coors Beverage Co. from the turn of the century until the pottery was destroyed by fire in the 1930s.

Copeland-Spode – The firm was founded by Josiah Spode in 1770 in Staffordshire, England. From 1847 W.T. Copeland & Sons Ltd. succeeded Spode, using the designation "Late Spode" to its wares. The firm is still in operation.

Copper Luster – See Lusterwares.

Cordey – Boleslaw Cybis was one of the founders of the Cordey China Company, Trenton, NJ. Production began in 1942. In 1969, the company was purchased by the Lightron Corporation, and operated as the Schiller Cordey Company. Around 1950, Cybis began producing fine porcelain figurines.

Cowan Pottery – Guy Cowan produced art pottery in Rocky River, OH, from 1913 to 1931. He used a stylized mark with the word COWAN on most pieces. Also, Cowan mass-produced a line marked LAKEWARE.

Crown Ducal – English porcelain made by A.G. Richardson & Co. Ltd. since 1916.

Cup Plates were used where cups were handleless and saucers were deep. During the early 1800s, it was very fashionable to drink from a saucer. Thus, a variety of fancy small plates were produced for the cup to rest in. The lacy Sandwich examples are very collectible.

Davenport pottery and porcelain was made at the Davenport Factory in Longport, Staffordshire, England, from 1793 until 1887 when the pottery closed. Most of the wares produced there – porcelains, creamwares, ironstone, earthenwares and other products – were marked.

Dedham (Chelsea Art Works) – The firm was founded in 1872, at Chelsea, Massachusetts, by James Robertson & Sons, and closed in 1889. In 1891, the pottery was reopened under the name of The Chelsea Pottery, U.S. The first and most popular blue underglaze decoration for the desirable "Cracque Ware" was

the rabbit motif – designed by Joseph L. Smith. In 1893, construction was started on the new pottery in Dedham, Massachusetts, and production began in 1895. The name of the pottery was then changed to "Dedham Pottery," to eliminate the confusion with the English Chelsea Ware. The famed crackleware finish became synonymous with the name. Because of its popularity, more than fifty patterns of tableware were made.

Delft – Holland is famous for its fine examples of tin-glazed pottery dating from the 16th century. Although blue and white is the most popular color, other colors were also made. The majority of the ware found today is from the late Victorian period and when the name Holland appears with the Delft factory mark, this indicates that the item was made after 1891.

Dorchester Pottery was established by George Henderson in Dorchester, a part of Boston, Massachusetts, in 1895. Production included stonewares, industrial wares and, later, some decorated tablewares. The pottery is still in production.

Doulton – The pottery was established in Lambeth in 1815 by John Doulton and John Watts. When Watts retired in 1845, it became known as Doulton & Company. In 1901, King Edward VII conferred a double honor on the company by presentation of the Royal Warrant, authorizing their chairman to use the word "Royal" in describing products. A variety of wares were made over the years for the American market. The firm is still in production.

Dresden – The term identifies any china produced in the town of Dresden, Germany. The most famous factory in Dresden is the Meissen factory. During the 18th century, English and Americans used the name "Dresden china" for wares produced at Meissen which has led to much confusion. The city of Dresden, which was the capital of Saxony, was better known in 18th century Europe than Meissen. Therefore, Dresden became a generic term for all porcelains produced and decorated in the city of Dresden and surrounding districts, including Meissen. By the mid-19th century, about thirty factories in the city of Dresden were producing and decorating porcelains in the style of Meissen. Therefore, do not make the mistake of thinking all pieces marked Dresden were made at the Meissen factory. Meissen pieces generally have crossed swords marks and are listed under Meissen.

Flowing Blue ironstone is a highly glazed dinnerware made at Staffordshire by a variety of potters. It became popular about 1825. Items were printed with Oriental patterns and the color flowed from the design over the white body, so that the finished product appeared smeared. Although purple and brown colors were also made, the deep cobalt blue shades were the most popular. Later wares were less blurred, having more white ground.

Frankoma – The Frank Pottery was founded in 1933, by John Frank, Sapulpa, OK. The company produced decorative wares from 1936-38. Early wares were made from a light cream-colored clay, but in 1956 changed to a red brick clay. This along with the glazes helps to determine the period of production.

Fulper – The Fulper mark was used by the American Pottery Company of Flemington, NJ. Fulper art pottery was produced from approximately 1910 to 1930.

Gallé – Emile Gallé was a designer who made glass, pottery, furniture and other Art Nouveau items. He founded his factory in France in 1874. Ceramic pieces were marked with the initials E.G. impressed, Em. Gallé Faiencerie de Nancy, or a version of his signature.

Gaudy Dutch is the most spectacular of the gaudy wares. Made for the Pennsylvania Dutch market from about 1785 until the 1820s, this soft paste tableware is lightweight and frail in appearance. Its rich cobalt blue decoration was applied to the biscuit, glazed and fired – then other colors were applied over the first glaze – and the object was fired again. No luster is included in its decoration.

Gaudy Ironstone was made in Staffordshire from the early 1850s until around 1865. This ware is heavier than Gaudy Welsh or Gaudy Dutch, as its texture is a mixture of pottery and porcelain clay.

Gaudy Welsh, produced in England from about 1830, resembles Gaudy Dutch in decoration, but the workmanship is not as fine and its texture is more comparable to that of spatterware. Luster is usually included with the decoration.

Gouda Pottery – Gouda and the surrounding areas of Holland have been one of the principal Dutch pottery centers since the 17th century. The Zenith pottery and the Zuid-Hooandsche pottery produced the brightly colored wares marked GOUDA from 1880 to about 1940. Many pieces of Gouda featured Art Nouveau or Art Deco designs.

Grueby – Grueby Faience Company, Boston, MA, was founded in 1897 by William H. Grueby. The company produced hand thrown art pottery in natural shapes, hand molded and hand tooled. A variety of colored glazes, singly or in combinations, were used, with green being the most prominent color. The company closed in 1908.

Haeger – The Haeger Potteries, Inc., Dundee, IL, began making art wares in 1914. Their early pieces were marked with HAEGER written over the letter "H". Around 1938, the mark changed to ROYAL HAEGER.

Hampshire – In 1871, James S. Taft founded the Hampshire Pottery Company in Keene, NH. The company produced redware, stoneware, and majolica decorated wares in 1879. In 1883, the company introduced a line of colored glazed wares, including a Royal Worcester type pink, blue, green, olive and reddish-brown. Pottery was marked with the printed mark or the impressed name HAMPSHIRE POTTERY or J.S.T. & CO., KEENE, N.H.

Harker – The Harker Pottery Company of East Liverpool, OH, was founded in 1840. The company made a variety of different types of pottery including yellowware from native clays. Whiteware and Rockingham type brown-glazed pottery were also produced in quantities.

Historical Staffordshire – The term refers to a particular blue-on-white, transfer-printed earthenware produced in quantity during the early 1800s by many potters in the Staffordshire district. The central decoration was usually an American city scene or landscape, frequently showing some mode of transportation in the foreground. Other designs included portraits and patriotic emblems. Each potter had a characteristic border, which is helpful to identify a particular ware, as many pieces are unmarked. Later transfer-printed wares were made in sepia, pink, green and black, but the early cobalt blue examples are the most desirable.

Hull – In 1905, Addis E. Hull purchased the Acme Pottery Company in Crooksville, OH. In 1917, Hull began producing art pottery, stoneware and novelties, including the Little Red Riding Hood line. Most pieces had a matte finish with shades of pink and blue or brown predominating. After a flood and fire in 1950, the factory was reopened in 1952 as the Hull Pottery Company. Pre-1950 vases are marked Hull USA or HULL ART USA. Post-1950 pieces are simply marked HULL in large

script or block letters. Paper labels were also used.

Hummel – Hummel items are the original creations of Berta Hummel, born in 1909 in Germany. Hummel collectibles are made by W. Goebel Porzellanfabrik of Oeslau, Germany, now Rodenthal, West Germany. They were first made in 1934. All authentic Hummels bear both the signature, M.I. Hummel, and a Goebel trademark. However, various trademarks were used to identify the year of production.

Ironstone is a heavy, durable, utilitarian ware made from the slag of iron furnaces, ground and mixed with clay. Charles Mason of Lane Delft, Staffordshire, patented the formula in 1823. Much of the early ware was decorated in imitation of Imari, in addition to transfer-printed blue ware, flowing blues and browns. During the mid-19th century, the plain white enlivened only by embossed designs became fashionable. Literally hundreds of patterns were made for export.

Jackfield Pottery – is English in origin. It was first produced during the 17th century; however, most items available today date from the last century. It is a red-bodied pottery, often decorated with scrolls and flowers in relief, then covered with a black glaze.

Jasperware – is a very hard, unglazed porcelain with a colored ground, varying from blues and greens to lavender, red, yellow or black. White designs were generally applied in relief to these wares, and often reflect a classical motif. Jasperware was first produced by Wedgwood's Etruria Works in 1775. Many other English potters produced jasperware, including Copeland, Spode and Adams.

Jugtown Pottery – This North Carolina pottery has been made since the 18th century. In 1915 Jacques Busbee organized what was to become the Jugtown Pottery in 1921. Production was discontinued in 1958.

King's Rose is a decorated creamware produced in the Staffordshire district of England during the 1820-1840 period. The rose decorations are usually in red, green, yellow and pink. This ware is often referred to as "Queen's Rose".

Leeds Pottery was established by Charles Green in 1758 at Leeds, Yorkshire, England. Early wares are unmarked. From 1775, the impressed mark "Leeds Pottery"

was used. After 1880, the name "Hartley, Greens & Co." was added, and the impressed or incised letters "LP" were also used to identify the ware.

Limoges – The name identifies fine porcelain wares produced by many factories at Limoges, France, since the mid-1800s. A variety of different marks identify wares made there including Haviland china.

Liverpool Pottery – The term applies to wares produced by many potters located in Liverpool, England, from the early 1700s, for American trade. Their print-decorated pitchers – referred to as "jugs" in England – have been especially popular. These featured patriotic emblems, prominent men, ships, etc., and can be easily identified, as nearly all are melon-shaped with a very pointed lip, strap handle and graceful curved body.

Lonhuda – In 1892, William Long, Alfred Day, and W.W. Hunter organized the Lonhuda Pottery Company of Steubenville, OH. The firm produced underglaze slip-decorated pottery until 1896, when production ceased. Although the company used a variety of marks, the earliest included the letters LPCP.

Lotus Ware – This thin, Belleek-like porcelain was made by the Knowles, Taylor & Knowles Company of Easter Liverpool, OH, from 1890 to 1900.

Lusterware – John Hancock of Hanley, England, invented this type of decoration on earthenwares during the early 1800s. The copper, bronze, ruby, gold, purple, yellow, pink and mottled pink luster finishes were made from gold painted on the glazed objects, then fired. The latter type is often referred to as "Sunderland Luster". Its pinkish tones vary in color and pattern. The silver lusters were made from platinum.

Maastricht Ware – Petrus Regout founded the De Sphinx pottery in 1835 at Maastricht, Holland. The company specialized in transfer printed earthenwares.

Majolica – The word "majolica" is a general term for any pottery glazed with an opaque tin enamel that conceals the color of the clay body. It has been produced by many countries for centuries. Majolica took its name from the Spanish island of Jamorca, where figuline (a potter's clay) is found. This ware frequently depicted elements in nature: birds, flowers, leaves and fish. English manufacturers marked their wares, and most can be identified through the English Registry mark and/or the potter-designer's mark, while most Continental pieces had an incised number. Although many American potteries produced majolica between 1850 and 1900, only a few chose to identify their wares. Among these were the firm of Griffen, Smith & Hill, George Morely, Edwin Bennett, Chesapeake Pottery Company, and the new Milford-Wannoppe Pottery Company.

Marblehead – This hand thrown pottery had its beginning in 1905 as a therapeutic program by Dr. J. Hall for the patients of a Marblehead, MA, sanitarium. Later, production was moved to another site and the factory continued under the management of A.E. Baggs until it closed in 1936. The most desirable pieces found today are decorated with conventionalized designs.

Matt-Morgan – By 1883, Matt Morgan, an English artist, was producing art pottery in Cincinnati, OH, that resembled Moorish wares. Incised designs and colors were applied to raised panels, and then shiny or matte glazes were applied. The firm lasted only a few years.

McCoy Pottery – The J.W. McCoy Pottery was established in 1899. Production of art pottery began after 1926, when the name was changed to Brush McCoy.

Meissen – The history of Meissen porcelain began in Germany in 1710 in the Albrechtsburg fortress of Meissen. The company was first directed by Johann Boettger, who developed the first truly white porcelain in Europe. The crossed swords mark of the Meissen factory was adopted in 1723.

Mettlach, Germany, located in the Zoar Basin, was the location of the famous Villeroy & Boch factories from 1836 until 1921, when the factory was destroyed by fire. Steins (dating from about 1842) and other stonewares with bas-relief decorations were their specialty.

Minton – Thomas Minton established his pottery in 1793 at Hanley, Stoke-on-Trent, England. During the early years, Minton concentrated on blue transfer painted earthenwares, plain bone china, and cream colored earthenware. During the first quarter of the 19th century, a large selection of figures and ornamental wares were produced in addition to their tableware lines. In 1968, Minton became a member of the Royal Doulton Tableware group, and retains its reputation for fine quality hand painted and gilded tablewares.

Mochaware – This banded creamware was first produced in England during the late 1700s. The early ware was light-weight and thin, having colorful bands of bright colors decorating a body that is cream colored to very light brown. After 1840, the ware became heavier in body and the color was often quite light – almost white. Mochaware can easily be identified by its colorful banded decorations – on and between the bands – including feathery ferns, lacy trees, seaweeds, squiggly designs and lowly earthworms.

Moorcroft – William Moorcroft established the Moorcroft Pottery, in Burslem, England, in 1913. The majority of the art pottery wares were hand thrown. The company initially used an impressed mark, MOORCROFT, BURSLEM, with a signature mark, W. MOORCROFT, following. Walker, William's son, continued the business after his father's death in 1945, producing the same style wares. Contemporary pieces are marked simply MOORCROFT with export pieces also marked MADE IN ENGLAND.

Newcomb – William and Ellsworth Woodward founded Newcomb Pottery at Sophie Newcomb College, New Orleans, LA, in 1896. Students decorated the high quality art pottery pieces with a variety of designs that have a decidedly southern flavor. Production continued through the 1940s. Marks include the letters "NC" and often have the incised initials of the artist as well. Most pieces have a matte glaze.

Niloak Pottery with its prominent swirled, marbelized designs, is a 20th century pottery first produced at Benton, Arkansas, in 1911, by the Niloak Pottery Company. Production ceased in 1946.

Nippon porcelain has been produced in quantity for the American market since the late 19th century. After 1891, when it became obligatory to include the country of origin on all imports, the Japanese trade-mark "Nippon" was used. Numerous other marks appear on this ware, identifying the manufacturer, artist or importer. The handpainted Nippon examples are extremely popular today and prices are on the rise.

Norse Pottery was founded in 1903 in Edgerton, WI. The company moved to Rockford, IL, in 1904, where they produced a black pottery which resembled early bronze items. The firm closed in 1913.

Ohr Pottery was produced by George E. Ohr in Biloxi, Mississippi, around 1883. Today Ohr is recognized as one of the leading potters in the American Art Pottery movement. Early work was often signed with an impressed stamp in block letters – G.E. OHR BILOXI. Later pieces were often marked G.E. Ohr in flowing script. Ohr closed the pottery in 1906, storing more than 6,000 pieces as a legacy to his family. These pieces remained in storage until 1972.

Old Ivory dinnerware was made in Silesia, Germany, during the late 1800s. It derives its name from the background color of the china. Marked pieces usually have a pattern number on the base, and the word "Silesia" with a crown.

Ott & Brewer – The company operated the Etruria Pottery in Trenton, NJ, from 1863 to 1893. A variety of marks were used which incorporated the initials O & B.

Owens – The Owens Pottery began production in Zanesville, OH, in 1891. The first art pottery was made after 1896, and pieces were usually marked OWENS. Production of art pottery was discontinued about 1907.

Paul Revere Pottery – This pottery was made at several locations in and around Boston, MA, between 1906 and 1942. The company was operated as a settlement house program for girls. Many pieces were signed S.E.G. for Saturday Evening Girls. The young artists concentrated on children's dishes and tiles.

Peters & Reed Pottery Company of Zanesville, Ohio, was founded by John D. Peters and Adam Reed about the turn of the century. Their wares, although seldom marked, can be identified by the characteristic red or yellow clay body touched with green. This pottery was best known for its matte glaze pieces – especially one type, called Moss Aztec, which combined a red earthenware body with a green glaze. The company changed hands in 1920 and was renamed the Zane Pottery Company. Examples marked "Zaneware" are often identical to earlier pieces.

Pewabic – Mary Chase Perry Stratton founded the Pewabic Pottery in 1903 in Detroit, MI. Many types of art pottery were produced here, including pieces with matte green glaze and an iridescent crystaline glaze. Operations ceased after the death of Mary Stratton in 1961, but the company was reactivated by Michigan State University in 1968.

Pisgah Forest Pottery – The pottery was founded near Mt. Pisgah in North Carolina in 1914, by Walter B. Stephen. The pottery remains in operation.

Quimper – Tin-glazed hand-painted pottery has been produced in Quimper, France, dating back to the 17th century. It is named for a French town where numerous potteries were located. The popular peasant design first appeared during the 1860s, and many variations exist. Florals and geometrics were equally popular. The HR and HR QUIMPER marks are found on Henriot pieces prior to 1922.

Redware is one of the most popular forms of country pottery. It has a soft, porous body and its color varies from reddish-brown tones to deep wine to light orange. It was produced in mostly utilitarian forms by potters in small factories, or by potters working on their farms, to fill their every-day needs. The most desirable examples are the slip-decorated pieces, or the rare and expensive "sgraffito" examples which have scratched or incised line decoration. Slip decoration was made by tracing the design on the redware shape with a clay having a creamy consistency in contrasting colors. When dried, the design was slightly raised above the surface.

Red Wing Art Pottery and Stoneware – The name includes several potteries located in Red Wing, MN. David Hallem established his pottery in 1868, producing stoneware items with a red wing stamped under the glaze as its mark. The Minnesota Stoneware Co. began production in 1883. The North Star Stoneware company began production in 1892, and used a raised star and the words Red Wing as it mark. The two latter firms merged in 1892, producing stoneware until 1920, when the company introduced a pottery line. In 1936, the name was changed to Red Wing Potteries. The plant closed in 1967.

Ridgway – Throughout the 19th century the Ridgway family, through partnerships, held positions of importance in Shelton and Hanley, Staffordshire, England. Their wares have been made since 1808, and their transfer design dinner sets are the most widely known product. Many pieces are unmarked, but later marks include the initials of the many partnerships.

Riviera – This dinnerware was made by the Homer Laughlin Company of Newell, WV, from 1938 to 1950.

Rockingham – See Bennington Pottery.

Rookwood Pottery – The Rookwood Pottery began production at Cincinnati, Ohio, in 1880 under the direction of Maria Longworth Nichols Storer, and operated until 1960. The name was derived from the family estate, "Rookwood," because of the "rooks" or "crows" which inhabited the wooded

areas. All pieces of this art pottery are marked, usually bearing the famous flame.

Rorstrand Faience – The firm was founded in 1726 near Stockholm, Sweden. Items dating from the early 1900s and having an Art Nouveau influence are very expensive and much in demand.

Rose Medallion ware dates from the 18th century. It was decorated and exported from Canton, China, in quantity. The name generally applied to those pieces having medallions with figures of people, alternating with panels of flowers, birds and butterflies. When all the medallions are filled with flowers, the ware is identified as Rose Canton.

Rose Tapestry – See Royal Bayreuth.

Roseville Pottery – The Roseville Pottery was organized in 1890 in Roseville, Ohio. The firm produced utilitarian stoneware in the plant formerly owned by the Owens Pottery of Roseville, also producers of stoneware, and the Linden Avenue Plant at Zanesville, Ohio, originally built by the Clark Stoneware Company. In 1900, an art line of pottery was created to compete with Owens and Weller lines. The new ware was named "Rozanne," and it was produced at the Zanesville location. Following its success, other prestige lines were created. The Azurine line was introduced about 1902.

Royal Bayreuth manufactory began in Tettau in 1794 at the first porcelain factory in Bavaria. Wares made there were on a par with Meissen. Fire destroyed the original factory during the 1800s. Many of the wares available today were made at the new factory which began production in 1897. These include Rose Tapestry, Sunbonnet Baby novelties and the Devil and Card items. The Royal Bayreuth blue mark has the 1794 founding date incorporated with the mark.

Royal Bonn – The trade name identifies a variety of porcelain items made during the 19th century by the Bonn China Manufactory, established in 1755 by Elmer August. Most of the ware found today is from the Victorian period.

Royal Crown Derby – The company was established in 1875, in Derby, England, and has no connection with the earlier Derby factories which operated in the late 18th and early 19th centuries. Derby porcelain produced from 1878 to 1890 carries the standard crown printed mark. From 1891 forward, the mark carries the "Royal Crown Derby" wording, and during the 20th century, "Made in

England" and "English Bone China" were added to the mark. Today the company is a part of Royal Doulton Tableware, Ltd.

Royal Doulton wares have been made from 1901, when King Edward VII conferred a double honor on the Doulton Pottery by the presentation of the Royal Warrant, authorizing their chairman to use the word "Royal" in describing products. A variety of wares has been produced for the American market. The firm is still in production.

Royal Dux was produced in Bohemia during the late 1800s. Large quantities of this decorative porcelain ware were exported to the United States. Royal Dux figurines are especially popular.

Royal Rudolstadt – This hard paste ware was first made in Rudolstadt, Thuringen, East Germany, by Ernst Bohne in 1882. The ware was never labeled "Royal Rudolstadt" originally, but the word "Royal" was added later as part of an import mark. This porcelain was imported by Lewis Straus and Sons of New York.

Royal Worcester – The Worcester factory was established in 1751 in England. This is a tastefully decorated porcelain noted for its creamy white lusterless surface. Serious collectors prefer items from the Dr. Wall (the activator of the concern) period of production which extended from the time the factory was established to 1785.

Roycroft Pottery was made by the Roycrofter community of East Aurora, New York, during the late 19th and early 20th centuries. The firm was founded by Elbert Hubbard. Products produced included pottery, furniture, metalware, jewelry and leatherwork.

R.S. Germany porcelain with a variety of marks was produced at the Tillowitz, Germany, factory of Reinhold Schlegelmilch from about 1869 to 1956.

R.S. Prussia porcelain was produced during the mid-1800s by Erdman Schlegelmilch in Suhl. His brother, Reinhold, founded a factory in 1869, in Tillowitz in lower Silesia. Both made fine quality porcelain, using both satin and high gloss finishes with comparable decoration. Additionally, both brothers used the same R.S. mark in the same colors, the initials in memory of their father, Rudolph Schlegelmilch. It has not been determined when production at the two factories ceased.

Ruskin is a British art pottery. The pottery, located at West Smethwick, Birmingham,

England, was started by William H. Taylor. His name was used as the mark until around 1899. The firm discontinued producing new pieces of pottery in 1933, but continued to glaze and market their remaining wares until 1935. Ruskin pottery is noted for its exceptionally fine glazes.

Sarreguemines ware is the name of a porcelain factory in Sarreguemines, Lorraine, France, that made ceramics from about 1775. The factory was regarded as one of the most prominent manufacturers of French faience. Their transfer printed wares and majolica were made during the nineteenth century.

Satsuma is a Japanese pottery having a distinctive creamy crackled glaze decorated with bright enamels and often with Japanese figures. The majority of the ware available today includes the mass-produced wares dating from the 1850s. Their quality does not compare to the fine early examples.

Sewer Tile – Sewer tile figures were made by workers at sewer tile and pipe factories during the late nineteeth and early twentieth centuries. Vases and figurines with added decorations are now considered folk art by collectors.

Shawnee Pottery – The Shawnee Pottery Company was founded in 1937 in Zanesville, OH. The plant closed in 1961.

Shearwater Pottery – was founded by G.W. Anderson, along with his wife and their three sons. Local Ocean Springs, MS, clays were used to produce their wares during the 1930s, and the company is still in business.

Sleepy Eye – The Sleepy Eye Milling Company, Sleepy Eye, MN, used the image of the 19th century Indian chief for advertising purposes from 1883 to 1921. The company offered a variety of premiums.

Spatterware is soft paste tableware, laboriously decorated with hand-drawn flowers, birds, buildings, trees, etc., with "spatter" decoration chiefly as a back-ground. It was produced in considerable quantity from the early 1800s to around 1850.

To achieve this type of decoration, small bits of sponge were cut into different shapes – leaves, hearts, rosettes, vines, geometrical patterns, etc. – and mounted on the end of a short stick for convenience in dipping into the pigment.

Spongeware, as it is known, is a decorative white earthenware. Color – usually blue, blue/green, brown/tan/blue, or blue/brown – was applied to the white clay base. Because the color was often applied with a color-soaked sponge, the term "spongeware" became common for this ware. A variety of utilitarian items were produced – pitchers, cookie jars, bean pots, water coolers, etc. Marked examples are rare.

Staffordshire is a district in England where a variety of pottery and porcelain wares has been produced by many factories in the area.

Stickspatter – The term identifies a type of decoration that combines hand-painting and transfer-painted decoration. "Spattering" was done with either a sponge or brush containing a moderate supply of pigment. Stickspatter was developed from the traditional Staffordshire spatterware, as the earlier ware was time consuming and expensive to produce. Although most of this ware was made in England from the 1850s to the late 1800s, it was also produced in Holland, France and elsewhere.

Tea Leaf is a lightweight stone china decorated with copper or gold "tea leaf" sprigs. It was first made by Anthony Shaw of Longport, England, during the 1850s. By the late 1800s, other potters in Staffordshire were producing the popular ware for export to the United States. As a result, there is a noticeable diversity in decoration.

Teco Pottery is an art pottery line made by the Terra Cotta Tile works of Terra Cotta, Illinois. The firm was organized in 1881, by William D. Gates. The Teco line was first made in 1885, but not sold commercially until 1902, and was discontinued during the 1920s.

UHL Pottery – This pottery was made in Evansville, IN, in 1854. In 1908, the pottery was moved to Huntingburg, IN, where their stoneware and glazed pottery was made until the mid-1940s.

Union Porcelain Works – The company first marked their wares with an eagle's head holding the letter "S" in its beak around 1876; the letters "U.P.W." were sometimes added.

Van Briggle Pottery was established at Colorado Springs, Colorado, in 1900, by Artus Van Briggle and his wife, Anna. Most of the ware was marked. The first mark included two joined "A's," representing their first two initials. The firm is still in operation.

Villeroy & Boch – The pottery was founded in 1841, at Mettlach, Germany. The firm produced many types of pottery including the famous Mettlach steins. Although most of their wares were made in the city of Mettlach, they also had factories in other locations. Fortunately for collectors, there is a dating code impressed on the bottom of most pieces that makes it possible to determine the age of the piece.

Walrath – Frederich Walrath worked in Rochester, NY, New York City, and at the Newcomb Pottery in New Orleans, LA. He signed his pottery items "Walrath Pottery". He died in 1920.

Warwick china was made in Sheeling, WV, in a pottery from 1887 to 1951. The most familiar Warwick pieces have a shaded brown background. Many pieces were made with hand painted or decal decorations. The word ILGA is sometimes included with the Warwick mark.

Watt Pottery – In 1935 the company began producing dinnerware with freehand decorations that has become very popular with collectors. Their most popular pattern is Apple which was produced in 1952. Early pieces in this pattern can be dated from the number of leaves. Originally, the apples had three leaves, but in 1958 only two leaves were used. Other popular patterns in this ware include Rooster (1955), Starflower and Tulip variations. New patterns were introduced annually until October, 1965, when the factory was destroyed by fire; it was never rebuilt.

Wedgwood Pottery was established by Josiah Wedgwood in 1759, in England. A tremendous variety of fine wares has been produced through the years including basalt, lusterwares, creamware, jasperware, bisque, agate, Queen's Ware and others. The system of marks used by the firm clearly indicates when each piece was made.

Weller Pottery – Samuel A. Weller established the Weller pottery in 1872, in Fultonham, Ohio. In 1888, the pottery was moved to Piece Street in Putnam, Ohio – now a part of Zanesville, Ohio. The production of art pottery began in 1893, and by late 1897 several prestige lines were being produced, including Samantha and Dickensware. Other later types included Weller's Louwelsa, Aurora, Turada and the rare Sicardo which is the most sought after and most expensive today. The firm closed in 1948.

Wheatley – Thomas J. Wheatley established the Wheatley Pottery in 1880. The Wheatley mark included joined letters WP with a dash below within a circle.

A-NH   **Northeast Auctions**

642 Dedham Pottery Experimental Volcanic Ware Vase of ovoid form w/incised mark & HCR cipher for Hugh Robertson, ht. 8¾in. **$2,000**

643 Marblehead Pottery Matte-Glazed Charger, mkd. #120, ca.1918, w/peacock perched upon a flowering branch & retains paper label, ht. 13¼in. **$500**

644 Merrimac Pottery Vase, Newburyport, MA, of cylindrical tapered form in gun-metal glazed w/imp. mark, ht. 9¾in. **$650**

645 Marblehead Pottery Model of the Hull of a Spanish Galleon, in cream glaze w/the scroll prow, foliate carved trim w/imp. ship mark, lg.

11½in. **$500**

646 Dedham Pottery Vase w/incised mark & N 06, in blue ink, ht. 3¼in. **$500**

647 Chelsea Keramic Art Works Vase, MA, of ovoid form & die-stamped CKAW, ht. 4½in. **$425**

648 Marblehead Pottery Bowl w/matte-glaze, inverted rim & impressed ship mark, dia. 8¾in. **$300**

1367

1368

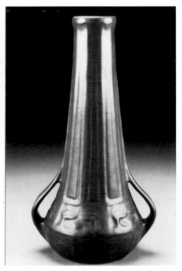

1369

1370

1371

1372

A-IA   **Jackson's International Auctioneers**

1367 Rookwood Pottery Vase by Sallie Coyne, ca.1906, stamped w/Rookwood flame mark & artist sgn., ht. 8¼in. **$940**

1368 Rookwood Vase, ca.1921, cylindrical form w/amethyst finish, ht. 10⅝in. **$235**

1369 Van Briggle Two-handled Pottery Vase, 20th C. & sgn. w/incised trademark, ht. 15¼in. **$352**

1370 Rookwood Trivet, ca.1927, dec. w/a Dutch pictorial of a mother & her children at the lake. **$235**

1371 Rookwood Figural Paperweight of a sitting nude, ca.1938, ht. 4¼in. **$205**

1372 Van Briggle Pottery Bowl, 20th C. w/incised trademark, Van Briggle Colo. Springs, ht. 4¼in. **$205**

A-NJ   **Craftsman Arts & Crafts Auction**
436 **North Dakota School of Mines Vase,** Indian Travois,
by Margaret Cable & Flora Huckfield, w/carved mark
Cable-Huck-Indian Travois 184, ht. 6¾in. **$4,750**

A-NJ   **Craftsman Arts & Crafts Auction**
438 **Pisgah Pottery Vases** w/band of cameo dec., one
w/a Native American buffalo hunt & village scene, the
other an ox-pulled covered wagon, ca.1930 w/potter's
wheel mark & WB Stephen, ht. 7½in. **$1,700**

A-NJ   **Craftsman Arts & Crafts Auction**
26 **North Dakota School of Mines Tall Vase**
w/sheaves of wheat mkd. w/indigo stamp &
ELH-750, S. Sorlie, ht. 8½in. **$5,500**
27 **North Dakota School of Mines Vase** by Julia
Mattson & dec. w/cowboys on brown ground &
mkd. w/indigo stamp, JM210, ht. 7½in. **$2,600**

528   529   530   531

532   533   534   535

A-NJ   **Craftsman Arts & Crafts Auction**
528 Rookwood Vases, four production Z-line-type, all mkd., tallest 9¼in. **$2,100**
529 Rookwood Vessels, three standard glaze, hairlines on each, all mkd. The ewer by A.M. Valentien, vase by C.F. Baker, & bud vase by I. Bishop. **$800**
530 Newcomb College Pottery Vase, ca.1923, cracked, carved by A.F.

Simpson, w/moonlit bayou landscape, mkd., ht. 9½in. **$1,000**
531 Newcomb College Low Bowl carved by Sadie Irvine, ca.1915, sgn. & mkd. Ht. 2½, dia. 5½in. **$650**
532 Newcomb College Art Deco Vase w/stacked leaves, sgn., ht.9½in. **$2,300**
533 Newcomb College Spherical Vase by H. Bailey, ca.1925, w/small

chip to base, sgn., ht. 3¾in. **$1,100**
534 Newcomb College Corseted Vase carved w/blossoms, ca.1919, ht. 7½in. **$1,700**
535 George Ohr Corseted Vessel w/two different ear-shaped handles, covered w/sponged ground & stamped G.E. Ohr, Biloxi, Miss., ht. 3¾in. **$4,750**

A-NJ   **Craftsman Arts & Crafts Auction**
701 Arthur Baggs Ovoid Vase w/stylized blue & green leaves, probably from Ohio State, w/two minor flakes to rim, mkd. AEB, ht. 5¼in. **$900**
703 Buffalo Deldare Teapot, Scenes of

Village Life & bowl, The Hunt, ca.1909. Hairline & restored chip to lid of teapot, both mkd. **$450**
705 Hampshire Vases, both mkd., the tall vase in rich earthy tones w/small chip to base, ht. 12in., the other

modeled w/tall leaves & buds in red & green, ht. 7in. **$850**
707 Paul Revere Vases, the taller in mottled green glaze, the shorter in black & yellow, both stamped, hts. 4½ & 10½in. **$850**

POTTERY / PORCELAIN

799   800   801   802

803   804   806   621

A-NJ   Craftsman Arts & Crafts Auction
799 Grueby Pottery Bowls, all w/glossy green interiors & mkd., dia. 5½ & 8in. **$750**
800 Grueby Vase carved w/full-height leaves under a leathery matte green glaze, bottom shaved flat & ¼in. chip on rim, ht. 6in. **$1,000**
801 Grueby Squat Vase w/matte indigo glaze & imp. pottery mark, ht. 3¼in. **$950**
802 Van Briggle Pottery Items in

Above opposite:
A-NJ   Craftsman Arts & Crafts Auction
873 Auguste Delaherche Four-handled Vase covered in mottled blue-green & brown glossy glaze, mkd. w/circular stamp & 6860, ht. 7¼in. **$1,100**
874 Newcomb College Vase by A.F. Simpson w/bayou scene of tall oak trees, Spanish moss & full moon, small chip at rim, mkd., ht. 8in. **$2,200**
875 Newcomb College Planter,

Opposite:
A-NJ   Craftsman Arts & Crafts Auction
881 Rookwood Wax Matt Vase sgn. Elizabeth Lincoln, ca.1920 w/flame mark, ht. 6in. **$700**
882 Rorstrand Porcelain Vase dec. w/white & purple lilies, small nick to foot ring & mkd.w/green stamp, ht. 7¼in. **$625**
883 Native American Indian Vase, sgn. Marie + Julian, burnished black

Mountain Craig Brown & turquoise glazes: an Indian-head vase, two bowls, small plate, flower frog & a cabinet vase, ca.1908-1911. **$1,300**
803 Rookwood Vase by Sallie Toohey w/standard glaze & dec. w/tulips. Flame mark/556C/ST, ca.1900, ht. 11¼in. **$1,600**
804 Two Vellum Rookwood Vases by Caroline Steinle & Edith Noonan. Taller one w/seconded mark, the other w/hairline, both mkd. & sgn.,

carved by M.W. Summey w/trees & landscape, ca.1910, mkd. ht. 4, dia. 11in. **$2,800**
876 Newcomb College Inkwell carved by A.F. Simpson, dec. w/jasmine, ca.1927, complete w/liner, hairlines & chip, sgn. paper label, ht. 3½in. **$750**
877 Rookwood Pitcher, dec. by Nat Hirsfield w/reeds & bats, ca.1882, mkd. w/remnants of Rookwood paper label & Chicago retailer, ht. 7½in. **$750**

clay w/geometric patt., ht. 4½in. **$1,400**
884 Two Pieces of Walrath Pottery incl. a vase w/green & red stylized blossoms on green-brown ground, together w/a small nude figurine in green & brown, ca.1912, both marked, vase ht. 4½in. **$1,800**
885 Van Briggle Bud Vase covered in matte chartreuse glaze, ca.1902, mkd., ht. 3¼in. **$1,300**

hts. 6 & 9in. **$700**
806 Four Rookwood Production Vessels, all mkd., incl. a covered jar w/ram emb. lid. Spiderline to body of yellow & green & small chip to brown vase w/pine cones, tallest 6¾in. **$800**
621 Two Rookwood Vases carved by S. Hentchel, early Production Z-line in turquoise & mauve, 1901, both mkd., ht. 3½in. **$2,300**

878 Black Rookwood Iris Vase by Sara Sax w/red-hot pokers, ca.1905 w/flame mark, artist's cipher/X & drilled bottom, ht. 11¾in. **$2,900**
879 Rookwood Porcelain Vase by L. Epply w/red cherry blossoms, ca.1919 w/ flame mark, ht. 4¾in. **$900**
880 Rookwood Painted Matt Vase by S. Toohey, w/red & yellow blossoms, ca.1901, ht. 5¼in. **$1,200**

886 Van Briggle Vase w/abstract floral design & covered in frothy matte blue glaze, mkd., ht.4in. **$700**
887 Pewabic Pottery Vase in unusual fire orange matte glaze & mkd. w/circular stamp, ht. 8in. **$1,200**
624 Rookwood Vase painted by E. Barrett w/full-height leaves in amber, red & blue-green w/1918 flame mark, ht. 8¾in. **$950**

873

874

875

876

877

878

879

880

881

882

883

884

885

886

887

624

A-ME   James D. Julia, Inc.

Roseville Pottery
1000   Two Handled Vase in Flower patt. unmkd., ht. 6in. **$387**
1001   Jardinière in Luffa patt., unmkd., ht. 7in. **$402**

1002   Two Handled Ball Type Vase in Morning Glory patt. **$575**
1003   Jardinière, unmkd., w/sharp shoulder, ht. 7in. **$201**
1004   Planter in the Sunflower patt., unmkd., ht. 6in. **$172**

A-NJ   Craftsman Arts & Crafts Auction
991   Five Pitchers w/Rockingham Glaze incl. a covered ale jug w/egrets; Gypsy patt.; two w/hunting scenes w/ greyhound handles. Several hairlines & chips, unmkd.,

tallest 10¾in. **$1,400**
992   Eight Pitchers w/Rockingham Glaze, four w/hunting scenes, two floral, one w/putto, Jeffers w/portrait, unmkd., chips & hairlines, tallest 10¾in. **$850**

A-ME   James D. Julia, Inc.
1006   Roseville Tea Set in the Freesia patt., mkd. **$230**
1007   Two Roseville Jardinières on stands in the Donatello patt. 3 unmkd. **$862**

473

476

463

464

465

466

467

468

A-NJ   Craftsman Arts & Crafts Auction
Dedham Crackleware Pottery
473 Two Crackleware Items, a bonbon covered dish in clockwise Rabbit patt., mkd. w/indigo stamp, ht. 5in., together w/a debris dish marked w/a blue dot & indigo stamp. $1,500
476 Four Crackleware Items in Rabbit design incl. a celery tray, two open nappies, nos. 2 & 5, & a large bowl no. 4, all mkd. w/indigo stamps. $1,200

463 Three Plates, nos. 1 and 2, in the Birds in Potted Orange Tree & Mushroom design, dia. 8½ & 10in. $750
464 Three Crackleware Plates in the Snow Tree design, incl. a saucer, shallow soup, and plate no. 1, all w/imp. & indigo marks, two by Davenport. $600
465 Four Dinner Plates incl. two Clockwise Rabbit, Pond Lily & Turkey

patt., all w/indigo & imp. marks. $950
466 Two Bowls in the Grape design, one scalloped, the other a whip cream bowl, dia. 7¼ & 9in. $850
467 Five Items in the Clockwise Rabbit patt. incl. a covered sugar bowl w/chips to lid & two milk pitchers, all w/indigo stamp. $800
468 Two Clockwise Rabbit patt. pitchers, mkd. w/indigo stamp. $600

POTTERY / PORCELAIN

A-MA   Skinner, Inc.

First Row

428 **Canton Soup Plates,** China, 19th C., one w/thin hairline, dia. 8½-9in. $881

Second Row

429 **Partial Assembled Set of Twenty-three Table Items,** Nanking patt., China, 19th C. incl. ten luncheon or salad plates, four handled teacups, four saucers, & five dessert plates, most w/gold rims, three plates w/rim chips. $823

430 **Chinese Export Ginger Jar,** 19th C. w/cover repr., ht. 12¼in. $1,116

431 **Canton Cider Jug,** early 19th C. w/foo dog finial, ht. 8¼in. $3,055

Third Row

432 **Two Chinese Export Plates,** 18th C., w/underglaze flower spray design, one w/minor rim chip, dia. 9⅛in. $558

433 **Two Scallop Rim Canton Bowls,** late 19th C., dia. 9½in. $1,058

434 **Three of Twelve Imperial Nanking Dinner Plates,** 19th C., w/imper., dia. 9½in. $823

Opposite:

A-NH   Northeast Auctions

1505 **Pair of Chinese Export Armorial Platters** w/The Arms of Temple Viscount Palmerston, each w/scalloped rim & gilt highlights, ca.1785, lg. 14¼in. $1,500

1506 **Chinese Export Punch bowl** w/hunt scenes, floral & swag motifs, int. painted w/basket of flowers & ext. w/four oval scenes, dia. 13½in. $1,300

1507 **Three Armorial Dishes & Tea Bowl** w/Arms of Temple, Viscount Palmerston, ca.1785. $900

1508 **Canton Punch Pot** w/associated lid w/foo dog finial, ht. 7½in. $1,250

1509 **Three Chinese Export Fitzhugh Pitchers,** each w/spearhead border, ht. of two 8in, third 5½in. $1,200

1510 **Chinese Export Fitzhugh Straphandled Covered Cider Jug** w/foo dog finial, ht. 9½in. $3,000

1511 **Nine Chinese Fitzhugh Strap-handled Pots de Crème** & two Canton examples, the Fitzhugh lids w/berry finials & spearhead borders. $1,700

1512 **Chinese Fitzhugh Partial Dinner Service,** each w/spearhead border incl. ten 9½in. plates, nine 7¾in. plates, five 7½in. plates & eight 6in. saucers. $2,400

1513 **Eleven Chinese Fitzhugh Soup Plates** w/spearhead border, dia. 9¾in. $700

1514 **Three Nanking Table Items** incl. a cut-corner salad bowl, gravy boat w/liner & a covered oval sweetmeat dish, lg. 5½in. $750

1515 **Group of Fitzhugh Cups, Saucers & Bowls** w/spearhead border incl. 12 cups, two w/wishbone handles & two small examples w/four saucers. $300

1516 **Four Chinese Export Fitzhugh Service Dishes** w/spearhead border incl. two oval platters, deep dish, rectangular dish & large 18¾in platter. $2,200

1517 **Six Fitzhugh Serving Dishes** incl. two soup tureens, oval platter, oval deep dish, gravy boat & sauce tureen. $900

1518 **Large Fitzhugh Oval Platter** w/crest of Beale, ca.1800, lg. 19in. $1,700

1519 **Three Fitzhugh Service Dishes,** each w/spearhead border incl. a covered vegetable w/berry knop & two hot water plates. $1,200

1520 **Four Export Pieces** incl. a strap-handled covered sugar bowl, creamer, circular covered butter dish & a strap-handled bowl. $6,000

1505-1507

1508-1511

1512-1516

1517-1520

POTTERY / PORCELAIN

A-NH   Northeast Auctions
Prattware
90 **Mischievous Sport & Sportive Innocence Jug,** ca.1795, ht. 7in. $400
92 **Pearlware Ruddy-faced Toby Jug,** ca.1810-20, ht. 10in. $600

Opposite:
A-IA   Jackson's International Auctioneers
129 **R.S. Prussia Bowl,** ca.1900 w/floral dec & red RSP mark. $235
130 **R.S. Prussia Bowl,** ca.1900 w/floral dec. & minor flake, red mark. $82
131 **R.S. Prussia Bowl,** ca.1900 w/floral dec. & red mark. $352
132 **R.S. Prussia Bowl,** ca.1900 w/floral dec. & red mark. $176
133 **R.S. Prussia Bowl,** ca.1900 w/double mold & floral border, red mark. $293
135 **KPM Porcelain Coffee Pot,** 20th C. w/hand painted floral dec. $58

136 **Noritake Owl Humidor,** ca.1926 & mkd. w/a green M in wreath. $200
137 **Two R.S. Prussia Bowls,** ca.1900 w/floral dec., the first unmkd., the second w/satin finish & red RSP mark. $146
138 **R.S. Prussia Cream & Sugar,** unmkd., together w/a hand painted Limoges sherbet, ht. 4in. $146
139 **Seven Porcelain Figures,** 19th & 20th C., incl. a Staffordshire spill vase, a blue & white Bavarian group, lg. 9in., and Japan figurals. $58
140 **Irish Belleek Porcelain Group,** late 20th C., incl. a vase, ht. 6in.;

two swan & two pigs w/green marks. $146
141 **Irish Belleek Porcelain Group** incl. an octagonal pot, shell cups & saucers, creamer, small vase & two cups. $165
142 **Eight-Piece Lenox Porcelain Group** incl. a covered jar, ht. 7in., three birds & four swans. $75
143 **Eleven Scuttle Mugs,** ca.1900 & later w/floral dec. $83
144 **Ten Scuttle Mugs,** ca.1900 & later w/floral dec. $94
145 **Nippon Porcelain Group,** early 20th C., incl. a coffee pot, bowl & two vases. $146

A-NH   Northeast Auctions
English Pearlware Mochaware unless noted
225 **Make-Do Jug** banded in dark-brown w/dark-brown, slate-blue & white looping earthworm on brown ground, groups of three cat's eyes forming stylized leaftips on a sand ground above a green-glazed herringbone border, ht. 7½in. $3,600
226 **Yorkshire Slipware Cake Dish,** Harwood Stockton, ca.1860, dia. 12¼in. $125
227 **Chamberpot Cover,** slip-banded

in dark brown w/rust & white cat's eyes on blue ground w/applied loop handle, dia. 9½in. $50
228 **Make-Do Jug,** slip-banded in black & slate-blue w/slate-blue & white cat's eyes, centering a row of parallel wavy white slip trailings on black ground & fitted w/a tin make-do handle, ht. 5⅞in. $1,500
229 **Bowl,** banded in dark-brown w/brown cinnamon & slate blue earthworm looping, dia. 7¼in. $200
230 **London Shape Bowl,** banded in

dark-brown, pale-blue & white slip twigs on sand ground, dia. 4½in. $175
231 **Half-pint Mug & Cover,** slip-banded in dark brown & surrounded by dark green dendritic trees, ht. 4½in. $200
232 **Mustard Pot & Cover** of drum form, slip banded in dark-brown & surrounded by dark green trees on blue ground, ht. 2¾in. $150
233 **An assembled English Toy Coffee Service** incl. a lighthouse coffeepot & cover, cream jug, waste bowl & cover, four handless cups & saucers. $400

129

130

131

132

133

134

135

136

137

138

139

140

141

142

143

144

145

A-PA **Freeman's**
English Liverpool Transfer-Decorated Pieces, 19th C.
1001 **Creamware Pitcher** dec. w/Washington in Glory-America in Tears & Peace & Plenty, and Independence w/eagle over bannerette inscribed E Pluribus Unum under spout, ht. 10in. **$1,912**
1002 **Creamware Pitcher** w/same as above dec., ht. 10in. **$2,031**
1003 **Creamware Pitcher** dec. w/Washington Monument & States, border & Peace & inscribed E Pluribus Unum under spout, ht. 10in. **$1,912**
1004 **Presentation Pitcher** dec. w/the name Joseph Babson & eagle w/shield, and Peace Commerce & Friendship with all Nations Under spout. Sides dec. w/floral sprigs enclosing Peace, Plenty & Independence w/a fully rigged ship flying the American flag, ht. 13in. **$3,883**
1005 **Creamware Pitcher** dec. w/Masonic emblems & wreath enclosing verse The World is Pain ... w/a tied ribbon & grape swag under spout, ht. 9in. **$717**
1006 **Creamware Pitcher** dec. w/Peace, Plenty & Independence & Washington Monument, enclosed by state border w/oval reserve enclosing woman & anchor under spout, ht. 9in. **$1,792**
1007 **Creamware Mug** dec. w/Peace, Commerce and Honest Friendship with all Nations Entangling Alliances with None - Jefferson, ht. 4¾in. **$2,868**
1008 **Presentation Pitcher** heightened w/gilt banding, vines & inscribed Hepsabeth Mannan and dec. w/fully rigged ship flying the American flag, & Apotheosis of Washington, ht. 8in. **$2,629**

Opposite:
A-NH **Northeast Auctions**
1460 **English Creamware Figure of a Recumbent Ram,** ca.1790-1800, lg. 5⅝in. Together w/a similar English creamware figure of a recumbent ram, ca.1790-1800 w/brown splotched border, lg. 5⅝in. **$700**
1461 **Pair of English Pearlware Figures of Sheep,** ca.1800-10, each standing on a green-washed oval base, lgs. 5⅝ & 5⅞in. **$2,800**
1462 **Creamware Figure of a Recumbent Ewe,** ca.1790 w/curly coat spotted in manganese-brown & ochre, lg. 6⅛in. Together w/a recumbent ewe, her coat sponged in brown stripes, lg. 6⅞in. **$900**
1463 **Pearlware Cow Creamer Milking Group,** ca.1800-10. The open-mouthed cow w/looped tail forming the handle & being milked by a seated milkmaid wearing a dotted dress, lg. 6⅞in. **$700**
1464 **Pearlware Recumbent Ram,** ca.1790-1800, lg. 5½in. Together w/a Staffordshire creamware recumbent ewe, spotted in manganese black, lg. 4⅞in. **$1,100**
1465 **Pratt-type Pearlware Figure of a Recumbent Ewe,** her coat spotted in dark brown, lg. 5⅝in. **$350**
1466 **Staffordshire Pearlware Figure of a Cock,** ca.1790-1800, streaked in ochre, brown & underglaze-blue & spotted in green, ht. 6⅝in. **$3,000**
1467 **Staffordshire Creamware Figure of a Lion,** ca.1780-90 w/brown spotted body, lg. 3$\frac{7}{16}$in. Together w/a recumbent lion, his main & haunches colored in pale tan & light brown lg. 6in. **$300**
1468 **Pratt-type Pearlware Figure of a Seated Lion,** ca.1800 w/coat spotted in ochre & underglaze-blue w/splotches of green on base, ht. 2¼in. **$140**
1469 **Two Pratt-type Pearlware Figures of a Lion & a Bear or Badger,** ca.1800, together w/a figure of a seated spaniel, 1790-1800; each w/an ochre sponged coat on a green-washed base, lgs. 2⅝ & 3½in. **$700**
1470 **Three Staffordshire Pearlware Recumbent Lions,** ca.1790-1800. One sponged in manganese & spotted in yellow w/cobalt blue; the second w/features & tail in ochre w/purple mane & body w/yellow spots; the third ochre w/ochre circlets, lgs. 3¾, 4 & 3¼in. **$1,100**
1471 **Wedgwood Majolica Hedgehog Crocus Pot,** 1865-75 w/white eyes, incised whiskers & a well-delineated coat pierced w/circular apertures in glazed shades of brown & green, unmkd. lg. 9½in. **$350**
1472 **Two Pearlware Allegorical Figures of Seasons,** ca.1790-1810. The larger representing Winter, the smaller with the title Spring, hts. 8¾ & 7$\frac{9}{16}$in. **$700**
1473 **Staffordshire or Yorkshire Creamware Quintal Flowerholder,** ca.1780-90 w/five apertures molded on their upper ends w/overlapping foliage, ht. 8¼in. **$350**
1474 **Staffordshire Dolphin Milk Jug,** ca.1790, lg. 7¼in. **$700**
1475 **Prattware Circular Portrait Plaque,** ca.1806 & molded w/bust of Charles J. Fox, dia. 5in. **$200**

A-NH   **Northeast Auctions**
**1448 Pair of English Pearl-Glazed Earthenware
Cow Creamer Milking Groups,** ca.1825-40,
being milked by a black-haired milkmaid, lgs. 7¾
& 8in. $1,400

1460-1462

1463-1466

1467-1470

1471-1475

A-NH Northeast Auctions

1001 Crown Derby Porcelain Dinner Service, Imari patt., ca.1884 & 1887, comprising an oval soup tureen, cover & stand, twelve soup plates & a dish. Marked w/an imp. crowned DERBY, printed underglaze-blue or enameled iron-red factory marks above year cipher, numeral 198 in red. Length of tureen 14½in., dia. of soup plates 10in. **$4,250**

A-IA Jackson's International Auctioneers

1468 Irish Belleek, Shamrock patt., 96 pieces including 6 mugs, 12 dinner plates, 12 cups & saucers, 12 luncheon & 12 salad plates, coffee and tea pot, sugars, creamers, salt & pepper sets, honey pot, egg cups, mustard jar, bowls & nappies. **$1,645**

1469 Copeland Spode Dinnerware, Gainsborough patt., including 118 pieces, service for twelve & comprising 15 dinner plates, 17 sq. breakfast plates & 12 each round breakfast, bread & butter, fruit dishes, 13 cups & 15 saucers, 11 soups, a compote, sugar, creamer, 2 platters, coffee & tea pots, two vegetables & a fluted tray. **$1,645**

1470 Hutschenreuter Bavarian Dinnerware including 91 pieces & comprising 17 dinner plates & saucers, 16 cups & luncheon plates, 15 sauce dishes and a sugar, creamer, gravy boat, coffee pot, nappy, platter, plus 4 vegetable bowls & a 25 piece chocolate set. **$587**

A-ME James D. Julia, Inc.

1181 Limoges Game Set, consisting of 15 pieces dec. w/game birds, heavy gold borders & several pieces sgn. Muville. Bottom mark includes L.R.& L. in red for Lazeyras, Rosenfeld, Lehman, ca.1920s. **$2,587**

A-NJ   **Craftsman Arts & Crafts Auction**
973   **Lenox Vases,** one leaf-shaped w/gilded branches; a bottle-shaped vase painted w/butterflies & roses; and one w/pink morning-glories & purple clematis, all stamped, tallest 11¼in. **$2,300**

A-NJ   **Craftsman Arts & Crafts Auction**
974   **Ott & Brewer Porcelain in the Dandelion patt.** Two pitchers, one basket w/branch handle & one small bowl w/branch base w/chips, all w/red crown & sword stamps, tallest 8in. **$1,100**

A-NJ   **Craftsman Arts & Crafts Auction**
981   **Assorted Service of Belleek** incl. three pitchers w/gilded flowers, two chocolate pots, one by CAC, the other by Willets w/dragon handle, an Ott & Brewer pitcher, Willets three piece sugar bowl, Ott & Brewer shell-shaped mustard jar & salt. **$1,000**

A-NJ   **Craftsman Arts & Crafts Auction**
963 Morris & Willmore Tankard & Two Mugs w/transfer-dec. scenes & applied gold foliage, mkd. w/MW stamp, ht. 14½ & 5½in. **$1,400**
964 Lenox Urn painted by W. Morley w/pink irises & gilded handles, mkd. w/ green Lenox CAC stamp/ W.H.Morley, ht. 13¼in. **$3,750**
965 Lenox Ovoid Vase dec. by Morley w/yellow primrose, mkd. w/green Lenox CAC stamp/Tiffany & Co./Primrose/ W.H. Morley, ht. 14½in. **$2,900**

A-ME   **James D. Julia, Inc.**
1287 Limoges Punchbowl Set, fourteen pcs., mkd. T&V Limoges, France, ca.1907-1919. Set consists of footed punchbowl w/stand & ten handled cups & a large under tray, all dec. w/multicolor grapes & leaves w/gold trim. The unmkd. ladle may be a later edition. Footed punchbowl ht. 6¼, dia. 14in. **$1,725**
1288 Limoges Punchbowl Set, twelve pcs. mkd. T&V Limoges, France, ca.1892-1907. Set includes a footed punchbowl & ten champagne style stems, all dec. w/heavy gold grapevine & leaves w/light blue trim. **$1,035**

Opposite top:
A-PA   **Alderfer's Fine Art & Antiques**
Meissen Blue Onion
1276 Covered Tureen w/two handles & mkd. w/crossed sword on underside, ht. 10in. **$977**

Opposite botom:
A-NH   **Northeast Auctions**
42 Two Sunderland Black Transfer-Printed Plaques, mottled pink & copper lustre. The first w/a fully rigged ship, 8 x 9in.; the second printed a brig w/mottled pink lustre frame molded w/shells & leaftips, 7½

1281 Compote w/lattice work around perimeter w/crossed sword mark. **$2,589**
1282 Covered Tureen w/two handles & mkd. w/crossed swords. ht. 6in. **$138**
1286 Electrified Oil Lamp w/white top

x 8¼in. **$754**
43 Two Sunderland Plaques, black or brown transfer-printed, the first w/a view or Retribution Steamer, and the second in brown w/a Brig. Each pink lustre frame molded w/shells & leaftips & the second edged in copper, the first 8¼ x 9¼in., the

globe w/fluted edge & mkd. w/crossed swords on underside, ht. 21½in. **$345**
1297 Divided Serving Dish mkd. on underside w/crossed swords, ht. 2½, dia. 13½in. **$230**

second 8 x 9in. **$348**
44 Two Sunderland Black Transfer-Printed & Mottled Pink Lustre Plaques, ca.1820. The first w/a view of a fully-rigged ship w/impressed mark MOORE & Co., 7½ x 8½in.; the second w/impressed crown mark, 7¼ x 8¼in. **$812**

1276, 1281, 1282, 1286 & 1297

A-NH   **Northeast Auctions**

33 Sunderland Pearlware Black Transfer Printed Jug w/verse Forget & Forgive, ht. 5¾in. **$580**

34 Sunderland Pearlware Jug w/printed verse beneath spout, another on side, and on the other a mariner's compass, ht.7½in. **$986**

35 Sunderland Creamware Jug w/black transfer & mottled pink lustre w/verses ht. 6½in. **$348**

36 Newcastle Pearlware Pink Lustre Jug, Tyneside School, ca.1826-30, & dec. w/flowers & leaves, ht. 4¾in. **$522**

37 Sunderland Creamware Teapot w/black transfer dec. & mottled pink lustre, w/matching cover,dec. w/verse & ship, ht. 4in. **$1,044**

A-NH   **Northeast Auctions**

707 Newcastle Pearlware Pink Lustre Jug, Tyneside School, dated 1837. Printed beneath the spout-Sailors Farewell- w/one side printed w/verse To a Friend, and on the other The sailor lost in stormy seas. ht. 7in. **$638**

708 Newcastle Pearlware Pink Lustre Jug, Tyneside School, ca.1830-40, w/printed verse beneath the spout, There is an hour of peaceful rest within a grapevine border. One side dec. w/the mariner's compass, the other w/verse Home is a name of more than magic spell…, ht. 7¾in. **$754**

709 Newcastle Pearlware Jug, Tyneside School, ca.1830-40 w/verse Still as through life our wear steps we bend, ht. 4¾in. **$464**

710 Newcastle Jug from Tyneside School w/printed verse beneath the spout, Long may you live…, one side w/ Sailors now are to 'd about… & the other side a printed ship, ht. 7⅛in. **$638**

A-NH   **Northeast Auctions**

748 Sunderland Creamware Presentation Mug w/black transfer dec. w/verse within floral wreath on each side, ht. 4in. **$464**

749 Sunderland Pearlware Presentation Oddfellows Jug w/black transfer dec. & pink lustre, dated 1832, ht. 5½in. **$406**

750 Sunderland Pearlware Presentation Jug dated 1843 w/black transfer & pink lustre dec. ht. 5½in. **$232**

A-NH   **Northeast Auctions**

971 Rose Medallion Covered Vase w/lion mask ring handles & lion knop w/painted flowers & butterflies on a gold ground, ht. 27in. **$1,160**

972 Chinese Export Mandarin Vase w/flaring scalloped rim, dog handles & dragons at shoulders. Back & front dec. w/two large figural patterns surrounded by a Chinese gilt meander, ht. 18in. **$696**

973 Rose Medallion Vase of square tapered form & mounted as a lamp, ht. 16in. **$1,276**

974 Chinese Export Rose Mandarin Temple Vase w/two pairs of facing foo dogs & dragons at shoulders, ht. 25in. **$1,508**

POTTERY / PORCELAIN

A-NH   **Northeast Auctions**
Rose Medallion
1373 **Fruit Basket & Stand** w/two shaped covered dishes & two bowls,

$580
1374 **Group of Tablewares** comprising a bottle vase, pr. of candlesticks, vase, brush pot & cup, together

w/three plates & a pr. of Chinese Export plates depicting figures in a garden, ht. of candlesticks 8¼in. $2,088

A-NH   **Northeast Auctions**
1376 **Chinese Export Porcelain Well & Tree Platter** & an oval Platter in Bird & Butterfly patt., lg. of first platter 15¾in. $1,160
1377 **Chinese Export Strap Handled Soup Tureen & Cover,** Bird & Butterfly patt.

w/polychrome dec., lg. 15in. $2,204
1378 **Shaped & Scalloped Footed Serving Dish,** Bird & Butterfly patt. w/poly. dec., lg. 15in. $1,044
1379 **Chinese Export Footed Round Tazzas,** Bird & Butterfly patt., ht. 4⅛in. $696

1380 **Chinese Export Tablewares,** Bird & Butterfly patt., incl. a covered hot water dish, two cups w/saucers, small vase, five soup & four dinner plates, leaf dish & a small dish w/damage. $1,392

A-NH   **Northeast Auctions**
977 **Chinese Export Rose Medallion Candlesticks** w/turquoise, gold & orange trellis form design on collars & bases, ht. 7½in. $1,044
978 **Pair of Chinese Export Mandarin Plates** each w/an Armorial, ca.1830

w/motto Aviso La Fin, & initials RAK, dia. 10in. $1,160
979 **Mandarin Well-And-Tree Footed Meat Platter** w/border & domestic scene in center w/figures, lg. 17½in. $1,508
980 **Early Chinese Export Mandarin Armorial Covered Soup Tureen**

w/strap handles, ca.1910. The lid & sides each w/two coat of arms of Grant w/mottos, lg. 13½in. $580
981 **Chinese Export Oval Platter,** lg. 11½in. & rectangular serving dish, together w/four plates, dia. 7¾in. not illus. $1,856

A-ME — James D. Julia, Inc.
481 Pair of Chinese Export Famille-Rose Armorial Plates,
c.1765 w/gilt outer edge, floral sprig border & the armorial

w/bound sheaves above motto. Chips, dia. 8¾in. $1,035
482 Chinese Export Armorial Punchbowl, Famille-Rose, late
18th C. w/motto, dia. 11½in. $1,955

A-NH — Northeast Auctions
Chinese Export Porcelain
1006 Mug, Tobacco Leaf patt.,
w/scalloped rim, late 18th C., ht.

5in. $7,540
1007 Pr. of Soup Plates, Tobacco Leaf
patt.,ca.1810, dia. 9½in. $4,640

1008 Garniture Vases w/Covers, late
18th C.,Tobacco Leaf patt., ht. 6½in.
$6,090

A-NH — Northeast Auctions
Chinese Export Porcelain unless noted
1010 Five Loped Bulb Vase dec.
w/flowers on a cracked ice ground.
The long neck vase is surmounted by
an open lotus bud, ht. 9⅜in. $319

1011 Japanese Blue & White Charger
dec. w/large basket of flowers, 18th
C., dia. 21½in. $1,180
1012 Two Saucers w/dec. of Ruins,
together w/a pair of blue & white
saucers, dia. of first 6½in. $468

1013 Pair of Hexagonal Salts, 18th
C., & dec. w/river scenes, ht. 2in.
$754
1014 Mantle Vases, dec. w/temples
in an extensive landscape. The covers
w/animal finials, ht. 10¾in. $812

548-550

551-554

555-560

561-566

A-PA
Conestoga Auction Company, Inc.
Spatterware
548 **Paneled Plate,** Acorn patt. w/red spatter, dia. 8⅜in. $4,510
549 **Red Spatter Paneled Plate,** Acorn patt., dia. 6in. $2,970
550 **Paneled Plate,** Acorn patt. w/red spatter, dia. 8½in. $3,410
551 **Handleless Cup & Saucer,** dec. w/blue spatter, Castle patt., cup w/tiny glaze flakes, ht. 2¾, saucer 5¾in. $220
552 **Green Spatter Cream Pitcher** w/Peafowl dec., & small glaze flakes on rim, ht. 3½in. $187
553 **Blue Spatter Footed Master Salt** w/hairline, ht. 2¼in. $165
554 **Rainbow Spatter Handleless Cup & Saucer** w/tiny base flake, Rose patt., dia. of cup 5¾in. $440
555 **Purple Spatter Teapot,** Rose patt., w/gooseneck spout & applied ear handle. Spout & handle has repair, ht. 6in. $110
556 **Rainbow Spatter Cream Pitcher** w/repr. to handle & hairline, ht. 5¾in. $357
557 **Teapot** w/red spatter dec., Rose patt. w/gooseneck spout & applied ear handle. Cover restored, ht. 5¾in. $192
558 **Red Spatter Handleless Cup & Saucer,** Peafowl patt. w/tiny hairline on rim of cup. $935
559 **Rainbow Spatter Paneled Plate** w/rim chip & glaze wear, dia. 7⅛in. $605
560 **Rainbow Spatter Handleless Cup & Saucer** w/spatter dot center. $632
561 **Blue Spatter Plate** w/four-color peafowl, mkd. Adams, dia. 9⅜in. $577
562 **Blue Spatter Bowl,** Rose patt., dia. 11⅜in. $220
563 **Red Spatter Peafowl Plate** w/tiny glaze flake on base rim, dia. 8½in. $412
564 **Purple Handleless Cup & Saucer,** Rose patt., cup ht. 2¼, dia. saucer 5⅞in. $220
565 **Blue Spatter Plate** in Pineapple patt. w/1¾in. crack extending from rim. Rare patt., dia. 8in. $3,575
566 **Rainbow Spatter Handleless Cup & Saucer,** Thistle patt. $577

A-PA Conestoga Auction Company, Inc.
505 Rabbitware Adams Rose Plate
w/center scene of rabbits in hayfield
w/split rail fence, dia. 9¼in. **$495**

A-PA Conestoga Auction Company, Inc.
633 Five Color Rainbow Spatter Pitcher
w/emb. swag dec. surrounding
border, rim & shaped scroll handle, ht.
9¾in. **$5,775**

A-PA Conestoga Auction Company, Inc.
766 Salopian Handleless Cup & Saucer, Stag patt. **$275**
765 Salopian Plate, Stag patt, dia. 7¼in. **$495**

A-PA Freeman's Red Staffordshire Spatterware
1378 Three Plates, Thistle patt., ca.1840, dia. 8¼in. **$1,912**
1379 Teapot in Thistle patt., ca.1840, ht. 7in. **$2,868**
1380 Four Thistle patt. Teabowls w/saucers. **$2,031**

POTTERY / PORCELAIN

A-PA Freeman's
Staffordshire Spatterware
1371 Blue & Red Rainbow, two
paneled plates, a teabowl & saucer in

Open Tulip patt. **$1,912**
**1372 Rainbow Octagonal Platter &
Plate** w/swag border, dia. 8¼, platter
lg. 12¼in. **$3,883**

1373 Five Teabowls w/Saucers, red &
blue Peafowl patt., ca.1840. **$3,465**
1374 Teabowl & Saucer, pink & blue
in Peafowl patt., **$2,270**

A-PA Freeman's
Staffordshire Spatterware
1390 Three Blue Plates, Castle patt., each w/varying
building groups & trees, dia. 9½ & 8in. **$750**
1391 Sugar & Waste Bowl, ca.1835, ht. 8¾in., dia. 6½in.
$500
1392 Two Toddy Plates, Castle patt., dia. 5in. **$425**

A-PA Freeman's
Staffordshire Spatterware
Schoolhouse Pattern Unless Noted
1393 Group Including two Teabowls, four saucers, two
dinner plates & two bread plates, dia. 6¼ & 8¼in. **$6,500**
1394 Pitcher, ca.1835, of paneled baluster form w/flaring
spout & foot, ht. 10¼in. **$4,500**
1395 Teabowl & Saucer, ca.1840. **$1,900**
1396 Teabowl & Saucer, Shed patt. w/teapot, 6in., not
illus. **$2,700**

A-PA   Freeman's
Staffordshire Pearlware
1045 **Partial Tea Service**, King's Rose patt., 19th C., incl. coffeepot, creamer & 13 plates & saucers w/pink borders. **$3,250**

A-PA   Freeman's
Staffordshire Spatterware
1383 **Five Teabowls** w/Saucer & an odd plate, ca.1840, Peafowl patt. **$1,100**
1384 **Four Teabowls** w/Saucer, Peafowl patt. **$900**
1385 **Dinner Plate**, dia. 10in. **$1,200**

A-PA   Conestoga Auction Company, Inc.
572 **Stick Spatter Plate** w/flow blue foliate stems & red rosettes, dia. 9⅛in. **$55**
573 **Stick Spatter Covered Bowl** w/spiral handles & shell terminals, minute rim flake, ht. 6¾in. **$357**
574 **Mush Cup & Underplate** w/stick spatter dec., cup has applied ring handle, plate dia. 8½in. **$220**
575 **Blue Spongeware Teapot** in Tulip patt., w/gooseneck spout & glaze flake on int. rim. **$330**
576 **Rainbow Spongeware Cup & Saucer** w/spatter dot center. **$82**
577 **Blue Spongeware Plate** w/peafowl center, dia. 8¾in. **$770**

A-PA   Conestoga Auction Company, Inc.
580 **Octagonal Spatterware Platter** mkd. MW, by Mary Weaver, ca.1975. **$55**

350   351   349   347   348   346   353

A-PA   Freeman's

Redware

350 Glazed & Slip-dec. Loaf Dish, 19th C. w/coggled edge & leafy trailings of white slip, 17 x 11in. **$956**

351 Glazed & Slip-dec. Serving Dish w/coggled rim & dec. w/wavy trailings of slip, 13½ x 8in. **$1,076**

349 Butter Stamp w/impressed design of a ewer. **n/s**

347 Sgraffito & Slip-dec. Charger, dec. w/a peacock & flower & heightened w/bittersweet, green & yellow slip, dia. 12in. **$3,346**

348 Manganese-slip Redware Reclining Sheep, ht. 4in. **$388**

346 Slip-dec. Charger w/coggled rim, dia. 13½in. **$3,107**

353 Ruffle-rim Glazed Dish w/slip dec. incl. white & brown banding w/flower heads, dia. 7¼in. **$2,390**

1302   1303   1304   1310   1305   1306   1304   1308   1310   1311   1310

A-PA   Freeman's

Redware

1302 Three Slip Dec. Plates w/coggled rims, dia. 8in. **$1,434**

1303 Three Glazed Manganese-dec. items incl. an ovoid crock illus. & an ovoid & bulbous pitcher not illus. **$5,079**

1304 Three Glazed & Slip-dec. Plates w/coggled rims, dia. 8in. **$1,673**

1305 Two Glazed & Incised Pitchers by Jacob Medinger, Montgomery Co. PA, 1856-1932, each w/eagle w/outstretched wings & shield at breast w/manganese spots, & inscribed Liberty, ht. 7¾in. **$3,107**

1306 Three Glazed & Slip-dec. Plates w/coggled rims, dia. 8in. **$1,075**

1308 Redware Vase, VA or PA w/flaring collar, belted foot & dec. w/ an applied rose blossom & stem, w/green & brown splotches & yellow banding, ht. 9¼in. **$21,510**

1310 Six Small Plates incl. a cup plate impressed w/an eagle, star & the date 1831 w/slip trailings & coggled rims, dia. of four, 4in., & one 3¼in. **$5,676**

1311 Glazed & Slip-dec. Bowl w/green banding, yellow-green ovals & diamonds, dia. 6in. **$3,226**

A-PA   Conestoga Auction Company, Inc.
Redware
29 **Slip Dec. Plate** mkd. J. McCully, Trenton, w/alternating pin stripes & squiggle bands & coggled rim, w/crack, dia. 11½in. **$1,320**
31 **Cream Pitcher** w/lid, pinched spout & applied ear handle, w/glaze loss, ht. 4¼in. **$495**
35 **Slip Dec. Plate** w/small dot dec. & rim flakes, dia. 6½in. **$357**
36 **Slip Dec. Plate** mkd. J. McCully, w/three bands of each squiggle lines & coggled rim w/chips, dia. 6½in. **$1,320**
30 **Plate** w/manganese dec. surrounding rim w/center dec., w/hairlines. **$302**
33 **Handled Crock** w/manganese splotching, incised lines & applied C scroll handle, minor rim flakes, ht. 5½in. **$203**
34 **Bulbous Jug** w/applied molded shaped handle & Albany slip glaze, w/base rim chip, ht. 6¼in. **$110**

A-PA   Conestoga Auction Company, Inc.
257 **Redware Rooster** w/dark manganese splotching resting on circular base w/gadrooned rim, ht. 5¼in. **$990**

A-PA   Conestoga Auction Company, Inc.
Redware
256 **Bird Whimsey Rattle** w/incised wing detail, manganese splotching & repeated pressed snowflake dec., ht. 2⅛in. **$2,860**
254 **Bird Whimsey Rattle**, att. to John Maize, Centre Co., PA, w/incised wing detail, manganese splotching, incised plume on top of head w/white glaze & resting on slab base w/repeated circle dec., ht. 2¾in. **$9,350**
255 **Redware Rabbit Whimsy** w/manganese splotching & resting on molded base, ht. 1¾, lg. 2¼in. **$880**

A-PA   Conestoga Auction Company, Inc.
28 **Shenandoah Valley Redware Harvest Jug** w/yellow, green & orange glaze w/center carry handle flanked by spout & air stem, ht. 6½in. **$1,870**

POTTERY / PORCELAIN

A-MA   Skinner, Inc.

First Row, Redware

367 **Two Slip-dec. Plates,** early 19th C., one w/pale yellow slip w.orangish brown, green & brown slip-glaze dec., together w/a pale yellow plate dec. w/a stylized blossom & leaf border w/wear, dia. 9½ & 10¼in. **$353**

368 **Redware Jar,** MA, early 19th C., ovoid w/applied lug handles w/streaks of brown manganese glaze on cover, rim & shoulder, chips, ht. 10⅜in. **$2,585**

369 **Pitcher,** early 19th C., w/applied reeded handle & sides dec. w/brown splotch stripes. Minor handle chip, ht. 6½in. **$176**

370 **Pottery Jar,** early 19th C., dec. w/streaks of brown manganese on shaded rust, gold & olive green glazed ground, chips, ht. 8in. **$1,528**

Second Row, Redware

371 **Rooster** w/modeled figure details delineated w/incised lines, clear lead glaze w/streaks of manganese, ht. 15⅞in. **$800**

372 **Cylindrical Jar** ornamented w/incised horizontal & wavy-line dec. around shoulder w/green copper oxide splotch dec. w/minor rim chips, ht. 7⅞in. **$940**

473 **Three Pottery Items,** probably N. Eng., including a speckled green glazed pitcher w/strap handle; a small pitcher w/applied strap handle & brown splotch dec.; and a large jar w/domed cover, applied lug handles & brown splotch dec. w/imperfections, ht. 12½in. **$382**

Third Row, Redware

374 **Jar,** ovoid form w/int. & ext. shades of glossy gold & olive green glaze streaked w/dark brown, ht. 8⅞in. **$1,998**

375 **Loaf Dish** w/slip dec., coggled rim & yellow bacon strip slip dec., chips, ht. 3, wd. 9⅛, lg. 13⅞in. **$940**

Fourth Row

376 **Slip Decorated Jar** dec. w/yellow & brown manganese brush splats, & incised line dec., ht. 6½in. **$1,293**

377 **Small Pitcher** w/applied strap handle, yellow spot slip dec. & tinged w/olive green,chips & crack, ht. 6½in. **$470**

378 **Covered Sugar Bowl** w/domed cover, applied handles, footed & dec. w/brown manganese splotch dec., minor chips, ht. 5in. **$1,528**

A-MA   Skinner, Inc.

14 **Molded & Incised Redware Pig Flask,** ca.1880, att. to Wallace & Cornwall Kirkpatrick, Anna Pottery, Anna IL, w/a hole at the rear & dec. w/incised inscriptions incl. Railroad & River Guide, with a little Good Old Rye In. Chip on one ear, lg. 7½in. **$7,638**

1400

1401

1402

1403

1404

1405

1406

1407

1408

1409

1410

A-IA   Jackson's International Auctioneers
Fiestaware
1400   Cobalt Blue Syrup w/green drip cup, ht. 6in. **$411**
1401   Two Yellow Pitchers incl. a tea pot, ht. 7in., & a high carafe w/ chip on foot, ht. 10in. **$176**
1402   Covered Coffee Pot, Creamer & Covered Sugar w/chip to the fitter on lid, ht. 10in. **$117**
1403   Two Water Pitchers, ht. 7 &

5¼in. **$70**
1404   Two Pitchers, one w/an ice lip, ht. 4¼in. w/chip on spout, together w/covered Kitchen Kraft Pitcher w/chips to underside of lid, ht. 6in., both by Homer Laughlin. **$23**
1405   Set of Mixing Bowls, some w/rim chips. **$323**
1406   Two Vintage Items incl. a compote & deco bud vase. **$146**
1407   Group of Eight Vintage Items

incl. two covered casseroles, losses, **$176**
1408   Large Vintage Relish Tray, dia. 11in. **$146**
1409   Homer Laughlin Footed Center Bowl, dia. 12in. **$176**
1410   Twelve Pieces of approximately 40, incl. a 14 & 12in. platter, two serving bowls & a 12in. oval platter. **$352**

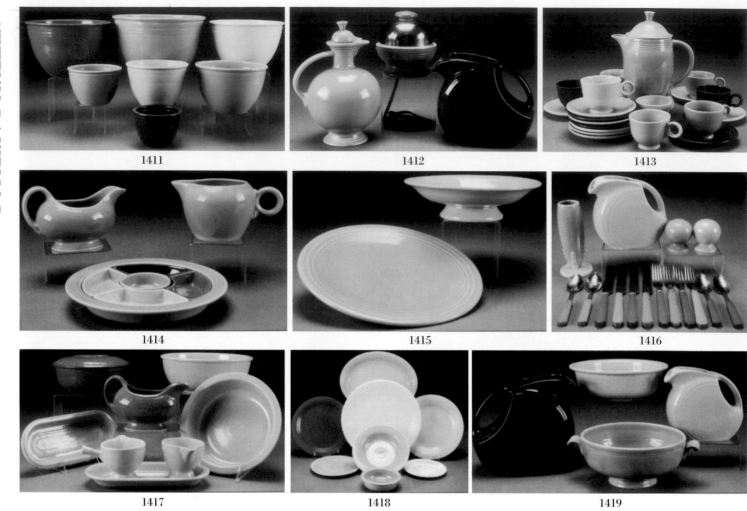

1411   1412   1413

1414   1415   1416

1417   1418   1419

A-IA   Jackson's International Auctioneers
Fiestaware
1411   Seven Vintage Mixing Bowls, a complete set. **$558**
1412   Green Carafe, Cobalt Water Pitcher & an egg cooker. **$146**
1413   Group of 21-Pieces of vintage ware incl. 8 cups, 12 saucers &

coffee pot. **$176**
1414   Eight Pieces of Vintage ware. **$411**
1415   Large Platter wd. 14in., together w/a footed center bowl. **$205**
1416   Juice Pitcher, bud vase & twelve pieces of flatware. **$264**
1417   Covered Bowl, Gravy Boat,

Celery, two large bowls, sugar & creamer w/under tray. **$293**
1418   Eight of a 63-piece group of vintage ware incl. five platters, ten plates & others. **$705**
1419   Two Bowls w/pitchers, losses. **$117**

A-PA   Conestoga Auction Company, Inc.
Yellowware
346   Water Cooler mkd. Powell, Bristol on upper rim w/band dec. in relief around body & metal spigot, ht. 15½in. **$93**
344   Large Mixing Bowl, ht. 6½, dia. 14¼in. **$110**
341   Harvest Jug in keg form w/spout flanked by loop handles in center of body w/incised lines. Small rim flakes, ht. 7in. **$357**
345   Figural Bulldog Bank w/chips, lg. 5⅛in. **$71**
343   Cream Pitcher w/pewter lid & thumb lift. Small flakes, ht. 5in. **$330**
342   Rolling Pin w/repl. wood handles, lg. 15in. **$374**

1442   1443   1444   1445

1446   1447   1448

1449   1450   1451

1452   1453   1454

1458   1459   1460

A-IA   **Jackson's International Auctioneers**
Hummel Figurines
1442 **Lamp, Out of Danger** w/full bee mark, No. 44/B., ht. 12in. **$146**
1443 Letter to Santa Claus, No. 340. **$146**
1444 **Blessed Event**, No. 333. **$176**
1445 **Two Figurines** Kiss Me, No. 311 & Doll Bath No. 319. **$188**
1446 **Stormy Weather**, No. 71. **$146**
1447 **Three Figurines** incl. Doll Mother, No. 67; The Botanist, No. 351; & Goose Girl, No. 47B. **$146**
1448 **Three Figurines** incl. Little Goat Herder, No. 200/0; Smart Little Sister, No.

346; & School Box, No. 82/0. **$117**
1449 **Three Figurines** incl. Apple Tree Box, No. 142/3/0; Apple Tree Girl, No. 141 3/0; & Be Patient, No. 197. **$117**
1450 Home From The Market, No. 198, together w/Mother's Darling No. 195. **$105**
1451 **Three Figurines** incl. Gay Adventure, No. 356; Volunteers, No. 50 2/0; & Playmates, No. 58. **$117**
1452 **Three Figurines** incl. Duet, No. 130; School Boy, No. 82/0; & The Lost Sheep, No. 68. **$117**
1453 **The Sensitive Hunter**, No. 6/0; To Market, No. 49/0, & Serenade

No. 85. **$117**
1454 **Goose Girl**, No. 47/10; Barnyard Hero, No. 195 2/0; & Strolling Along, No. 5. **$117**
1458 **Group of Nineteen Facsimile Hummel Figurines**, WWII period & later, the tallest 6in. **$117**
1459 **First Edition Hummel Plate**, Heavenly Angel, No. 264. **$300**
1460 **Group of Twenty-one Goebel Figurines**, all in the Friar Tuck pattern incl. a large water pitcher, ht. 8in., & a condiment set. **$264**

The Shaker movement in America began in 1774 when Mother Ann Lee, an untutored English textile worker, arrived in this country with a small group of ardent followers. By the time of the Civil War membership had increased to around 8,000 brothers and sisters living in eighteen communities from Maine to Ohio. Shakers believed in celibacy and lived in communities that were largely self-supporting. They were very traditional, believing in simplicity and conservatism which were heightened by religious strictures against any type of unnecessary decoration. Deliberately withdrawing from the world around them, members of this religious communal sect have left us a heritage of simplicity and beauty in their furniture, as well as every other Shaker craft. Their lifestyle is wholly without parallel in American history.

Shaker furniture is a major creative force in our decorative arts heritage because it is the only truly original American style of furniture. Harmony and quiet simplicity came naturally to the Shaker craftsman. His ambition was to produce works of the highest quality with the best materials to be found. Most Shaker pieces have simple, geometric lines and ingenious features such as complex drawer arrangements. Oftentimes, surfaces were left unpainted or covered with a thin coat of stain.

Since the "discovery" of Shaker designs during the 1920s, a number of American museums and collectors have amassed distinguished collections of the sect's furniture and artifacts. The word "Shaker," as in every other Shaker craft, is now being very appreciated at its true value and has become a magic term to collectors these days. Recent auctions have attracted serious collectors, as well as museum representatives, and their frenzied bidding has literally driven prices upward until many new heights have been realized in recent years.

A-MA   **Willis Henry Auctions, Inc.**
45 Cupboard Over Drawers, butternut & poplar w/orig. ochre varnish finish, signed in pencil – J. Munson, Mt. Lebanon, NY — ca.1840-1850. The single inset panel doors open to a small cupboard int., probably used for bonnets, over six dov. & lipped drawers, ht. 63½, wd. 43, dp. 20in. **$80,000**

A-MA   **Willis Henry Auctions, Inc.**
50 Sewing Table, birch w/pine secondary woods w/orig. brown/red stain, ca.1840, single board scrubbed birch top, lipped & dov. drawers w/orig. pulls. The case is pegged at the drawer supports on the front & double pegged at the tenon on pine sides, from Enfield, NH, overall ht. 28½, wd. 35½, dp. 23¼in. **$26,000**

A-MA
Willis Henry Auctions, Inc.
65 **Small Sewing Desk,** butternut, walnut, birch & pine w/orig. varnish finish ca.1870, Canterbury, NH, ht. 39, wd. 26 at case & 29in. at the writing surface. **$13,000**

A-MA   **Willis Henry Auctions, Inc.**
91 **Tall Chest,** pine w/hard rubbed varnish finish, simple molded top board over seven full length lipped & dovetailed drawers w/replaced cherry pulls, Mt. Lebanon, NY, ca.1840-1850, ht. 5ft.10½, wd. 45in. **$10,500**

A-MA   **Willis Henry Auctions, Inc.**
80 **Drop Leaf Work Table,** cherry & maple w/old reddish stained varnish finish, pegged one-board top, hinged drop leaves & boxed rect. leaf supports, w/square tapered legs, Canterbury, NH, ca.1820-1830, ht. 26½, wd.16½, dp. leaf 8in. **$3,600**

A-MA   **Willis Henry Auctions, Inc.**
70 **Cobbler's Bench,** pine, oak & birch, dov. case, sgn. & dated Jan. 13, 1819 – Mt. Lebanon, NY, ht. 24½, wd. 23½, lg. 27in. **$2,500**

A-MA   **Willis Henry Auctions, Inc.**
95 **Storage Chest,** walnut & poplar w/natural varnish finish, hinged lift lid compartment over small inset panel door cupboard on left & two dov. drawers on right. Union Village, OH, ca.1840-1850, ht. 30, wd. 36in. **$9,000**

A-MA   **Willis Henry Auctions**

115 **Hanging Cupboard,** pine w/orig. gray/green painted finish, four-shelf int. & six vertical backboards symmetrically nailed, MA ca.1840, ht. 41, wd.36in. **$5,500**

142 **Candlestand,** maple w/orig. red painted surfaces, adjustable threaded arm & two brass candle cups, ca.1785-1871, ht. 34, dia. 15in. **$4,000**

A-MA   **Willis Henry Auctions, Inc.**
118 **Stack of Oval Fingered Boxes,** lg. 3½ to 15in. **$8,500**

A-MA   **Willis Henry Auctions, Inc.**

195 **Blanket Chest,** pine, poplar old hand-rubbed varnish finish w/snipe hinged lift lid, single dov.& lipped drawer & early drawer pulls. An early homespun blanket found in chest is incl. w/lot, ca.1820-1830, ht. 34, wd.36, dp. 19in. **$7,500**

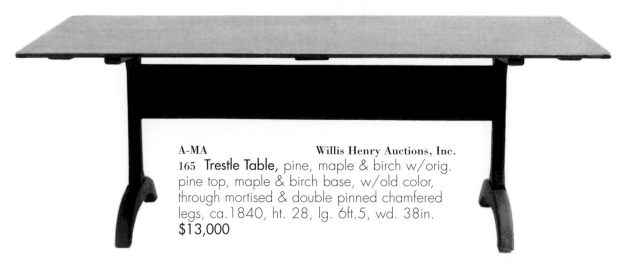

A-MA   **Willis Henry Auctions, Inc.**
165 **Trestle Table,** pine, maple & birch w/orig. pine top, maple & birch base, w/old color, through mortised & double pinned chamfered legs, ca.1840, ht. 28, lg. 6ft.5, wd. 38in. **$13,000**

A-MA **Willis Henry Auctions, Inc.**
35 Work Stand, walnut, cherry, pine & poplar w/orig. dark stained finish & black stained cherry pulls, att. to Orren Haskins, 1815-1892, Mt. Lebanon, NY, ca.1860-1870, ht. 42½, wd. 32½, dp. 22¾in. **$420,000**

A-MA **Willis Henry Auctions, Inc.**
81 Oval Carrier, maple & pine w/orig. chrome yellow painted finish, fixed handle & finely carved three fingers w/copper points, ht. to top of handle 7, lg. 9⅛, dp. 6½in. **$9,000**

A-MA **Willis Henry Auctions. Inc.**
36 Revolver Chair, maple, pine & hickory w/orig. red/brown stained finish, ca.1840, New Lebanon, NY, ht. 28in. **$9,000**

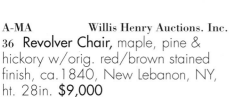

A-MA **Northeast Auctions**
Shaker Oval Boxes
305 Three Finger Box, fitted for a pincushion w/cover & painted chrome yellow, lg. 4½in. **$580**
307 Three Finger Covered Box w/chrome yellow paint, lg. 7⅜in. **$512**
308 Brown Stained Covered Box w/three fingers, lg. 7½n. **$348**
308A Red Stained Oval Box w/three fingers & mkd. Robert Barn, lg. 9in. **$522**
309 Blue-Gray Painted Box w/four

fingers, lg. 10¼in. **$2,320**
310 Robin's Egg Blue Four Finger Box, lg. 11in. **$1,276**
311 Small Covered Two Finger Box w/opposing fingers, from Harvard Shaker Community, lg. 3in. **$232**
312 Deep Red Covered Two Finger Box from Harvard Shaker Community, lg. 5½in. **$406**
313 White Painted Covered Box, three-finger w/opposing fingers w/handwritten inscription, lg. 9in. **$2,784**

314 Oval Carrier, two finger const. w/stationary handle, lg. 8½in. **$232**
315 Cherry Covered Box w/five fingers & in orig. finish, lg.13½in. **$928**
316 Cherry Covered Box w/five fingers in orig. finish, lg. 13¼in. **$1,044**
317 Bittersweet Stained Covered Box w/six fingers. The int. of lid & base w/paper covering, lg. 14¾in. **$1,508**
318 Mt. Lebanon Shaker No. 0 Rocking Chair w/stencilled label, ht. 22in. **$2,784**

A-MA   **Willis Henry Auctions, Inc.**
126 Armchair, maple w/orig. varnish finish, mushroom capped arms & orig. rush seat, Mt. Lebanon, NY, ca.1920-1925, overall ht. 45in. **$1,900**

A-MA   **Willis Henry Auctions, Inc.**
01 Weaver's Chair, maple & tiger maple w/orig. red stained varnish finish & rush seat, Harvard, MA, ca.1830-1840, overall ht. 41½in. **$4,400**

A-MA   **Willis Henry Auctions, Inc.**
40 Elder's Rocking Chair, maple w/orig. walnut brown stained finish & rush seat appears to be orig. showing traces of orig. yellow paint indicative of the Harvard community, w/interesting provenance. **$24,000**

A-MA   **Willis Henry Auctions, Inc.**
30 Rocking Chair & Footstool, maple chair w/orig. dark walnut stain w/shawl bar, orig. green & red taped seat & w/red plush covers on back, seat & stool, Mt. Lebanon, NY, ca.1880, overall ht. 41½in. **$1,000**

A-MA
Willis Henry Auctions, Inc.
05 Child's Rocker, maple w/orig. dark walnut stained finish w/orig. red & green taped seat No.0, Mt. Lebanon NY, ca.1870-1880, ht. 23½in. **$3,600**

A-MA   **Willis Henry Auctions, Inc.**
175 **Work Table,** cherry & pine w/round top & dov. drawer under, turned shaft & cherry snake legs w/repr. to one foot, Mt. Lebanon, NY, ca.1880, ht. 27½, dia. 36in. $6,500

A-MA   **Willis Henry Auctions, Inc.**
219 **Candlestand,** unusual form w/round blistered poplar top, turned cherry shaft & arched spider legs fitted into an octagonal block w/turned knob below, ht. 27½, dia. 21½in. $6,700

A-MA   **Willis Henry Auctions, Inc.**
218 **Cheese Basket Ladder,** oak & ash w/orig. red painted finish, 20 carved spokes w/circular rim & latticework base, ca.1850, ht. 6½, lg.33½, dia. 21in. $1,900

A-MA   **Willis Henry Auctions, Inc.**
117 **Utensil Carrier,** maple w/orig. finish, finely dov., canted sides, & cut-out heart handle, ca.1850, ht. 5, lg. 13¾, wd. 7in. $1,200

A-MA   **Willis Henry Auctions, Inc.**
19 **Revolving Spool Holder,** walnut w/orig. varnish finish, two circular tiers, fifteen Shaker spools, maple & cherry, a strawberry emery & pincushion top, ht. 11, dia. 8½in. $400

A-MA   **Willis Henry Auctions, Inc.**
125 **Set of Four Side Chairs,** maple w/orig. finish & rush seats, Mt. Lebanon, NY, ca.1920-1925, ht. 41in. $3,400

A-MA   Willis Henry Auctions, Inc.
02 **Shaker Dressed Doll** w/porcelain head, kid body, white wool pleated dress w/fringed bib, white wool cape & satin fringed palm leaf bonnet, ht. 13in. **$1,100**

A-MA   Willis Henry Auctions, Inc.
217 **Flax Wheel**, maple & oak w/orig. finish & stamped SRAL, ht. 34in. **$450**

A-MA   Willis Henry Auctions, Inc.
06 **Sister's Work Basket**, black ash w/carved side handles, single wrapped rim & three runners on base, ht. 34, wd. 21, dp. 16in. **$1,300**

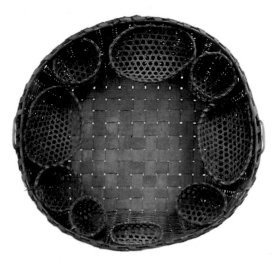

A-MA   Willis Henry Auctions, Inc.
18 **Sewing Basket**, black ash splint w/two carved heart-shaped side handles, cat's head form, nine attached int. small baskets to hold sewing items, ht. 4¾, dia. 16in. **$1,600**

A-MA   Willis Henry Auctions, Inc.
29 **Gathering Basket**, woven black ash w/double wrapped rim, carved heart-shaped handles & inverted base, ht. 15, dia. 21in. **$500**

A-MA   Willis Henry Auctions, Inc.
155 **Cast Iron Stove** w/turned wood knob on door, lipped front, stepped down back & four dov. legs numbered, New Lebanon, NY, ca. 1830-1840, ht. 17, lg. 29½, wd. 13½in. at lip. **$1,600**

A-MA   Willis Henry Auctions, Inc.
119 **Herb Carrier**, poplar w/orig. red/brown stained finish, fixed ash handle, copper angle braces on corners & small copper backing braces for handle, ht. 10¾, wd. 10, lg. 11¼in. **$3,000**

768 Small New Lebanon Shaker Oval Box in pale gray-green paint, ca.1840. The underside of lid w/applied red paper initials El, ht. 2in., top 3⅜x5¼in. **$7,450**
769 Shaker Covered Oval Box in orig. dark salmon paint, ca.1840, ht. 4in., top 7⅛x10½in. **$11,600**
770 Sabbathday Lake Covered Box w/meeting house blue paint, inscribed on lid Sister Eva, 1872-1966. Ht. 4⅞in., top 8⅛x11½in. **$20,300**
771 Large New Lebanon Shaker Covered Oval Box w/orig. pale-bittersweet stain, mid-19th C., retains Bees Wax label, ht. 6½in. top 11x15in. **$23,200**

766 Mt. Lebanon Shaker No. 6 Slatback Armed Rocker w/trademark decal, ca.1880, w/orig. dark Indian red finish & later red & black taped seat. **$1,160**
767 Mt. Lebanon Community No. 5 Armed Rocker in dark-red finish. **$1,044**

STONEWARE

Stoneware is another type of country pottery that has swung into prominence. Its production in America got underway around the mid-1700s and, because of its popularity, it was mass produced until the late 1800s.

Stoneware is a weighty, durable, dense pottery made from clay mixed with flint or sand, or made from very siliceous clay that vitrifies when heated to form a nonporous base. The common household vessels were glazed inside and/or outside to prevent porosity and resist chemical action. Most of the ware produced is salt-glazed. To produce this type of glaze, common table salt was heated and then thrown into the ware-filled kiln when firing was at the maximum temperature. The intense heat caused the salt to vaporize instantly, covering the objects with a clear, thin glaze; hence the term "salt-glaze". Frequently, the salt particles hit the vessels before being transformed into vapor, creating a pitted or pebbly surface on the stoneware.

When not salt-glazed, stoneware was coated with a slipglaze, often referred to as brown "Albany" slip, which consisted of a mixture of clay mixed with water. When applied as a finish, the mixture would fuse into a natural smooth glaze at certain firing temperatures.

The earliest stoneware was plain and unadorned but, by the turn of the 19th century, potters were using splashes of cobalt blue to decorate the gray and tan jugs and crocks. Gradually, their first squiggles evolved into the highly sophisticated freehand figures of the mid-1850s and '60s, then to the usage of stenciled patterns as interest declined.

Interest in stoneware today is not in its beautiful forms or colors, but in its decoration, the maker's name, location, and in rare instances a date, painted or incised into the clay. But, as a general rule, the more fanciful cobalt blue decorated vessels continue to increase in value, forcing the serious collector to be more discriminating.

A-PA   **Freeman's**
328 Two Stoneware Pitchers w/cobalt stylized floral dec., ht. 7¼ & 9in. **$2,510**
329 Stoneware Crocks, two late 19th C. w/cobalt dec., PA, one dec.

w/Leafy flourishes, together w/one dec. w/wisteria blossoms, ht. 10½ & 13in. **$478**
330 Three Items, PA, late 19th C. including a tin capped batter jug dec. & mkd. F.H. Cowden, Harrisburg,

together w/an ovoid jar dec. w/leafage & mkd. H. Wilson & Co., & a crock dec. w/flower on stem & mkd. Mark Cowden & Wilcox, Harrisburg, PA. **$3,346**

Opposite
A-MA   **Skinner, Inc.**
First Row
343 Jar w/blue dec. by J.& E. Norton Pottery, Bennington, VT, 1850-1861, rim chips & hairline, 3 gal., ht. 12¾in. **$9,420**
344 Jar by L. Norton & Son, late 19th C., w/stylized flower & Albany slip int., ht. 11⅛in. **$1,645**
345 Water Cooler by L. Norton, late 19th C., barrel-form w/incised lines & dec. w/an applied cobalt blue eagle figure, crazing, ht. 14in. **$1,998**

Second Row
346 Crock w/impressed mark of L. & L.P. Norton, Bennington, VT, 4 gal. w/cobalt blue bird on branch, minor hairline & chips, ht. 11in. **$588**
349 Two Cobalt Blue Items, the first a cylindrical jar w/hairline & chips, together w/late 19th C. butter crock w/cover, illus. on third row, ht. 6½in. **$764**
347 Jar w/stylized cobalt blue bird, 19th C., w/impressed mark of J. North & Co., 2 gal. w/Albany slip int., chips & hairline, ht. 11¾in. **$1,058**
Third Row
348 Salt Glazed Jug by New York

Stoneware Co., Fort Edward, NY, late 19th C. w/hairlines & chips, ht. 11in. **$323**
350 Salt Glazed Jug w/applied strap handle & inscr. w/merchant's name & address, rim chips & hairline, ht. 11¼in. **$382**
Fourth Row
351 Crock & Jug, 1 gal. mkd. Nichols & Boynton, Burlington, VT, ht. 11in., together w/jar mkd. B.C. Milburn, ht. 10¼in. **$1,763**
352 Pitchers w/blue dec.w/strap handles, chips & hairlines. **$1,528**

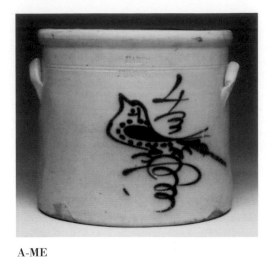

A-ME   James D. Julia, Inc.

680 **Crock** w/cobalt blue dec., 4 gal., mkd 1878-1895, Hart's Fulton, Fulton, NY, ht. 11in. **$402**

681 **Jug** w/blue dec. & mkd. N. Clark & Co., Lyons, NY, ca.1822-1852, ht. 13½in. **$390**

682 **Crock** w/blue leaf dec., mkd N.A. White & Son, Utica, NY, 2 gal. w/Albany slip int. ht. 9in. **$210**

A-ME   James D. Julia, Inc.

679 **Crock** w/blue stylized bird on branch & mkd. F.B. Norton Sons, Worcester Mass. ca.1865-1885, 4 gal., ht. 11in. **$575**

A-PA   Conestoga Auction Co., Inc.

384 **Water Pig** w/blue dec. surrounding entire body resting on applied feet, mkd. w/an incised S. Chip at spigot hole & hairlines, ht. 9¼, lg. 12in. **$467**

A-MA   Skinner, Inc.

First Row

205 **Two Crocks**, one w/cobalt blue dec., 19th C. by Nathan Clark, Jr., Athens, NY, 1843-1892, 3 gal. w/Albany slip int. The second crock made by Noah White & Sons, Utica, NY, 1840-1853 & dec. w/a large cobalt blue bird sitting on branch, 4 gal. Illustrated on third row. **$470**

206 **Crock** w/blue leaf dec., rim chips & indistinct maker's mark. n/s

Second Row

209 **Jug** w/cobalt blue dec. & mkd. Riedinger & Caire, Poughkeepsie, NY, 1856-96, w/applied ridged strap handle & minor rim chip, ht. 13in. **$529**

208 **Crock** w/cobalt blue dec. of bird on branch, mkd. S.L. Pewtress & Son, 19th C., 2 gal., ht. 8in. **$441**

207 **Jug** mkd. Riedinger & Caire, Poughkeepsie, NY, 1856-96, w/minor rim chip, ht. 13in. **$1,528**

Third Row

210 **Jar** mkd. John B. Caire & Co. Po'keepsie, New York, 1842-52, w/applied lug handles, freehand painted blue flower blossom & Albany slip int., rim chips, 3 gal., ht. 12in. **$588**

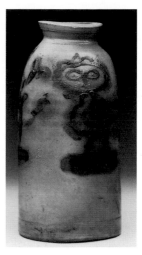

A-PA

Conestoga Auction Co., Inc.
54 **Jug** by Cowden & Wilcox, Harrisburg, PA, 3 gal., w/two chips on strap handle, ht. 15¼in. **$12,000**

A-PA Conestoga Auction Co., Inc.
128 **Bulbous Crock** w/bold cobalt blue dec. of a bird perched on branch w/flowers, 2 gal., w/base chip, ht. 10¾in. **$3,300**

A-PA

Conestoga Auction Co., Inc.
347 **Jug** dec. w/profile of gentleman wearing top hat, goatee & mustache w/neckerchief around his neck, 3 gal. w/small flakes & spider line around rim, ht. 15¼in. **$7,975**

A-ME

James D. Julia, Inc.
602 **Tall Jar** w/cobalt blue image of a very large owl type bird, mid-19th C., ht. 10½in. **$1,955**

A-PA

Conestoga Auction Co., Inc.
56 **Pitcher** by Sipe-Nicols & Co., Williamsport, PA w/cobalt blue dec., chips & hairline, ht. 8½in. **$3,080**

55 **Crock** by Cowden & Wilcox w/cobalt dec. of Man in the Moon face, w/repairs, ht. 10½in. **$3,520**

57 **Jug** by Cowden & Wilcox w/single blue drooping bell flower & minor rim abrasion, ht. 10½in. **$385**

A-PA Conestoga Auction Co., Inc.
126 **Crock** w/Lid by New York Stoneware Co. w/cobalt dec. of bird perched on branch, 2 gal. w/old rim chip & chips to lid, ht. 11¼in. **$467**

127 **Crock** w/cobalt dec., stamped 1½ gal., by Sipe, Nicols & Co., w/rim chips & hairlines, ht 9¼in. **$121**

A-PA

Conestoga Auction Co., Inc.
385 **Batter Jug** w/blue dec., stamped Evan R. Jones, Pittston, PA, w/bail handle & wooden hand grip, tin lid & spout cover, ht. 6in. to shoulder. **$1,375**

A-PA
    Conestoga Auction Co., Inc.
390 Strainer in basket form w/pierced body, overall ht. 11½in. **$605**

A-PA   Conestoga Auction Co., Inc.
123 Crock w/folky cobalt dec. of bird resting on branch, by W. Roberts, Bingham, NY, 2 gal., w/base rim chip & hairline, ht. 9½in. **$385**
124 Jug by W. Roberts w/applied handle & cobalt blue dec., ht. 10½in. **$330**
125 Crock w/blue dec. & imp. B. Norton Sons, Worcester, MA, ht. 9¼in. **$137**

A-PA
    Conestoga Auction Company, Inc.
299 Chicken Feeder w/blue foliate dec. surrounding the hooded opening, rim chip & hairline, ht. 11¾in. **$935**

A-PA
    Conestoga Auction Company, Inc.
303 Pitcher w/tall blue floral branches & accents surrounding rim, ht. 10½in. **$1,540**

A-PA   Conestoga Auction Company, Inc.
297 Water Cooler w/blue dec. accents, applied handles, w/minor flake on handle, ht. 14½in. **$2,530**
298 Churn by Chart & Son w/blue stylized flower & foliate design, name stamped under rim w/#3. Several upper rim chips & hairline, ht. 15¼in. **$220**

A-PA   **Conestoga Auction Company, Inc.**
132 Crock w/cobalt blue dec. of a bird perched on stump, 4 gal., w/rim chips & hairlines, ht. 11in. **$192**
133 Jug w/cobalt blue dec. of a bird w/flowing tail perched on branch & stamped New York Stoneware Co.,

Fort Edward, 4 gal., rim chip & hairline, ht. 16in. **$385**
134 Crock w/cobalt blue dec. of stylized bird & branch, mkd. New York Stoneware Co., 4 gal. w/rim chip & hairlines, ht. 11½in. **$308**
135 Crock w/heavy cobalt dec. bird

on floral branch, 3 gal., mkd. N.A. White & Co., Binghamton, NY, ht. 12¼in. **$1,265**
137 Crock w/blue floral dec., mkd. A. O. Whittemore, Havana, NY, 2 gal. w/rim chip & hairline, ht. 9¼in. **$93**

The early settlers brought to these shores the best handworked patterns and techniques of their native lands. Women were accomplished with the needle and their creations were a matter of pride, as well as necessity. They literally threaded themselves into the patchwork of a new American life-style as they settled into their new environment. Every handcrafted, surviving example is an expression of their talent, and textiles are among the more diverse of American collectibles.

It has become increasingly difficult to find an early colorful quilt or woven coverlet these days. Coverlets remain among one of the more expensive of American textiles. The quilt collector focuses on the quality and vintage of the needlework, the diverse forms and condition. Within the past thirty years, prices for fine quilts and coverlets have escalated dramatically... yet good buys remain for the resourceful collector.

Many collectors have turned to other forms of bed covers such as the embroidered blanket, bedspreads of the white variety, stenciled spreads and all forms of embroidery including show towels made by the Pennsylvania Germans.

Colorful hooked and braided rugs command much attention these days, and fetch very substantial prices ... especially those with original designs.

Samplers and needlework pictures became popular during the 18th and 19th centuries. More of these works of art have survived than any other type of fancy American needlework. The most intricately stitched American samplers and needlework, including elaborate mourning pictures, are extremely pricey. Many less elaborate pieces are still available ... and, like other fine American textiles, very good investments.

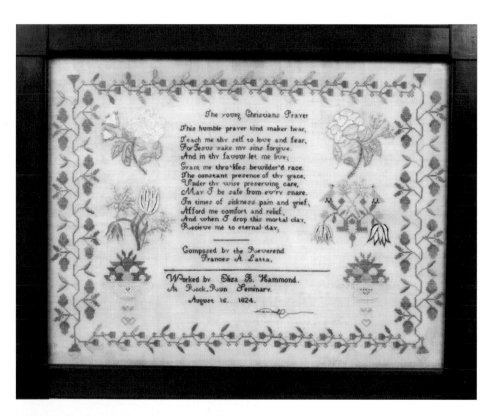

A-PA   Conestoga Auction Co., Inc.
816 Needlework Sampler by Eliza B. Hammond at Rock Run Seminary, August 16, 1824, titled A Young Christian's Prayer, composed by the Rev. Frances A. Latta. Provenance in pocket mounted to back of the contemporary molded corner block frame, 21x16in. **$22,000**

A-PA   Freeman's
1518 Wool & Cotton Coverlet by C. Yordy, Willow Street for Martin Rohrer, 1848, two pieces, 98x82in. **$507**
1523 Double Woven Coverlet, ca.1830, two pieces, 72x78½in. **$538**
1522 Jacquard Coverlet by B. Lichty, Bristol, Wayne Co., Ohio, dated 1844, w/steamboat & tree border, 93x75in. **$2,074**
1519 Jacquard Coverlet w/corner block inscr. Manu. by Martin Hoke, York, PA, AD 1845, 98x86in. **$956**

TEXTILES

A-MA   Skinner, Inc.

Clockwise from upper left:

492 Blue & White Wool & Cotton Coverlet, two-piece double weave w/corner block inscr. DELHI 1851, minor toning, Am., 97x78in. **$1,116**

493 One-piece Beiderwand Coverlet, wool & cotton w/sgn. corner blocks P.E. 1856. Sparsely fringed on ends & yarn losses, 91x89in. **$1,998**

495 Beiderwand Coverlet, wool & cotton, two-piece, bordered on three sides w/peacocks & flower filled urns, minor fringe loss & toning, excluding fringe 102x84in. **$323**

494 Wool & Cotton Two-color Coverlet w/corner blocks inscr. Isaac Brubaker 1837 DC Diller. Two pieces w/minor fringe loss & toning, excluding fringe, 100x82in. **$1,293**

491 Wool & Cotton Four-color Beiderwand Coverlet, two-piece w/corner block inscr. Made by D. Beil For_____with 1851 date, w/fringe losses excluding fringe, 87x70in. **$1,293**

A-MA   Skinner, Inc.

Clockwise from upper left:

475 Pieced & Appliquéd Calico Cotton Quilt, late 19th C., backed w/red printed patt. fabric & diagonal line quilt stitching, 85x73in. **$705**

476 Calico Cotton Quilt, pieced & appliquéd, late 19th C. w/green binding, backed w/very black patt. fabric and quilted w/diamond & concentric outlining stitches, 79x79in. **$1,116**

477 Album Quilt, cotton, pieced & appliquéd, ca.1860 w/sixteen blocks, four signatures, white cotton backing & diagonal line quilting. Minor light stains & toning, 78x74in. **$3,173**

478 Pieced Triangle Pattern Quilt, cotton, mid-19th C., w/natural cotton backing, quatrefoil & outline stitches w/toning & scattered small stains, 92x76in. **$1,175**

479 Pieced Amish Geometric Quilt, cotton, probably PA, late 19th/early 20th C. w/intersecting line stitches, wear & stains, 81½x 80in. **$588**

A-PA Conestoga
Auction Co., Inc.
**820 Needlework
Picture of Kitten**
playing w/quill pen
w/some staining in
upper right corner,
9⅞x6⅞in. **$660**

A-PA Conestoga Auction Co., Inc.
173 Pin-cushion, silver plate over brass clamp w/velvet cushion, screw end mkd. G.K., ht. 10in. **$797**
174 Sewing Clamp Pin-cushion, burled walnut w/cylinder form & turned wooden screw, ht. 5¼in. **$137**
175 Sewing Ball w/vibrant colors, dia. 2½in. **$220**
176 Two Tiered Turned Spool Caddy w/pin-cushion top & six lift wire spool supports w/ball finials, paint not orig., ht. 6½in. **$330**

A-PA Conestoga
Auction Co., Inc.
**298 Tulip
Appliqué Quilt,**
hand stitched
w/plain & printed
fabric on yellow
ground. Pencil
lines still visible,
82x80in. **$605**

A-PA Pook & Pook, Inc.
244 Wrought Iron Sewing Clamps,
three, all w/cutwork dec., one dated
1838 & mkd. SF, a second dated
1841 & mkd. S&L, & another mkd. JH.
$878
245 Wrought Iron Spring Clamp in the
form of an insect, 18th C. w/punched
face dec., together w/a wrought iron
spring clamp w/pin-cushion. **$761**

A-PA Pook & Pook, Inc.
246 Sewing Boxes, w/single drawer,
PA, w/pin-cushion tops & wrought iron
clamps, overall ht. 7¼&7in. **$644**
267 Satinwood Sewing Box, 19th C.
w/inlaid woods, pin-cushion top &
wrought iron clamp; together w/a
turned wooden sewing clamp w/pin-
cushion top. **$351**
248 Three Sewing Clamps, wrought
iron, early 19th C. w/pin-cushion tops
& unusual clamps, one initialed L, &
one MB. **$468**

A-MA   Skinner, Inc.

59 Silk Needlework Picture attrib. to Sara White, under the instructions of Abby Wright, South Hadley, MA, ca.1805, w/silk, silver & gold metallic threads on silk ground w/a watercolor painted paper face depicting Liberty, imper., unframed 16¼x13½in. **$15,275**

A-PA   Freeman's

169 Needlework Picture, ca.1825, depicting a biblical scene of Moses found in bulrushes by Pharaoh's daughter. worked w/silk threads & watercolor on silk ground, 22x20in. **$956**

A-PA   Conestoga Auction Co., Inc.
Pin-cushions
First Row

943 Starburst Shaped Needlework, underside w/blue cotton fabric & minor wear on underside, dia. 4¾in. **$55**

942 Round Needlework Cushion, underside blue silk w/minor wear, 4¾in. **$137**

941 Starburst Cushion w/multi-colored flower, underside with blue silk fabric, dia. 6½in. **$440**

Second Row

940 Shaped Needlework Cushion w/central flower, underside w/blue chintz fabric & edge lined with clear drop beads, 7x6¼in. **$550**

939 Turtle Form Cushion, underside w/brown chintz fabric & edge lined w/clear drop beads, 7½x 5in. **$880**

A-PA   Freeman's

1461 Woven Blue & White Plaid Bed Linens, PA, 19th C. incl. two-piece sheet, small plaid fringed throw 40x40in., and a window-pane plaid tick cover 73x70in. **$388**

1462 Woven Bed Linens, dark blue, light blue & white, PA, 19th C. incl. light & dark blue tick w/bolster & navy blue & white two-piece sheet, 92x75in. **$418**

1463 Group of Plaid Bed Linens, blue & off-white incl. two pillow cases w/matching tick cover & two ticks, 73x62, 58x71 & 66x59in. **$567**

1464 Woven Bed Linens, blue & white plaid & check woven incl. a check tick, plain sheet & another plaid tick. **$448**

1465 Woven Linen Bittersweet & Off-white Plaid Tick Cover, together w/tick two-piece sheet w/two lengths of pumpkin & tan check fabric & a tan striped woven tick. **$6,572**

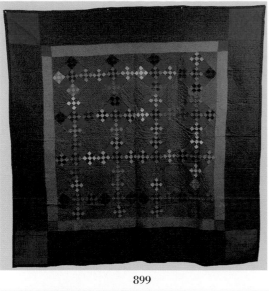

899

900

902

904

A-PA   Conestoga Auction Co., Inc.
899 Hand Stitched Amish Double
Nine Patch Quilt, 84x90in. $2,200
900 Hand Stitched Amish Bar Quilt,

84x90in. $990
902 Bowmansville Star Hand Stitched
Quilt, Lancaster, County PA, 88in.
square. $1,430

904 Sunburst Quilt, hand stitched in
pieced printed fabrics w/bear paw
border, 82x78in. $2,475

A-PA   Pook & Pook, Inc.
253 Virginia Indian Plumes Quilt, mid-19th C.,
101x91in. $2,574

A-PA   Pook & Pook, Inc.
261 Vibrant Mennonite Postage Stamp Quilt, early 20th C.,
106x83in. $2,574

A-PA   Pook & Pook, Inc.

Samplers

263 **Silk on Linen Needlework**, PA, dated 1825 w/verse, buildings, doves, etc. 15½x17in. **$878**

264 **Philadelphia Silk on Linen Needlework** dated 1805 w/verse above house, lawn, figure & animals within floral border, 21x21in. **$5,616**

A-MA   Skinner, Inc.

244 **Wool & Cotton Penny Rug** w/flower motifs, Am. or Canada, late 19th/early 20th C., composed of rows of wool circles, backed w/burlap & minor imper.31x44in. **$235**

245 **Wool & Cotton Penny Rug** w/hearts, Am. or Canada, late 19th/early 20th C., composed of rows of black wool circles edged w/contrast stitching, each centered w/a woven colored cotton field. Backed w/burlap bag w/printed Montreal flour mill label, miner imper. 31x44½in. **$235**

246 **Penny Rug** w/dove motifs, an elongated hexagonal rug composed of rows of navy wool circles w/pink thread blanket stitching, each centered w/a stylized dove, backed w/a Montreal flour mill burlap bag, 30¼x46in. **$235**

247 **Two Wool Felt Penny Rugs**, Am., early 20th C., each composed of multi-colored lapped felt circles outlined w/contrasting blanket stitching w/scalloped felt borders & minor stitch losses, 47½x28, 44x25½in. **$705**

A-PA   Pook & Pook, Inc.

First Row
62 **Two Sewing Clamps,** wrought iron w/pin-cushion tops, one w/punched dec. dated 1823 & initialed ELE; the other w/cutwork dec. dated 1837 & mkd. w/initials MH. **$1,287**
63 **Two Wrought Iron Sewing Clamps,** one w/punched dec. dated 1827 & initialed PS; the second w/cutwork dec., dated 1829 & initialed SL. **$995**

Second Row
64 **Three Clamps,** wrought iron, one dated 1857, Sarah Adams; the second w/ cutwork dec. & initialed FH; the third w/dec. pin-cushion top. **$1,638**

A-PA   Pook & Pook, Inc.

58 **Silver Mounted Queen Stitched Pinball & Hanger,** probably Chester Co., PA, mkd. HW on silver band, dia. 2¼in.; together w/another pinball w/silver mounts & floral embroidery, dia. 2in. **$1,287**
59 **Silver Mounted Silk Embroidered Pinball & Chain** w/floral & bird dec., dia. 2¼in.; together with silver mounted knitted silk pinball & chain, 1¾dia. **$3,510**
60 **Silver Mounted Silk Pinball** w/beaded rimmed band inscr. Hannah Brown, 25n7mo1801, 2¼ dia., together w/a smaller pinball w/silver band inscr. HK & SR, dia. 1¾in. **$1,112**
61 **Silver Mounted Silk Pinball** w/chain & hook, 18th C., w/initials ED & the silver mark DH on back, possibly D. Henchman, Boston. The ball retains remnants of tulip & floral embroidery. **$1,287**

A-PA   Pook & Pook, Inc.
541 **Scottish Silk on Linen Needlework** dated 1823 w/verse over fenced brick house & trees, 16¾x12½in. **$2,106**

A-PA   Pook & Pook, Inc.
262 **Silk Needlework,** late 18th C., depicting Wilton House in Salisbury, Eng. w/couples wandering on grounds, 17¾x25½in. **$5,850**

Toys

Early, interesting old toys – especially the hand-carved examples – are truly vivid expressions of the American craftsman's art of imagination. They are continuously in demand, and prices increase sharply each year. Those worthy of consideration as a "folk art" are very pricey, even though some are crudely whittled; others show fine craftsmanship and detailing. Among the most interesting of the early toys are the carved wooden dolls, squeak toys, wood and metal jumping figures, wood and chalk animals, whistles, miniatures, and the ever-popular "Sunday" toys when boisterous play was banned. The carved "Noah's Arks" were especially designed for this purpose. They oftentimes contained as many as fifty minutely carved and decorated animals, in addition to human figures.

The American toy industry was brought into being during the first decades of the nineteenth century. William S. Tower of South Hingham, MA, a carpenter by profession, has often been called the founder of the toy industry in America. In spite of the availability and wide usage of wood during this period, an increasing number of tin and iron toys were made. Many of the mass-produced toys were made during the 1870s, including the popular cast iron mechanical banks.

Because of the scarcity of earlier toys, today there is a rapidly growing band of enthusiasts buying up toys, almost regardless of the era – sometimes the items haven't been around as long as those doing the prospecting! But, whether it is indicative of a universal yearning for the good old days, or simply a case of monkey-see, monkey-do, the rush goes on.

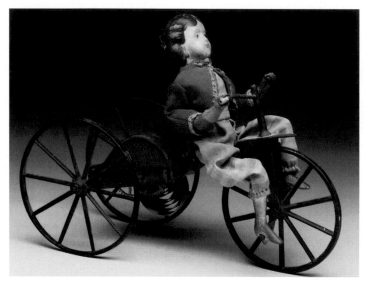

A-ME   James D. Julia, Inc.
63 Althof Bergmann Velocipede, cast iron, tin, is driven by a woman w/comp. head, a tin & cloth body. When wound, she steers the bike in a circle, pat. 1870, toy appears to be all orig. w/slightly soiled clothing. The accentuating rod from gearbox is lacking, lg. 11½in. **$977**

A-ME   James D. Julia, Inc.
61 Horsehead Perambulator Clockwork Toy by Ives Blakeslee Co., of CT, in all orig. cond. The toy has a tin horse head & retains a partial paper label on rear, w/minor overall wear. **$20,125**

A-ME   James D. Julia, Inc.
581 Carved & Painted Wood Rocking Horse, 19th C., w/saddle & bridle in orig. unrestored cond. w/damage to saddle, mane & leather parts, ht. 31, lg. 33in. **$862**

A-ME   James D. Julia, Inc.
582 Rocking Horse On Stand w/metal frame, removable saddle & some paint loss, ht. 27, lg 33in. **$287**

A-ME   James d. Julia, Inc.
199 Fischer Penny Toy, when pushed boy on horse sways back & forth, near excellent cond., lg. 3in. **$720**

A-PA   **Pook & Pook, Inc.**

198 **Victorian Pram,** late 19th C. w/blue painted surface & dec. w/gold & red pinstriping. **$575**

199 **Victorian Surrey,** wood & wrought iron, late 19th C., retaining a plaid & black painted carriage wired frame, ht. 41, wd. 45in. **$2,185**

200 **Carved & Painted Hobby Horse,** ca.1900, ht. 29in., together w/a cast metal example not illus. **$575**

201 **Two Sleds,** carved & painted, early 20th C., one illus. inscribed Annie, lg. 31in. **$1,725**

202 **Reindeer Sled,** painted pine & cast iron, late 19th C., retaining its orig. poly. dec. surface, lg. 55, wd. 13½in. **$1,495**

A-PA   **Pook & Pook, Inc.**

First Row

181 **Carved Wood Horse & Cart Pull Toy,** lg. 29in. **$510**

182 **Pair of Black Felt Horse Pull Toys,** ht. 9, lg. 12in. **$510**

Second Row

183 **Hide Covered Horse Pull Toy** w/leather harness & wooden platform, ht. 14½, lg. 15in. **$660**

184 **Carved Wooden Horse Pull Toy** w/poly. dec. surface, ht. 11, lg. 11in., together w/a smaller example, ht. 7, lg. 6in. **$480**

185 **Felt Covered Horse Pull Toy** w/wooden platform & iron wheels, ht. 18½, lg. 19in. **$575**

A-PA   **Freeman's Americana**
613 Painted & Grained Firkin, 19th C. w/lid & wire swing handle, ht. 7⅛in. **$2,868**
615 Pair of Children's Buckets, staved & painted, 19th C. w/bail handles, one inscribed Good Boy & dec. w/stars & crossed Am. flag, the other dec. w/ a horse, Am. flag, drum & inscribed Good Boy, Truth. **$2,032**
614 Miniature Blanket Chest, N. Eng.,

early 19th C. w/green-gray painted combed dec. Ht. 9¾, wd. 12¾in. **$2,510**
616 Miniature Painted & Dec. Sled, 19th C., & inscribed MAE, lg. 6¾in. **$1,912**
626 Miniature Arrowback Chair w/painted dec. & dated 1842, ht. 6¾in. **$1,434**
627 Miniature Slant Front Desk, ca.1835 w/painted dec. &

cubbyhole int., ht. 18½, wd. 14¼in. n/s
619 Painted & Decorated Doll's Chair dated 1895, the seat is decorated w/ flowers in gold, green & black. Chair has indecipherable inscription on underside. **$2,032**
620 Miniature Classical Chest of Drawers, ca.1845 w/rectangular top fitted w/two covered boxes w/rust & red dec., ht. 12, wd. 10in. **$269**

A-ME   **James D. Julia, Inc.**
862 Marx Fresh Air Taxi & Black Funny Dancer; when wound the taxi moves erratically, Amos 'N' Andy stop & shake, then continue again. Sold w/ a Marx Funny Dancer; when wound the dancer's eyes move up & down & shake, fashioned after Harold Lloyd, ht. 10½, car 7in. **$833**

A-PA   **Freeman's Americana**
629 Printed Cotton Stuffed Cat, late 19th C. w/pat. July '92 at underside, ht. 19in. **$179**
630 Wooden Cow Pull Toy, hide covered & mounted on wooden platform, moos when head is turned,

ht. 7in. **$239**
633 Boy Doll, African-American, early 20th C. w/cloth body & legs, ht. 11½in. n/s
634 Stuffed Mohair Bear on Wheels w/glass eyes & cast iron wheels, lg. 10in. **$598**

A-PA   **Pook & Pook, Inc.**

First Row

16 **Dayton Mechanical Animal Car,** painted, pressed steel, early 20th C., lg. 14½in. **$173**

17 **Three Early Toys** by Ives Blakeslee incl. high wire monkey, ht. 9in.; a dancing monkey on platform pull toy, ht. 9in., & a clockwork bear not illus. **$1,955**

18 **Tin Doll Windmill,** early 20th C., ht. 15in. **$450**

19 **Kenton Cast Iron Overland Circus Wagon** w/driver, a lion in cage, a hitch & two white horses, together w/a Kenton cast iron Overland circus wagon driver & two white horses (illus. on bottom row), wagon lg. 14in. **$748**

Second Row

20 **German Painted Mechanical Bird,** tin, ca.1900, ht. 9in. **$1,725**

21 **Muhler & Kadater Tin Go-round Toy** w/zeppelins & airplanes, painted, ht. 22in. **$5,290**

22 **Martin Tin Mysterious Ball Toy,** painted, ht. 13½in. **$920**

23 **Hubley Royal Circus Animal Cage,** cast iron w/two horses, a rhinoceros, black bear & driver, lg. 16in. **$805**

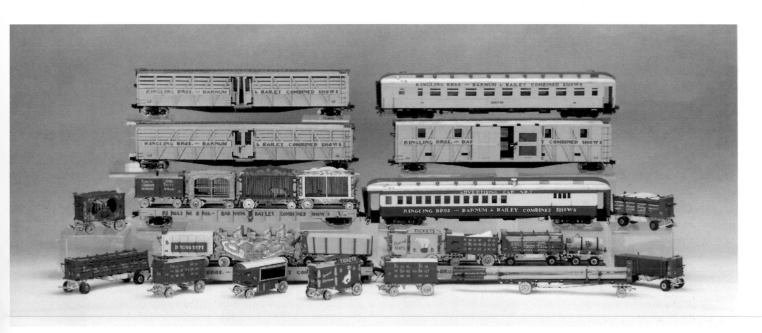

A-PA   **Freeman's Americana**

635 **Ringling Brothers & Barnum & Bailey painted & carved Circus Train,** ca.1940, incl. passenger cars, cattle cars, one band wagon, large tent pole wagon, calliope wagon, cage, advertising, water & black cattle ramp. 29 pcs. **$1,673**

A-PA   Pook & Pook, Inc.
142 Ives 3235 Three-piece Passenger Train set in green, incl. observation &

dining car, lg. 36in. $575
143 Three Lionel Engines & Tenders to

include Lionel 773, 2055 & 736. $1,035

A-PA   Pook & Pook, Inc.
Top Row
160 Electroplated P.R.R. Passenger Train mfg. by Dent Hardware, lg. 33in. $288

Middle Row
161 Marklin Engine, Tender & Box Car, early 2-2-0, w/spring loop couplers, lg. 12in., together w/a Marklin baggage trolley & an early engine

mkd. FV w/passenger car. $1,920
Bottom Row
162 Ten Pieces of 0 Gauge 1930s Marklin Trains to include two engines & tenders w/six freight cars. $480

Opposite:
A-PA Nov. 2005   Pook & Pook, Inc.
138 Alice in Wonderland Lithograph, on wood set w/10 characters. $2,300

756 **Long Bill Donald On Rocking Horse,** early celluloid Donald sitting on a wooden rocking horse, ht. & lg. 7½in. **$900**

451 **Carved & Painted Dappled Rocking Horse,** late 19th C. w/horsehair tail & mane, ht. 48½, wd. 88in. **$2,760**

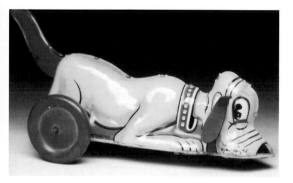

846B **Disney Tin Pluto Mechanical Toy** dated 1939 w/orig. rubber ears. Tail not working properly, lg. 8½in. **$57**

769 **Lehmann Quack Quacks,** when wound duck simulates walking while the three chicks bob back & forth, lg. 8in. **$948**

Toys

Jackson's International Auctioneers

A-IA
831 Ives Phoenix Cast Iron Fire Patrol Wagon, ca.1885 w/poly. dec. w/hinged tool box in rear, lg. 21in. $2,350

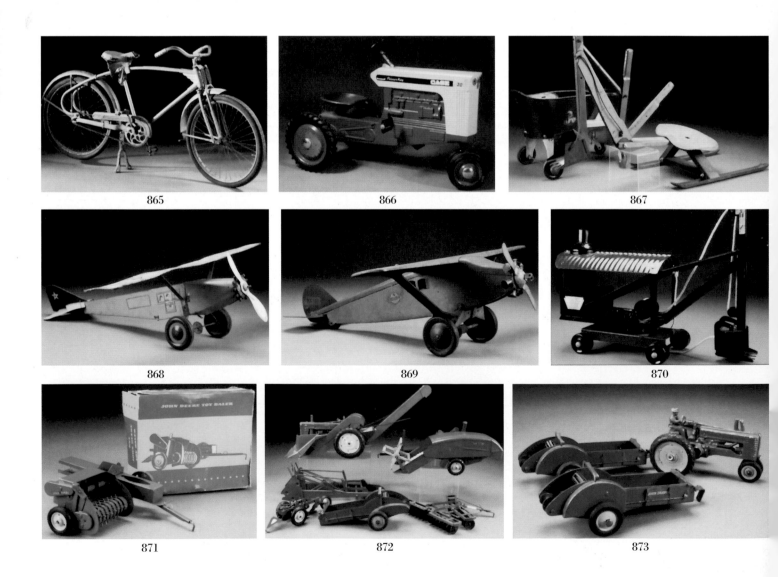

865

866

867

868

869

870

871

872

873

A-ME   James D. Julia, Inc.
733 Nifty Jiggs In His Jazz Car, lithographed. When car is wound
Jiggs' head turns steering wheel, lg. 6½in. **$1,897**

A-ME   James D. Julia, Inc.
73 Howdy Doody Band w/orig. box,
When wound, Howdy Doody toy
dances while Buffalo Bob plays the
piano, ht. 8¼in. **$1,320**

A-ME   James D. Julia, Inc.
**59 Ives Hook-Behind
Toy** depicting a country
woman in horse-drawn
cart being chased by a
young man w/cast iron
legs, comp. head &
orig. fabric clothing. The
woman is attired in orig.
clothing, w/clockwork
motor. **$20,125**

Opposite:
A-IA   Jackson's International Auctioneers
865 Silver King Aluminum Bicycle,
ca.1940s, together w/a Silver King
woman's frame. **$705**
866 Case 30 Pedal Tractor w/some
rest., steering not functioning. **$489**
867 Buddy-L Toy Dandy Digger w/a
Turner walker. **$50**

868 Schieble #220 Tin Plate Toy night
plane, lg. 29in. **$411**
869 Steelcraft Toy Plane w/US Army
stars on wings, lg. 24in. **$381**
**870 Keystone Ride 'Em Toy Tin Steam
Shovel,** repainted. **$35**
871 John Deere Toy Hay Baler,
pressed steel, mint & in orig. box.

$352
872 John Deere Farm Equipment Set
incl. tractor w/corn picker, disk, plow,
manure spreader, combine & orig.
canvas. **$528**
873 John Deere B Tractor, cast
aluminum w/two manure spreaders.
$117

A-ME   James D. Julia, Inc.
192 Elastolin Hansel & Gretel Set, depicting the childhood story, incl. a brilliantly painted gingerbread house, forest background & five orig. figures, including the witch, black cat & crow, near mint, lg. of base 18¼in. **$2,880**

A-ME   James D. Julia, Inc.
191 Marx Haunted House Toy, battery operated, figures incl. a skeleton in the chimney, spooky sounds, whistling winds & a ghost at window plus other features. **$540**

A-ME   James D. Julia, Inc.
771 Jazzbo Jim Toy, dancer on roof holding a tin guitar, ht. 10½in. **$420**

A-ME   James D. Julia, Inc.
772 Jazzbo Jim Store Display used to promote & sell the Jazzbo Jim toy. The toys were common, but the display is rare. The display has an electric motor & the dancer could dance for hours. The figure is dressed in silk w/comp. face & hands holding a wood & tin banjo, ht. 32in. **$862**

A-PA   Pook & Pook, Inc.
306 Painted & Cast Gaming Wheel, ca.1900 by H.C. Evans & Co. **$2,106**
307 Clown Circus Figure, carved w/poly. dec., 20th C., ht. 77in. **$4,212**
308 Carved & Painted Rocking Horse, late 19th Cl, wd. 44in. **$341**

734 Superman Rollover Plane by Marx, lg. 6½in. $1,200

322 Hubley Do-X Airplane w/nickel plated wheels, & crack running through one side at the pin, lg. 6½in. $230

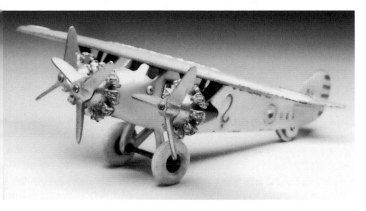

93 Questionmark Airplane by Dent Hardware Co., w/rubber tires. Finish is of recent vintage, 12in. $1,840

91 Hubley Airplane, Am., one of the largest cast iron planes produced w/pilots in an open cockpit, ca.1930s, w/rubber tires; when pushed along all props spin. 17in. $2,070

127 Marx Popeye The Pilot w/litho. plane marked 47 on both sides, plane runs erratically when toy is wound & Popeye's head nods, lg. 8¾in. $517

323 Four Cast Iron Airplanes incl. a red Lindy, orange Hubley Giro, orange Tat w/nickel plated wings & Lucky Boy. $402

92 Hubley Friendship Seaplane w/ribbed cabin, cast piston heads on the motors, pontoons & rubber tires, paint all orig. & one front prop is an old repl., wingspan 13in. $2,070

116 Tin Air France Airplane w/four props which turn when wound, mkd. Popeye's Air France & F. Anny, lg. 16in. $345

T O Y S

A-PA   Pook & Pook, Inc.
First Row
48 **Buddy-L Model-T Dump Truck,**
pressed steel, early 20th C., lg.

11½in. $1,265
49 **Buddy-L Model T Dump Truck,**
pressed steel, lg. 12in. $805

Second Row
50 **Two Buddy-L Model-T Cars,**
pressed steel, early 20th C., lg.
11½in. $1,150

A-PA   Pook & Pook, Inc.
First Row
63 **Buddy-L Dump Truck,** lg. 23in.
$240
64 **Painted Wood Roadster,** early

20th C., lg. 38in. $1,150
65 **Converse Tin Roadster,** painted,
lg. 15in. $2,990
Second Row
66 **Buddy-L Hook & Ladder Truck,**

pressed steel, early 20th C., lg. 25in.
$546
67 **Sonny Police Patrol Wagon,**
pressed steel, early 20th C., lg. 28in.
$978

A-PA   Pook & Pook Inc.

First Row

05 **Bing Roadster,** painted tin, early 20th C., lg. 11in. **$2,300**

06 **Lehmann Lila Toy,** painted tin, ca.1900, lg. 6in., together w/a Lehman motor car. **$1,265**

07 **German Tin Roadster,** painted,

early 20th C., lg. 9in. **$1,265**

08 **Metalcraft Tin Coca-Cola Truck,** ca.1930, lg. 10½in. **$690**

Second Row

09 **Lehman Mandarin,** painted tin, ca.1900, lg. 5½in. **$1,725**

10 **Carl Bubb Early Tin Roadster**

painted, lg. 10½in. **$1,680**

11 **Caretted Tin Limousine,** painted, early 20th C., lg. 15in. **$3,680**

12 **Caretted Tin Roadster,** painted, early 20th C., lg. 10½in. **$1,955**

13 **Carl Bubb Limousine,** painted tin, early 20th C., lg. 11in. **$690**

A-PA   Pook & Pook, Inc.

First Row

79 **Ives Phoenix Pumper Truck,** cast iron w/driver & rear fireman, lg. 18in. **$748**

80 **Hubley Police Patrol Wagon** w/two horses, driver & six policemen,

lg. 20in. **$920**

Second Row

81 **Harris or Hubley Hook & Ladder Truck,** cast iron w/nickel plated back end, lacking ladder, lg. 30in. **$1,955**

Third Row

82 **Oversize Dent Hose Reel Wagon,** cast iron, lg. 21½in. **$4,600**

83 **Ives Phoenix Fire Patrol Truck,** cast iron w/six firemen, two hanging on to rear platform & lacking driver, lg. 20in. **$1,840**

242 Game of Aladdin by Singer, ca.1890, featuring a brightly lithographed cover depicting Aladdin descending into the crypt. The game board itself is equally impressive featuring danger at every turn, w/box lg. 18, wd. 9½in. **$4,312**

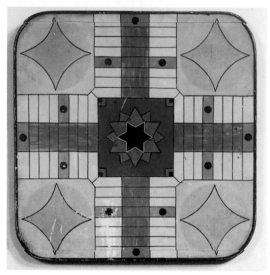

A-MA   Skinner, Inc.
191 Painted Parcheesi/Checkers Double-sided Wooden Game Board, late 19th or early 20th C. w/applied molding, 20⅝in. square, **$2,403**

A-MA   Skinner, Inc.
185 Painted Wooden Parcheesi Game Board, Am., 19th C. w/poly. playing field outlined in black w/black borders, 18⅛ x 18½in. **$6,463**

A-ME   James D. Julia, Inc.
810 Chein Amusement Toy w/four brightly litho. rockets & two children riding each one. Two of the celluloid propellers missing parts & some denting, ht. 18in. **$402**

A-ME
   James D. Julia, Inc.
243 Stanley Africa Game by Bliss w/box, beautifully lithographed historical game, lg. 18¾, wd. 9½in. **$7,475**

Game Boards

164 Wooden Double-sided
Checkerboard, Am., 19th C.
w/scattered paint wear, 17¼ x 26in.
$441

165 Checkerboard, Am., 19th C.,
rec., pine w/applied mitered molding
& dividers w/loss on one divider,
15½ x 27½in. $235

166 Yellow & Black-painted Wooden
Board, 19th C., w/applied mitered
molding & dividers w/cracks, 17 x
25in. $1,293

167 Small Red-washed Wooden
Board w/black checks, square panel
w/applied mitered molding, 13 x
12¾in. $1,116

168 Carved & Painted Game Board
Paddle, Am., 19th C. w/integral

handle & stippled inscription on the
arch: J 1838 B. lg. 15½, wd. 6½in.
$2,233

169 Double-sided Checkerboard,
Am., 19th C., rec. w/applied
molding & game piece dividers,
w/cracks, warp & paint wear, 15¼ x
24¼in. $705

170 Pine Checkerboard w/painted
mustard field & black painted checks,
19th C. w/applied mitered molding
& dividers, cracks, 16½ x 24½in.
$353

171 Painted Pine Square Game
Board w/cut corners, late 19th/early
20th C., wear & crack, 19½ x 20in.
$1,293

172 Pine Checkerboard w/applied
molding, painted yellow w/large
black dots in the holding area, minor

wear, 19¼ x 31¼in. $999

173 Canadian Wooden
Checkerboard, 19th C., w/applied
mitered molding & dividers. The field
is painted dark blue w/dark red
painted checks, 19½ x 30¾in. $529

174 Red & Black-painted Wooden
Board, 19th C., w/applied mitered
molding & dividers, 17¾ x 28in.
$411

175 Inlaid Double-sided Wooden
Game Board, Am., 1876 w/applied
dov. molding inlaid w/diamond
motifs, one side inlaid w/a
contrasting wood, w/geometric
borders & sgn. SJH 1876 w/inlaid
letters & numerals. The reverse w/a
Nine Men's Morris game also called
Merels, w/crack & paint loss, 14½ x
15in. $470

A-ME   **James D. Julia, Inc.**
245 Game of Going To The Klondike,
ca.1898, by McLoughlin Bros.,
involving the lust for gold during the
great Northwest in the 1890s. Int.
shows the great Northern lights, &
a series of mountain passes, near
excellent condition w/only slight
wear, 18¾ x 10¼in. **$4,600**

A-ME   **James D. Julia, Inc.**
**244 Election Game from J.H. Singer
Co.,** portraying early political
concerns. Interior consists of six
miniature litho. ballot boxes. Two
boxes contain various cards for votes
& game cards of different character
w/ orig. directions, lg. 13, wd. 7in.
$3,450

A-ME   James D. Julia, Inc.
195 Fischer Rabbit In Cart Penny Toy, w/some minor wear, lg. 3in. **$900**

A-ME   James D. Julia, Inc.
939 Gendron Pedal Car, unrest. w/leather seat, rubber grip steering wheel, art deco hood ornament, steel bumpers, balloon tires w/two spares and retains the orig. Gendron decal on hood & license plate, lg. 56, wd. 23, ht. 28in. **$9,200**

A-ME
James D. Julia, Inc.
298 Hubley Parcel Post Motorcycle, Harley Davidson delivery cycle w/orig. decal on tank & black rubber tires w/clicker intact, lg. 9¾in. **$2,875**

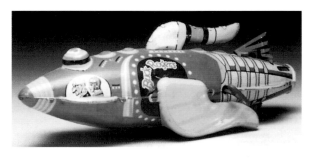

A-ME   James D. Julia, Inc.
190 Marx Buck Rogers Space Ship, when wound sparks come out of the back of space ship, making a twanging sound, lg. 12in. **$450**

A-PA   Conestoga Auction Company, Inc.
167 Composition Rooster Squeak Toy w/poly. dec. on canted base w/linen bellows, not working, ht. 6⅝in. **$153**

A-ME   James D. Julia, Inc.
51 Dent Cast Iron Battleship The New York, modeled after an 1890s Am. battleship w/copper flash cannons, anchors & tin masts, w/minor chipping of paint & one mast repl., lg. 20in. **$4,485**

Toys

A-ME   James D. Julia, Inc.
957 **Keystone Wrecking Car**
w/rubber tires & steel hubs &
Keystone Wrecker decal on back bed
w/emergency decal on both sides of
seat, and a Packard decal on grill, lg.
27in. **$1,140**

958 **Buddy L Moving Van** w/two
opening back doors, minor scratches
to roof, edge wear to fenders & some
flaking to tires & sides of truck, lg.
25in. **$780**
959 **Buddy L Express Line** w/decal on
side of van & two opening back

doors. Truck is professionally restored,
lg. 25in. **$1,020**
960 **Buddy L Railway Express Truck**
w/decal on both sides w/steel disc
wheels, some paint loss to top of truck
& fenders, lg. 25in. **$1,020**

A-ME   James D. Julia, Inc.
693 **Strauss Inter-State Bus,** brightly
lithographed w/some wear to wheels &
minor scuffing, lg. 10½in. **$603**

A-ME James D. Julia, Inc.
35 **Lehmann Autobus** in
original box, near mint
cond., German litho.
toy w/tan spoke
wheels & a tin figure,
lg. 8in. **$3,335**

A-ME James D. Julia, Inc.
853 **Marx Mack U.S.
Mail Truck** w/painted
signs on each side U.S.
Air Mail Fast Freight
Information Furnished
by Post Office. Has a
back door, front bumper
& litho. driver. Minor
chipping to truck &
wear, lg. 9¾in. **$420**

A-ME   James D. Julia, Inc.
306 **Arcade Yellow Taxi Cab,** ca.1927 &
stamped Yellow Cab Co., Main 7171 on
both sides, w/nickel plated driver & cast
iron disc wheels, lg. 9in. **$660**

A-ME   James D. Julia, Inc.
22 **Blank Button White Steiff Bear** w/shoe button eyes, red flossing on nose, mouth & paws, blank button in ear & slight hump. Retains orig. felt pads & straw stuffing, ht. 13in. **$5,400**

A-ME   James D. Julia, Inc.
51 **Steiff Cinnamon Bear,** straw stuffed w/Steiff button in ear, shoe button eyes, brown felt pads, floss nose & small hump. Some hair loss to nose & back of legs & 1in. split at base of head, ht. 24in. **$4,485**

A-ME   James D. Julia, Inc.
21 **Steiff Sheep On Wheels,** stuffed w/straw, shoe button eyes, brass bell & orig. Steiff button in left ear. Some wool missing & one ear partially detached. Stands on four wooden wheels, ht. 11, lg. 12in. **$747**

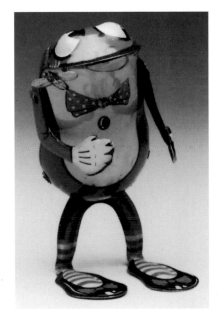

A-ME   James D. Julia, Inc.
71 **Pre-WWl White Mohair Bear** w/shoe button eyes, brown stitched nose, mouth & claws. Hair loss on lower back & left ear partially detached, ht. 16in. **$920**

A-ME   James D. Julia, Inc.
72 **Two Early Fully Jointed Mini Steiff Bears** w/Steiff buttons, glass bead eyes & never had felt pads, ht. of both 4in. **$316**

A-ME James D. Julia, Inc.
728 **German Frog Tin Windup by CKO**...George Kellerman. When wound, frog sways & vibrates as fly flits avoiding capture, ht. 4½in. **$1,150**

A-ME James D. Julia, Inc.
726 **Distler Windup Monkey Car,** brightly lithographed w/flowers. When wound, monkey tips his hat as car rolls along, ht. 4¾, lg. 6in. **$1,322**

136-153

A-NH   **Northeast Auctions**
616 Twelve English Pewter Plates, dia. 10in. **$2,100**
617 Assembled Set of Five Banister Back Side Chairs w/heart-pierced crest, all in black paint w/rush seat & sausage turned legs & one w/silvered disk on crest inscribed NSM, 1740.

$17,000
618 William & Mary Banister Back Side Chair, black painted w/shaped crest, urn finials, rush seat, block & ball turned legs. **$400**
619 Charles II Style Country Cherry Drop-leaf Gate-leg Table

w/rectangular top, drawer, shaped ends, raised on bobbin & reel turned legs joined by box stretcher, ht. 28, lg. 53½in. **$2,000**
620 Fereghan Sarouk Carpet, North Persia, ca.1900, 14ft.x9ft.6in. **$6,000**

Opposite:
A-MA   **Skinner, Inc.**
136 Small Whale-end Shelf, mah., Am., 19th C. w/three shelves, ht. 20½, wd. 19in. **$1,763**
137 Tin Candlestick, Am., early 19th C., painted black w/green & yellow leaf dec. w/wavy line border, ht. 5⅛, base 5¾in. **$881**
138 Tinware Items, five w/painted dec.incl. a cannister, apple basket & three domed trunks. **$1,116**
140 Portrait of Woman wearing white lace bonnet, unsgn., pastel on paper, ca.1820 in period giltwood frame, 22x17½in. **$1,528**
141 Portrait of Woman holding a book, unsgn., pastel on paper, ca.1820, att. to Micah Williams, 1782-1837, w/two repr. tears, upper right, sight size 25¾ x 21in. **$49,350**

142 Porcelain Presentation Pitcher w/poly. & gilt dec. n/s
143 Redware Plate w/slip dec, early 19th C. w/coggled rim & yellow slip, w/glaze wear & old rim chip, dia. 9in. **$823**
144 Mochaware Mug, England, 19th C., banded in light blue & dark brown w/earthworm dec. in blue, white & brown, ht. 3⅝in. **$382**
145 Mochaware Bowl, England, early 19th C. banded in brown w/earthware dec. in blue, white & black on light blue ground & w/hairlines, ht. 3½, dia. 6½in. **$646**
146 Chest w/two drawers, repainted red w/rest., ht. 40, wd. 38in. n/s
147 Redware Loaf Dish w/slip dec., possibly Norwalk CT, early 19th C. w/coggled rim, yellow slip & minor rim chips, 10¾x 15½in. **$3,819**
148 Chalkware Stag Figure w/painted

poly. dec., early 19th C. w/paint loss & hairline, ht. 9¼, lg. 8¼in. **$764**
149 Chippendale Slant-lid Desk, red painted, N. Eng., late 18th C. w/stepped int., bracket feet, repl. brasses & old surface, reprs. & imper., ht. 45, wd. 40in. **$3,525**
150 Wash Stand, N. Eng., ca.1825-35 w/orig. paint, ball feet & minor imper. ht. 37, wd. 18in. **$999**
151 Paint Dec. Leather Fire Buckets, pr., Am., c.1821 & mkd. No. 1 & No. 2 w/handles & paint losses, ht. 12½in. **$8,813**
152 Fireman's Parade Hat, paint dec. dated 1823, mkd. Monroe Fire Company, Philadelphia w/repairs, ht. 6, dia. 12½in. **$4,113**
153 Fancy Painted Chairs, pr., possibly N. Eng., ca.1825, w/ shaped rush seats & minor imper., ht. 35in. **$1,763**

A-OH   **Garth's Arts & Antiques**
595 Child's Farm Wagon inscribed Blue Grass Farm Wagon on both sides, w/orig. paint in green w/yellow & red. Wooden wheels have iron rims and room for two on adjustable buckboard seat, ht. 30, lg. w/handle 76in. **$1,955**

A-NH   **Northeast Auctions**
832 Georgian Inlaid Reading Table, mah., w/two adjustable accordion tops & swiveling candle trays, on tripos arched cabriole legs on pad feet w/platforms, ht. closed 29in. **$11,000**

A-OH   **Garth's Arts & Antiques**
411 Decorated Blanket Chest, PA, poplar w/orig. smoke graining, dov., till & turned feet. Some paint loss & touch-ups, ht. 24, wd. 41in. **$402**
412 Set of Eight Assembled Copper Measures, ht. 10½ to 1½in. **$345**
413 Child's Barrel Back Rocker dec. w/old green paint & mustard stringing, minor wear & one rocker repl. **$86**

A-OH   **Garth's Arts & Antiques**
591 Child's Four-drawer Chest, cherry, pine & poplar w/paneled sides, turned feet & old alligatored brown finish, ht. 25, wd. 22in. **$1,762**
592 Child's Highchair, maple, hickory & pine w/bamboo turnings, ref. & repl. footrest, ht. 22in. **$115**
593 Footstool, painted green & top stenciled w/melons & pineapple w/minor wear on top, ht. 7½in. **$345**
594 Burl Bowl w/flared rim, mellow ref. & two small old rim chips, wd. 14in. **$977**

A-MA   Skinner, Inc.
89 Pair of Portraits, 19th C.,
unsigned, oil on panel, ca.1820 in
later molded frames, 28 x 22½in.
$4,113

90 Pine Stencil Dec. Box in the manner
of Moses Eaton, early 19th C.,
w/dov. const., interior lined
w/colorful wallpaper, the top
stenciled w/two hearts, all w/apple
& leaf border, old surface & imper.,

ht. 12, wd. 29¾in. **$3,055**
91 Six-board Chest w/painted dec.,
ca.1825 w/cut-out ends, lidded till &
original surface dec. & minor imper.,
36x 31in. **$3,525**

A-MA   Skinner, Inc.
82 Federal Sideboard, NY, ca.1815-20, mah. & mah. veneer w/inlay, reeded faux columns continuing to tapering feet on brass-cap casters & repl. lion's ring pulls, ref. & imper., ht. 50½, wd. 75in. **$2,350**

83 Assembled Six-piece Coin Silver Tea Service, Am. 19th C., w/engraved monograms. **$3,525**

84 Brass & Iron Faceted Lemon-top Andirons, J. Davis, Boston, ca.1800, mkd. behind log stops, ht. 22, wd. 12½, dp. 11in. **$5,875**

A-OH   Garth's Arts & Antiques
18 Country Hepplewhite Drop-leaf Table, OH, the top & two leaves made from solid pieces of burl w/exceptional figure & color, two tiger maple aprons, the rest made of walnut w/pegged mortise joints. Both leaves have age splits, ht. 27½, wd. 42in. **$9,315**

19 Historical Blue Staffordshire Platter, North Carolina state arms in dark blue transfer w/floral border, mkd. Mayer Stone Warranted, w/prof. repr. 11½x14¾in. **$1,955**

20 Redware Pie Plate w/coggled rim & the name Ann in yellow slip & minor edge flakes, dia. 8in. **$977**

21 Painted Splint Basket w/orig. green paint & minor paint wear, 10½x15in. **$920**

A-NH   Northeast Auctions
118 Assembled Set of Six Birdcage Windsor Side Chairs & Armchair. $3,250

119 N. Eng. William & Mary Tiger Maple Gate-leg Table w/single drawer raised on ring & baluster turned legs, on ball feet. **$20,000**

120 Rooster Form Weathervane in mustard paint, fitted in wooden base, ht. 17in. **$500**

A-ME   James D. Julia, Inc.
1059 Pair of Cloisonné Vases, dec. w/berry laden branches, green & blue leaves & two sparrow like birds, unsgn. w/silver rims & bases, ht. 7½in. **$1,840**

A-SC   Charlton Hall Auctions
002 Continental Marquetry Inlaid Letter Box, 19th C. w/divided compartments, w/some minor losses, ht. 7½, wd. 10in. **$150**

003 English Apple-form Tea Caddy, ca.1900, w/ivory escutcheon & key, ht. 6¼in. **$600**

004 Tortoiseshell Tea Caddy w/silver stringing & bound w/ ivory, int. lidded compartments & on bun feet, int. relined, ht. 6½in. **$1,100**

005 Regency Style Inlaid Tea Caddy, mah., w/double lidded int. & inlaid w/satinwood, ht. 4¾, wd. 6⅞in. **$200**

006 English Tea Caddy w/brass bail form handle on stepped hinged lid w/bombé form mah. body, key & four divided compartments, ht. 6, wd. 10in. **$300**

A-SC — **Charlton Hall Auctions**

001 Sterling Tea Caddy, Am., Starr & Marcus, NY, ca.1864 w/inset relief panels depicting hummingbirds & framed by etched designs, mkd. English sterling, ht. 4½, lg. 6½in. $2,300

Opposite:

A-MA   Skinner, Inc.

158 **Portrait of a Ship's Captain,** unsgn., oil on panel w/a three-masted ship flying an Am. flag sail in the distance, w/period frame & retouched, 24x20in. **$3,525**

159 **Ivory, Whalebone & Baleen Veneer Model of the Clipper Ship** *Rainbow*, late 19th, early 20th C., maker unknown, w/minor imper. ht. 15¾, lg. 25in. **$1,998**

160 **Nantucket Purse Basket,** mid-20th C. by José Formoso Reyes, w/walnut oval lid medallion, sgn. & lacking closure peg, ht. 6½, lg. 9½in. **$1,293**

161 **Nantucket Light-ship Purse Basket,** Am., mid-20th C. w/carved ivory whale figure mounted on oval walnut lid medallion, carved ivory pins, peg & latch, ht. 7, lg. 10½in. **$411**

162 **Carved Painted Ship in Bottle,** late 19th/early 20th C. w/three-masted ship flying an Am. flag, lg. 9¼in. **$392**

163 **Small Ship Diorama,** late 19th/early 20th C., the scene depicting a two masted brigantine on a molded putty sea w/painted background, ht. 7¼, lg. 12⅛in. **$558**

164 **Carved Wooden Ship in Bottle,** 19th/early 20th C., depicting a three-masted bark floating by a wharf w/houses & lighthouse, lg. 11in. **$176**

165 **Ship in Bottle,** mid-20th C., depicting a rigged three-masted ship model, flying an Am. flag on a molded & painted putty sea next to a steamer & mounted in a gallon-size bottle on wooden stand, lg. 12¼in. **$235**

166 **Sailor's Seashell Valentine,** Barbados, late 19th C., mounted in an octagonal glazed wood case, 14¼in. sq. **$5,581**

167 **Schooner in Bottle,** mid-20th C., w/two masted vessel w/sails & lifeboats on deck in a gallon-size bottle, lg. 11¼in. **$382**

168 **Cased Ship Diorama,** 19th C., depicting a rigged four-masted bark, the hull painted white w/carved wooden accoutrements w/putty sea & painted mountains in background, w/imper. ht. 8¾, lg. 11¼in. **$411**

169 **Ship in Bottle,** early to mid-20th C., a four-masted bark w/sails & rigging, flying an Am. flag w/lighthouse & trees, in a gallon-size bottle on stand, lg. 11¾in. **$411**

170 **Harbor Scene w/Ships in Bottle,** depicting four vessels incl. the triple decker steamer *Barrymore*, a three-masted bark labeled *Ruth*, the sloop *Trenton* flying an Am. flag & British schooner *Doria*, lg. 10in. **$588**

171 **Sailor's Seashell Valentine,** Barbados, late 19th C. featuring an eight point star w/central round reserve w/shellwork lettering HOME AGAIN w/ fanciful shell border & mounted in an octagonal glazed wood case, 14¾x14⅛in. **$5,288**

172 **Group of Six Sailor Items,** probably 19th C., incl. five needlecases, three covered w/knotwork, & a small telescoping brass spyglass. **$441**

A-NH   Northeast Auctions

668 **Treenware,** comprised of six plates, four bowls of various sizes, two footed vessels, a scoop & spoon. The largest plate w/note. Made before 1818 at Mill of Jearns Haskell at Otis, Mass. 15 items. **$8,500**

A-NH   Northeast Auctions

669 **Slat-back Chair** in old paint, the armrests w/mushroom supports & rush seat, ht. 48½in. **$1,300**

670 **Two Redware Plates** w/mustard stylized leaf motif, dia. 9in. & an 8-in. plate w/straight & serpentine black lines. Each w/coggled edge. **$650**

671 **Redware Plate** w/house motif, dia. 7¾in. **$600**

672 **Large Redware Serving Plate** w/slip glaze swirling motifs, dia. 13⅛in. **$800**

673 **Two Redware Plates** w/slip dec., dia. of larger plate 9¼in. **$750**

674 **Pine & Poplar Work Table** w/two drawers in red wash & sq. tapering legs, ht. 29½, top 48 x 26in. **$800**

675 **N. Eng. Country Q.A. Side Chair** w/rush seat & Spanish feet. **$400**

676 **Oblong Bride's Box,** red painted w/overall floral dec., lg. 19in. **$400**

677 **Two Large Woven Splint Gathering Baskets,** one a feather basket w/sq. base, ht. 30in.; the second w/push-up base & carved D-form handles, dia. 20in. **$200**

A-MA   Skinner, Inc.

52 Convex Gilt-carved Mirror, Eng. or Am., ca.1800-10, w/minor imper., ht. 41, wd. 25in. **$5,875**

53 Chippendale Easy Chair, mah., Eng. or Am., late 18th C., w/Marlborough legs, ref. & reupholstered, ht. 45, wd., seat ht. 17in. **$3,525**

54 Q.A. Cherry Tilt-top Tea Table, CT w/birdcage & cabriole legs ending in pad feet, old finish & imper. ht. 27¼, dia. 37in. **$2,500**

55 Two Pairs of Brass Candlesticks, those illus. possibly English, ca.1750 w/slender tapered shaft, ht. 3¾in., the second pair possibly Spanish, 18th C. w/sq. footed bases. **$1,116**

56 Rose Medallion Porcelain Water Bottle, China, 19th C. w/gilt & enamel wear, ht. 13in. **$470**

57 Q.A. Side Chair, MA, walnut, ca.1740-60 w/an overupholstered compass seat, frontal cabriole legs, turned stretchers & ref., ht. 41in. **$1,765**

A-PA   Pook & Pook, Inc.
444 **Sterling Silver Tea Service,** five piece together
w/a silver plated tray w/grapevine dec. **$1,170**
445 **Late Federal Breakfast Table,** Phil., mah.,
ca.1825, w/animal paw feet, ht. 29½, wd. 24in.
$644

A-PA   Pook & Pook, Inc.
187 **Federal Pillar & Scroll Clock,** CT, ca.1820 by Eli Terry,
mah. case, ht. 31in. **$2,223**
188 **N. Eng. Hepplewhite Card Table,** ca.1800 w/demi-lune
top over a frame w/three paterae & line inlaid panels,
supported by sq. tapering legs, ht. 29½, wd. 37in. **$3,042**

A-PA   Pook & Pook, Inc.
612 **English Salt Glaze Pottery,** late 18th C., to include bowl,
dia. 12in., two plates, dia. 7in., sauce boat & teapot, ht. 5in.
$995
613 **Chippendale Dressing Table,** Phil., ca.1770, mah. w/shell
carving & drop, cabriole legs, shell carved knees & ball &
claw feet. **$81,900**
614 **Chippendale Armchair,** Phil., mah. ca.1770 w/pierced
splat, slip seat cabriole legs terminating in ball & claw feet.
$2,340

A-NH   Northeast Auctions
740 **Wirework Compote** w/ten pieces of stone fruit incl. peaches, three apples, pear, lemon & a pomegranate, ht. of compote 7¾in, dia. 9in. **$956**

A-NH   Northeast Auctions
793 **Two Stone Pears,** over-size, hts. 7½ & 7¼in. **$812**
791 **Stone Melon & Two Over-Size Red Delicious Apples,** hts. 5, 4½ & 3¾in. **$812**
792 **Large Stone Peach** ht. 6in. & the large grapes lg. 16in. **$1,508**
790 **Turned Maple Bowl** in orig. green paint, PA, mid-19th C. w/molded rim, ht. 10½, dia. 27¼in. **$9,280**
795 **Over-size Stone Peach,** ht. 8in. **$1,508**
796 **Over-size Stone half Golden Delicious Apple,** wd. 7in. **$1,508**

A-PA   Pook & Pook, Inc.
644 N. Eng. Ladderback Armchair, ca.1810, w/overall red & black grain dec w/yellow highlights. **$1,755**
645 Pr. of Brass Candlesticks, 18th C.

w/sq. bases, ht. 63¼in., together w/a single brass stick w/circular base, ht. 7¾in. **$585**
646 Q.A. Bible Box, walnut, PA, ca.1750 w/turned feet, ht. 9½, wd.

14½in. **$2,340**
647 Tavern Table, cherry & walnut, ca.1770 w/rectangular top, splayed legs & box stretcher, ht. 26, wd. 38¾in. **$8,190**

A-PA   Pook & Pook, Inc.
468 Writing Arm Windsor Chair, Phil., ca.1790, branded I.B. Ackley, the crest w/scrolled ears, above knuckled arm supported by turned legs. **$9,945**
469 Document Box Dated 1882, painted pine & front dec. w/leaping stag flanked by tulips, ht. 9, wd. 17¾in. **$995**
470 Carved Bird Figure w/poly. dec.,

early 20th C. **$1,287**
471 Carved Hollow Bodied Bird Form Tobacco Box, late 19th C., ht. 14½in. **$439**
472 N. Eng. Mule Chest, painted pine, ca.1760, retaining old salmon surface, ht. 35, wd. 42½in. **$1,220**
473 English Oak Table Top Desk dated 1673, ht. 10½, wd. 21in. **$936**

A-PA   Pook & Pook, Inc.
643 Miniature Ladderback Armchair, PA, 18th C., retaining an old green surface, ht. 11in. **$8,190**

MISCELLANEOUS

A-MA   Skinner, Inc.
258 Wrought Iron Six-branch Chandelier, Am., late 18th/19th C. w/adjustable ratchet w/finial depicting head of woman, candle sockets & shallow round drip pans, drop 26-39in. **$7,050**
259 Q.A. Side Chair, painted & carved, Boston, mid-18th C. w/leather overupholstered seat & minor imper. **$3,819**
260 William & Mary Gate-leg Table, probably MA, ca.1730-50 w/ring-turned legs, drawer & old brown painted surface, imper. ht. 25½, wd. 30in. **$14,100**
261 Redware Loaf Dish w/yellow squiggle-line dec.& coggled rim, minor rim chips & hairlines, ht. 3, wd. 10, lg. 14½in. **$1,528**
262 Wrought Iron Candlestand, probably France, 18th C. w/adjustable candleholder on vertical shaft, ht. 29¼in. **$881**
263 Q.A. Side Chair, painted & carved, Boston w/over-upholstered seat & old dark brown paint, minor imper. **$3,819**

A-NH   Northeast Auctions
649 Miniature Woven Splint Baskets w/C-form handles, nest of seven, Columbia Co. NY, early 20th C. w/old surface. Each w/double wrapped rim & push-up base, dia. of largest 5½, smallest 1¼in. **$5,800**

A-NH   Northeast Auctions
646 Blown Clear Glass Vase w/twelve assorted pieced leather & painted oil cloth toy balls of various sizes, 19th C. **$1,856**

A-NH   **Northeast Auctions**
517 Seven N. Eng. Banister Back Side Chairs w/rush seats. $1,856

518 Pine Sawbuck Table in orig. red paint w/rectangular top & sawbuck ends joined by stretchers, ht. 28½, top 84x25in. **$5,220**

A-PA   **Pook & Pook, Inc.**
282 N. Eng. Candlestand, late 18th C., retaining an old salmon surface, 26¼in. **$702**
283 N. Eng. Turned Candlestand, late 18th C. w/adjustable candleholders & dish, ht. 41in. **$2,574**

A-OH   **Garth's Arts & Antiques**
619 Child's Rocking Horse, pine w/orig. floral stenciling & red striping on black w/whip & wear, lg. 46½in. **$1,265**
620 Jacquard Coverlet, blue wool & natural cotton, two loom widths, double weave, by Jay A. Van Vleck, Gallipolis, OH. Van Vleck is listed in the 1850 Ohio Census as a 23 year old weaver born in NY. Minor wear. 80 x 92in. **$402**

A-MA   **Northeast Auctions**
800 Empire Mahogany & Gilt Stenciled Overmantel Mirror, 23x44in. **$900**
801 Sheraton Birch Chest of Drawers, mahoganized w/backsplash, ht. 51, wd. 43½in. **$800**
802 Sheraton Bedstead w/ball & tassel finials, mah., headboard arched w/scrolled ears, ht. 68, wd. 81in. **$1,200**
803 Pr. of European Brass Candlesticks w/drip pan, ht. 7¾in. **$650**
804 Q.A. Tilt-top Candlestand, walnut w/cabriole legs ending in pointed feet, ht. 28¾, wd. 22in. **$900**
805 Chippendale Birch Side Chair w/serpentine crest rail, over-upholstered seat, legs joined by stretchers. **$800**

A-MA   **Skinner, Inc.**
201 Late Federal Work Table, mah. & mah. veneer, probably Salem, MA, ca.1825, w/two drawers, ovolo corners, fitted int. & bag drawer, ref. & minor rest., ht. 28, wd. 21½in. **$2,820**
202 Classical Work Table, mah. & mah. veneer, MA or NY, ca.1825 w/acanthus carved & turned support & carved molded legs ending in brass hairy paw feet on casters, repl. brasses & old finish, ht. 28, wd. 19in. **$1,293**
203 Federal Work Table, mah. & mah. veneer, ca.1820 w/ovolo corners, cockbeaded drawers, repl. pulls & turned reeded tapering legs w/casters, minor imper., ht. 28½, wd. 20in. **$1,525**

Opposite:
A-MA   **Skinner, Inc.**
220 Painted Wood & Iron Fishing Spear, Am., 19th C. w/four-tined cast iron spear head w/barbed terminals, lt. 9ft. 4¾in. **$558**
221 Painted Wood & Tin Ship Weather Vane, Am., early 20th C., & mounted on a wood stand w/weathered surface, ht. 22¼in. **$559**

222 Painted Wooden Flying Goose Whirligig, Am., early 20th C., no stand, ht. 11, lg. 31½in. **$353**
223 Blue Clothes Closet, PA, early 19th C., blue-painted w/hinged door, clockbeaded flush panels, two flaking recessed panels, orig. surface & imper., ht. 74, wd. 63in. **$7,638**
224 Sheet Copper & Wood Bannerette Weather Vane, att. to J.W. Fiske, NY,

late 19th C. weathered wooden spire atop copper shaft supporting the sheet copper scrolled banner motif, w/traces of gilt & verdigris, ht. 23¾, lg. 34½in. **$2,115**
225 Wooden Architectural Element, green painted, semi wheel-shaped w/ seven spokes, ht. 33¼, wd. 35in. **$881**

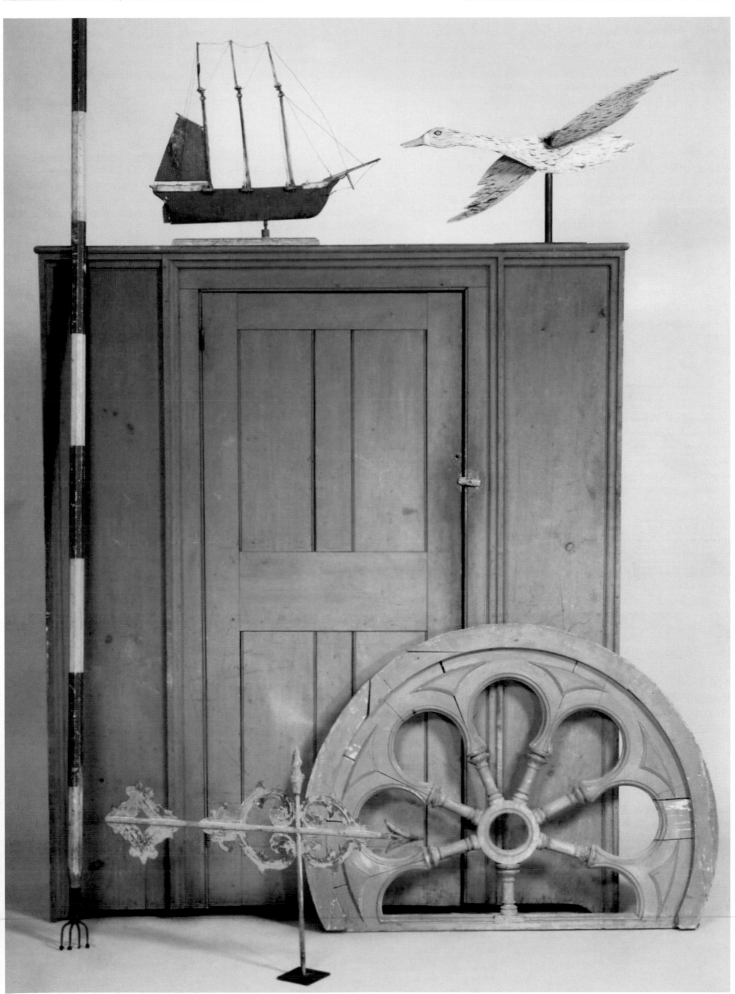

A-NH   **Northeast Auctions**
833 Pine Wall Pocket, midwestern, red painted, small size, 19th C., ht. 8, wd. 7in. **$928**
834 Three Amish Men's Straw Hats, a boy's hat in black straw, lady's bonnet & a girl's w/fancy weave (first four illus). **$522**
835 Open Box, red painted w/eight composition apples, ht. 2¼, top 10 x 11¾in. **$522**
836 N. Eng. Country Wood Bin, walnut & pine, 19th C., ht. 34, wd 30in. **$464**
837 Small Mic-Mac Porcupine Woven Basket & a covered example, 4⅜ & 3½in. **$348**
838 Country Pine Bench in old red surface, ca. 1840, ht. 19, lg. 60¼in. **$406**
839 Matched Set of Three Rattan Woven Baskets w/stationary handles, 19th C. w/push-up base & wrapped footrim, hts. over handles 8½, 11½, & dia. of largest 11in. **$2,320**
840 Red Painted Stool w/raked tapering legs, ht. 22¼in. **$232**

A-NH   **Northeast Auctions**
777 Sixteen Lady's Hair Combs of various sizes, 19th C., most are tortoiseshell. **$2,552**

A-NH   **Northeast Auctions**

9 **Early Pine Blanket Chest** in red stain, till & bootjack ends, ht. 22, wd. 48in. **$900**

10 **Q.A. Tap Table** w/one drawer & pad feet, ht. 28, wd. 42½in. **$3,000**

11 **Am. Blue Painted Blanket Chest** w/till, probably NY, dov. const. w/cotter pin hinges, lg. 36in. **$1,500**

12 **Tin Sconces,** two prs. w/single candleholder, dia. 9¼in. **$3,500**

13 **Metal Porringer,** pierced tab handle stamped Bellevue, together w/an iron Betty lamp w/undertray & other utensils including an iron pipe tongs & trammel hooks, one w/spiral twist, five items. **$1,100**

14 **Iron Skewer Holder & Five Meat Skewers,** together w/a bird roaster w/an adjustable trammel & two food choppers, each w/wooden handle. **$2,000**

15 **Adjustable Tree Table-top Candleholder,** together w/a candle dryer fitted w/drying spokes. **$2,000**

16 **Two Similar Oval Tin Sconces,** together w/two circular reflecting sconces, each w/single candleholder. First two w/crimped edge, ht. 13 & 13½in.; dia. of the last two 9½in. **$8,000**

17 **Roasting Oven,** two-part & a tinned candlebox w/hanging tabs, lg. 13½in. **$200**

18 **Three Tinned Fluid Lamps** w/handles, two w/saucer bases, one w/cylindrical font & the other w/teardrop font. **$700**

19 **Three Lanterns,** incl. two half-round examples. The first Revere type, pierced overall & w/conical cap; the others include one w/star punch motif & the other w/ribbing. **$1,400**

20 **Three Adjustable Table-top Candleholders** w/conical base & one w/crimped drip pan. **$800**

21 **Iron Kettle** w/tilter, lid attached by chair w/swing handle & ring. **$500**

22 **Children's Toys** incl. two marble boards w/marbles, a pair of skates, two trivets, chopping bowl & chopper,

tin oven, two stencilled pans, a mini. cast iron chair & painted wood mini. houses. **$600**

23 **Four Treen Plates, a Bowl & Noggin,** dia. of plates 7-8in. **$2,250**

24 **Clock-Jack Spit** w/crank handle, Am., wrought & cast-iron on penny feet, ht. 19½in. **$3,800**

25 **Wrought Iron Swivel Toaster** w/Christmas tree motifs, lg. of first 16½in., together w/another example. **$1,100**

26 **Iron Hearth Cooking Utensils** incl. a brazier, trivet & bird roaster. **$1,000**

27 **Carved Woodblock** w/bird & flowers, 8x15½in.; a diamond carved box for knitting needles w/lollipop bookplate for wall mount, & an English iron lion, lg. 7in. **$1,600**

28 **Francestown, NH Soapstone Container,** sq. w/cut corners, lg. 6in. **$450**

29 **Tin Nine-light Chandelier,** Am., w/curved candle arms joining a disk w/conical drop, dia. 21in. **$10,000**

MISCELLANEOUS

A-PA
Pook & Pook, Inc.
516 N. Eng. Whale's Tail Hanging Shelf, mid-19th C. w/scalloped sides, ht. 33, wd. 27in. **$3,978**

A-NH
Northeast Auctions
593 Early High Back Pine Settle in red wash, New Haven Colony, w/storage compartment, ht. 69¾, wd. 48in. **$11,000**

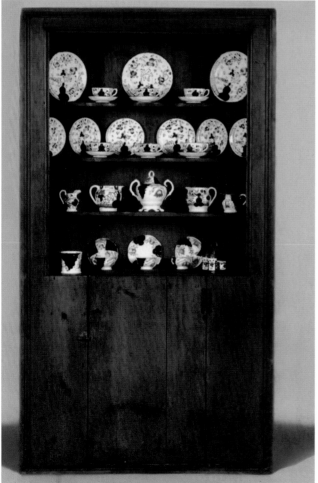

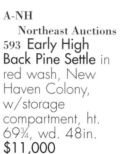

A-PA Alderfer's
1408 George II Pole Fire Screen, mah., English, ca.1750, ht. 58, wd. 27½in. **$4,025**

A-PA Pook & Pook, Inc.
328 Gaudy Welsh Porcelain, 19th C. incl. plates, cups & saucers, etc. 54 pcs. **$761**
329 Gaudy Welsh Porcelain, 19th C., incl. covered sugar, creamers, cups & saucers, etc. 25 pcs. **$351**
330 N. Eng. Pine One Piece Corner Cupboard, early 19th C. w/scalloped shelves above single door w/H-hinges, ht. 76, wd. 41in. **$2,808**

A-NH   Northeast Auctions
744 **Wirework Compote** w/six velvet fruits & vegetables, late 19th C., incl. two over-size appliquéd & embroidered strawberries, pear, eggplant & an apple w/partial ink inscription w/1906 date & a large carrot, dia. of compote 10in. **$3,828**

A-NH   Northeast Auctions
745 **Chalkware Bank**, PA, in the form of a rabbit w/collar & bell, 19th C, ht. 8¼in. **$6,264**

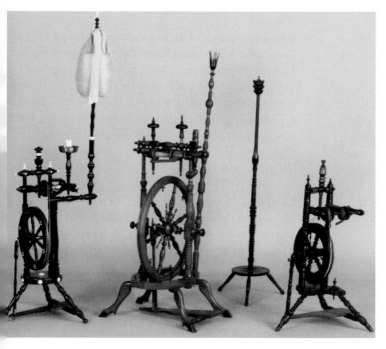

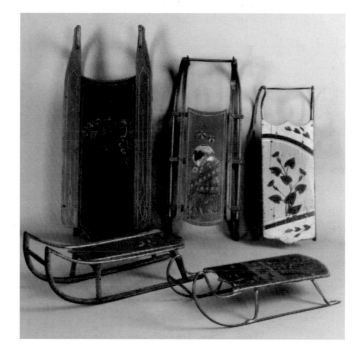

A-PA   Pook & Pook, Inc.
705 **Complete Spinning Wheel**, ebonized, 19th C. w/ivory mounts & original watercups, ht. 32½in. **$410**
706 **English or Scottish Carved & Turned Spinning Wheel**, 19th C. w/ebonized highlights & hoof feet, ht. 47½in. **$1,287**
707 **Continental Spinning Wheel**, carved & turned, 19th C. w/pewter rings & matching pole distaff, hts. 29½ & 43in. **$351**

A-PA   Pook & Pook, Inc.
498 **Large Sled** w/painted dec., ca.1900, inscribed Willie on brown ground, lg. 44in. **$556**
499 **Sled** w/painted yellow & black stenciled dec. on orange ground, lg. 37in. **$761**
500 **Painted Sled**, ca.1900 w/floral dec., lg. 32in. **$644**
501 **Two Painted Sleds**, ca.1900 & retaining their original dec., lg. 21½in. **$936**

A-ME   James D. Julia, Inc.
1300 **J.& P. Coats Four Drawer Spool Cabinet**, rests atop treadle operated sewing table, cabinet ht. 15½, wd. 21in. **$345**
1301 **J.& P. Coats Spool Cabinet**, walnut w/paneled sides & Eastlake styled drawers, ref. & original drawer front inserts possibly repl., ht. 20½, wd. 24in. **$460**

A-PA   Pook & Pook, Inc.
502 Cast Iron Rooster Weathervane, 20th C., ht. 31, wd. 34in. **$8,775**
503 Earthenware Mastiff, late 19th/early 20th C., retaining its original cream, brown & salmon poly. dec., ht. 9½, wd. 17in. **$1,112**
504 N. Eng. Sheet Iron Rooster Weathervane, 19th C. w/old black over red painted surface, ht. 26, wd. 21½in. **$4,446**
505 N. Eng. Sheraton Drop-leaf Table, birch, ca.1820, ht. 28, wd. 60½in. **$976**
506 Rocking Horse Sleigh, carved & painted, ca.1900 w/orig. poly. surface, ht. 20½, wd. 31½in. **$1,638**

A-MA   Skinner, Inc.
001 Brown Painted Cherry Pipe Box, CT, early 19th C. w/cut-out shaped & pierced backboard & sides, single dov. drawer w/brass pull, ht. **$8,813**

A-ME   James D. Julia, Inc.
1295 Merrick's Round Spool Cabinet, oak table top cabinet w/curved tambour door & patent date July 20, 1897, ht. 20, dia. 18in. **$1,156**

A-ME   James D. Julia, Inc.
1298 Clark's O.N.T. Spoon Cabinet, walnut w/paneled back & sides w/orig. pulls. ht. 23, wd. 26in. **$1,207**

A-ME   James D. Julia, Inc.
1296 Clark's Ribbon Cabinet, maple w/walnut top featuring a pair of mirror paneled sides, ht. 36, wd. 20in. **$345**

A-PA   Conestoga Auction
                    Company, Inc.
925 Stenciled Hardware
Cabinet, octagonal case
w/66 vertical pie shaped
drawers w/size information,
ht. 56, wd. 30½in. $990

A-ME   James D. Julia, Inc.
1294 Clark's O.N.T. Spool
Cabinet which turns on
turntable base w/orig. finish
& labels, ht.23, wd. 20¼,
dp. 16in. $2,040

A-PA   Pook& Pook,Inc.
288 Two Ladderback Side Chairs, PA,
18th C., both w/turned finials &
medial stretchers. $819
289 N. Eng. Pine Firkin, 19th C.,
retaining an old yellow surface. $584
290 Copper Kettle, mkd. John Getz,
PA, 19th C. w/swing handle &
gooseneck spout, ht. 12⅜in. $1,287

291 Stoneware Crock, 19th C., four
gallon w/cobalt floral dec., ht.
13½in. $585
292 Tavern Table, PA, walnut,
ca.1760 w/two drawers & box
stretchers, ht. 30¾, wd. 53¾in.
$2,223
293 N. Eng. Swell Bodied Rooster

Weathervane, ca.1900, retaining a
later yellow & red surface over orig.
gilding, ht. 24¼in. $3,744
294 Stoneware Jug, 19th C. w/cobalt
bird dec., 3 gal., ht. 15in. $468
295 Stoneware Jug, 19th C. , NY, 3
gal., w/cobalt inscription, ht. 16in.
$410

A-PA **Pook & Pook, Inc.**

130 Am. Gameboard, painted pine, 19th C. w/orig. dec. surface, 17½ x 29¾in. $1,342

131 Toleware Coffeepot, 19th C. w/red, yellow & green floral dec., ht. 10½in. $468

132 Redware Crock, 19th C. w/green & orange mottled glaze, ht. 10in. $263

133 Sheraton Tiger Work Table, tiger maple & cherry, ca.1825 w/lift lid over a case w/two drawers, ht. 29, wd. 23in. $854

134 PA. Corner Cupboard, early 19th C., one piece w/old red stain surface, ht.79, wd. 32in. $5,148

135 Portrait, Am. School, ca.1830, oil on canvas, 26x21in. $351

136 Candlebox w/slide lid, painted & sgn. on underside D.Y. Ellinger, 1913-2003, ht. 5, wd. 15in. $1,586

137 Sheraton Chest of Drawers, PA, ca.1830, cherry w/scalloped skirt, ht. 29, wd. 27¼in. $2,808

A-PA **Freeman's**
110 George III Terrestrial Library Globe, 18in., by W.& T Bardin, dated 1807 & dedicated to the Royal Society w/an inset compass. Mah. w/spade feet, ht. 41in. $35,850

A-PA **Freeman's**
288 George IV Terrestrial Library Globe, 18in., by W. & T.M. Bardin, ca.1829, w/mah. stand & spiral turned legs, ht. 45, dia. 24in. $26,680

A-ME   James D. Julia, Inc.
1056 Inlaid Victrola Cabinet w/wood horn that is fitted inside behind, the top two grill front doors, inlaid case. No mechanism present. ht. 51½in. **$1,322**

A-ME   James D. Julia, Inc.
616 Concert Roller Organ w/Six Cylinders, walnut case w/gold stenciling in good orig. cond., ht. 12, wd. 18in. **$460**

A-ME   James D. Julia, Inc.
1057 Italian Inlaid Music Cabinet w/beveled mirror & decorative inlaid panels w/music motif. Some minor imper. in mirror & inlay, ht. 59in. **$460**

A-ME   James D. Julia, Inc.
605 Tabletop Disc Music Box Stella 17, w/mah. case, brass hdw. & record storage drawer. Music Box is double comb & includes two discs. Case has been ref., winding crank of period, but not orig. **$4,500**

A-ME   James D. Julia, Inc.
606 Stella 17 Disc Console Music Box, mah. case w/large door for record storage. Music box has a double comb & incl. three discs, all brass hdw. & all teeth intact. Winds nicely, w/orig. crank & key, ht. 36in. **$2,990**

A-ME   James D. Julia, Inc.
614 Victor III Talking Machine w/external horn phonograph w/oak case & 30in. brass horn, repl. crank & reproducer; **$1,380**

615 Papier-mâché Victor Mascot Nipper in orig. paint & retains most of the orig. decal on underside. One back leg repr., ht. 14in. **$920**

A-PA   Pook & Pook, Inc.
Scrimshaw
1128 Carved Shell, 19th C. w/dec. of a sidewheeler, inscribed The Grt Eastern's first trip to N. York, arrived June 28 1860 & Purchased on board, ht. 3¼, wd. 5¼in. **$633**
1129 Two Whale's Teeth, 19th C., one w/dec. of a woman, the other

w/gentleman standing above two grape bunches, ht. 5 & 6in. **$633**
1130 Continental Carved Ivory Pencil Box, 19th C., w/inset watercolor of hunt scenes, duels, portraits, etc., together w/a similar domino box, ht. 4½, wd. 11in. **$403**
1131 Whale's Tooth, 19th C., one side w/church inscribed A Sperm

Whale Tooth Caught Near the Bahamas 1871, ht. 5¼in. **$1,093**
1132 Sailor's Carved Bone Pie Crimper, 19th C. w/pierced heart dec., lg. 8¼in. **$115**
1133 Three Sailor's Carved Bone Pie Crimpers, 19th C., longest 6¼in. **$1,150**

Opposite:
A-MA   Skinner, Inc.
555 The Sailor's Farewell, 19th C., unsgn., reverse painting on glass in orig. molded wood frame w/paint loss, 8x10in. **$1,645**
556 Glazed Whalebone Candle Lantern, 19th C., w/arched copper top, wire handle & ball feet, ht. 10½in. **$3,290**
557 Painting, watercolor on paper, unsgn. depicting a woman standing before an anchor…the symbol of hope… and title of painting, 8x10in. **$2,585**
558 Ivory & Mah. Scrimshaw Carpenter's Plane. n/s
559 Sailor's Inlaid Pine Box, 19th C. w/inlaid whalebone panel engraved w/a scene of a three-masted ship flying an Am. flag. The panel & sides inlaid w/m.o.p., baleen & ivory. Interior w/lift-out tray & three compartments, ht. 7¼, wd. 14½in. **$3,819**
560 Carved Ivory & Poly. Paper Fan, China, late 18th/early 19th C. The

other side painted w/scenes of courtly figures w/applied cut-out painted ivory faces, in a lacquered rectangular wooden box w/brass inlays, fan 11x20in. **$2,703**
561 Engraved Whale's Tooth, 19th C., the obverse portraying a bust-length portrait of a military officer, the reverse depicting a whaling scene, mounted on a shaped walnut base, w/imper. **$764**
562 Sailor-made Inlaid Wooden Heart-shaped Sentiment Box w/an inscription. The box int. w/inlaid crucifix w/poly. painted floral dec. **$411**
563 Inlaid Wooden Sailor's Puzzle Box w/hinged lid over three compartments. Box is inlaid w/contrasting stars, hearts crucifixes & scrolls, ht. 2¾, wd. 13¼in. **$353**
564 Carved Whalebone Carpenter's Plane, 19th C. w/iron blade & mustard paint, lg. 8⅛in. **$2,233**
565 Engraved Whale's Tooth, mid-19th C., one side depicting a military

officer, the reverse showing a woman standing on the shore & a sailing vessel in the distance, w/minor imper., ht. 4⅞in. **$1,293**
566 Engraved Whale's Tooth, 19th C., depicting the steam vessel SS *Indiana* & inscribed, w/minor age cracks, ht. 5⅛in. **$411**
567 Engraved Whale's Tooth, 19th C. depicting a stag in a landscape w/tall grass, house & hills in background, ht. 4⅞in. **$353**
568 Pr. of Turned Whalebone Candlesticks, 19th C. w/oval candlecups & incised ring-turned dec., ht. 6¼in. **$2,820**
569 Engraved Whale's Tooth, engraved w/a ship carrying an American flag off the stern, & a distant lighthouse topped w/an arrow weathervane, **$1,528**
570 Engraved Walrus Tusk, 19th C., engraved w/grapevines, an urn of flowers, a portrait of a gentleman within a leafy & bowknotted wreath, lg. 15¼in. **$382**

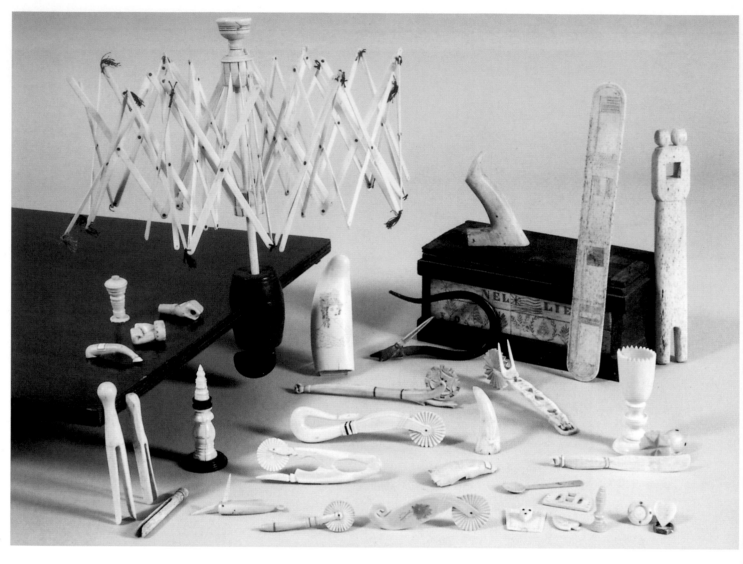

A-MA   **Skinner, Inc.**

Scrimshaw

533 Yarn Swift w/a mah. table clamp, 19th C. w/turned ivory yarn cup, an expanding yarn winder made of flat carved bone ribs & whalebone shaft, ht. 13in., expanding to a dia. of approx. 23in. **$1,116**

534 Engraved Whale's Tooth, late 19th C., one side depicting portrait of a young woman, highlighted by red sealing wax, w/cracks from base edge, lg. 5½in. **$176**

535 Two Scrimshaw Items, a 19th C. hook device made of carved wood bound w/a carved ivory barb, together w/a baleen busk engraved w/a heart, foliate medallion, a two-masted sailing vessel & potted plant, lg. 6½ & 12in. **$264**

536 Wood & Bone Sailor-made Inlaid Box, 19th C. w/hinged lid inlaid w/a five point star & flanked by two smaller stars, front w/four inlaid bone panels engraved w/British & American flags, shield & leafy branches & name Nellie Young, heightened w/red & blue sealing wax, losses, ht. 5, wd. 11⅜in. **$881**

537 Carved Whalebone Wall Hook,
19th C., ht. 3¾, lg. 4¾in. **$382**

538 Engraved Whalebone Busk, 19th C., one side engraved w/church, Am. flags, flowers, sailing vessel & Am., France, a Confederate flag & engravings, lg. 14¼in. **$881**

539 Four Carved Bone & Ivory Items, 19th C. including a carved bone wrench device, carved bone butter knife, butter stamp w/inlaid baleen disks & a whale ivory cup w/imper. **$1,116**

540 Four Carved Whale Ivory Items, 19th C., incl. two fists, a horse leg & a stamp w/incised line hand turned shaft, lg. 1¼, ⅞in. **$470**

541 Three Carved Whalebone Clothes-pins, 19th C., lg. 3 & 5in. **$499**

542 Turned Ivory & Rosewood Pick Wick, 19th C. & highlighted w/red sealing wax, cracks, ht. 4½in. **$823**

543 Carved Ivory & Whalebone Whale-form Folding Toothpick, 19th C., lg. 2½in. **$705**

544 Small Whale Ivory Jagging Wheel, 19th C. w/shaft dec. w/incised lines filled w/red & black sealing wax, lg. 3⅜in. **$470**

545 Carved Ivory Jagging Wheel, 19th C., A-form w/carved fork on
one end, lg. 5⅛in. **$499**

546 Carved Ivory Snake-form Jagging Wheel, 19th C. The shaft has two baleen bands & serpent's neck is engraved w/diamond design & red sealing wax, cracks on shaft, lg. 6¾in. **$4,700**

547 Whalebone & Baleen Jagging Wheel w/fist finial, 19th C. The shaft has two baleen bands w/loss & cracks, lg. 8⅛in. **$1,880**

548 Carved & Engraved Whale Ivory Jagging Wheel, 19th C. The handle has scrolled terminal w/one engraved side w/rose stem, red & green sealing wax, lg. 4⅞in. **$1,880**

550 Carved & Engraved Whalebone & Ivory Jagging Wheel, 19th C., the handle w/fork, heart & trefoil cut-outs & engraved berry sprigs w/break on prong, lg. 7in. **$2,233**

551 Six Small Carved Bone Items, 19th C., including a spoon, stamp, a fid & three possibly knitting needle sheaths. **$323**

552 Three Carved Ivory Rings, 19th C., one w/carved heart, one circular w/abalone dots, & one w/engraved diamonds & dots filled w/red wax. **$176**

A-MA   Skinner, Inc.

737 Three Carved & Painted Animal Plaques, VT, by Elbert S. Stevens & dated 1914, an owl, coyote & a fox, ht. 20,16 & 16in. **$2,938**

738 Carved & Painted Wooden Owl Decoy, att. to Frank Finney, 20th C., ht. 19¾in. **$1,528**

739 Bufflehead Duck Decoy, carved & painted, early 20th C. w/paint wear, ht. 3¾, lg. 9⅝in. **$441**

740 Shorebird Decoy, late 19th/early 20th C. w/painted eyes & mounted on wooden base, carved & painted, ht. 8¼in. **$382**

471 Carved & Painted Owl Decoy, Am., 20th C. w/inset eyes & bear-claw bill, ht. 12⅜in. **$646**

472 Shorebird Decoy, carved & painted w/flattened full-body figure mounted on wooden base w/scattered paint loss, ht. 9¼in. **$441**

743 Passenger Pigeon Decoy, carved & painted, 20th C., w/elongated tail & mottled painted plumage, no stand, ht. 3⅝, lg. 13¾in. **$176**

744 Folk Art Carved & Painted Bird on Branch, 19th C., ht. 6in. n/s

745 Hooded Merganser Drake Duck Decoy, carved & painted, w/tack eyes, ht. 6½, lg. 23in. **$764**

746 Three Carved & Painted Duck Decoys incl. two canvasbacks & possible scoter decoy. The canvasbacks carved w/initials LD on base, ht. 8½, 5¾in. **$8,813**

747 Sleeping Mallard Hen Decoy, carved & painted w/inset glass eyes, the initials J.H. incised on base w/later repaint. n/s

748 Wood Duck Decoy, carved & painted w/inset glass eyes, ht. 6½, lg. 16¼in. **$59**

749 Two Duck Decoys att. to Ken Harris, third qtr. 20th C., a mallard drake & a broadbill hen, both w/inset glass eyes, carved & painted. **$235**

A-MA   **Skinner, Inc.**
184 Blown Glass Goblet w/Stone Fruit incl. painted & carved nuts, vegetable & fruit, ht. 12in. **$499**
185 Painted Tin & Glass Make-do Goblets, Am. 19th C. w/red painted tin bases ht. 7in. **$705**
186 Two Tin & Glass Make-do Compotes, Am. 19th C., one w/blown molded glass bowl on round tin base containing marbles together w/a round tin tray supported by a press-molded glass base, ht. 6, 7¾in. **$1,763**

187 Large Blown Glass Bowl on stand w/bell-form base, together w/a small bowl & goblet not illus. **$235**
188 Three Make-do Goblets w/blown molded bowls on turned wooden bases **$382**
189 Large Blown Glass Goblet w/stone fruit, vegetables & nuts, ht. 8in. **$470**
190 Four Make-do Strawberry Pincushions, Am., 19th C. incl. pincushions made w/bases of molded & blown glass candlesticks, goblets, or lamps, covered w/wool, silk or

velvet textiles, the largest embellished w/glass beads & suspending three strawberry pincushions, wear, ht. 4½-16¾in. **$823**
191 Collection of Eight Pincushions, fashioned from lamp or goblet bases & topped w/colorful fabric, wear, ht. 3, 6, 8in. **$294**
192 Ten Assorted Pincushions, fabric covered, silk, wool & velvet incl. one w/emery-filled strawberry & one sq. red & brown velvet patchwork pot holder, wear. **$881**

Opposite:
A-MA   **Skinner, Inc.**
1032 Turned Tiger Maple Crib, possibly PA, ca.1825, ref. & minor imper., ht. 42½, wd. 28¼in. **n/s**

1033 Chippendale Tiger Maple Tilt-top Tea Table, late 18th C. w/birdcage support & vase & ring-turned post & tripod cabriole legs w/pad feet, ref.

& rest., ht. 29, dia. 33½in. **$999**
1034 Tiger Maple Drop-leaf Table, N. Eng., ca.1800 w/straight skirt, ref., ht. 23½, dp. 30in. **$1,998**

A-MA   Skinner, Inc.
1028 Tiger Maple & Bird's-eye Maple Tilt-top Candlestand, Federal, ca.1810/15 w/octagonal top on vase & ring-turned support w/tripod base & stringing on legs w/spade feet,

old ref. & imper., ht. 29½in. **$5,581**
1029 Set of Six Classical Tiger Maple Side Chairs, ca.1820 w/caned seats, old surface, ht .33½in. **$3,055**
1030 Federal Tiger Maple Drop-leaf Table, N. Eng., ca.1810 w/straight

apron, ref. w/minor imper. ht. 28¼, wd. 36¾in. **$2,233**
1031 Flint Enamel Pottery Chamber Pot, Bennington Pottery, 1849-58 maker's mark on base, lacking cover & minor base hairline, ht. 13¾in. **$353**